The Founding Fathers of Sephardic Jewry

From Rav Saadia Gaon (882-942 C.E.)
to Shemuel ibn Tibbon (1150-1232 C.E.)

The Founding Fathers of Sephardic Jewry

*From Rav Saadia Gaon (882-942 C.E.)
to Shemuel ibn Tibbon (1150-1232 C.E.)*

YAMIN LEVY

MHC Press
New York
2024

MHC Press
Published by Maimonides Heritage Center
26 Steppingstone Lane
Kings Point, NY 11024

Copyright 2024 © Yamin Levy

All rights reserved. No part of this publication may be reproduced, stored in a retrieval system, or transmitted in any form or by any means electronic, mechanical, photocopy, recording, or otherwise without the prior written permission of the publisher.
The paper used in this publication meets the minimum requirements of the American National Standard for Information Sciences—Permanence of Paper for Printed Library Materials, ANSI/NISO Z39/48-1992

Cover design by: Gina by Design, Inc.

ISBN 979-8-9877500-2-5 (Hard Cover)
ISBN 979-8-9877500-3-2 (Paperback)

Manufactured in the United States of America

The publication of this book was made possible by
Edna and Saeed Amirian
In Loving Memory of
Turan and Elyahoo Amirian ZL

Turan and Elyahoo Amirian were pillars of the Persian Jewish community in Iran and the United States of America. Their kind spirit, affectionate manner, and welcoming personality enriched the lives of everyone with whom their paths crossed. They raised a loving and generous family and left a legacy rich in Jewish values and principles.

May their memory be a source of inspiration to all.

With appreciation to
Edna and Saeed Amirian
And in memory of
Turan and Elyahoo Amirian

Yamin Levy
2024 / 5784

Acknowledgments

THIS BOOK IS AN OUTGROWTH to my previous book **The Mysticism of Andalusia: Exploring HaRambam's Mystical Tradition**. One of the primary themes of my research has always been confirming the direct linkage between the teachings of geonim who, were the most authoritative transmitters of rabbinic Judaism, and the teachings of HaRambam. That is precisely what I do in this book. That is why the preparation of this book for publication simply involved organizing the many index cards, notebooks and word files of the research that had already been done. Therefore, all those who read, commented, and helped produce my last book deserve to be thanked here as well.

I do want to especially thank my dear friends Edna and Saeed Amirian and the entire Amirian family for sponsoring the publication of this book in memory of Turan and Eliyahoo Amirian z'l. Touran and Eliyahu Amirian were beloved members of our community. Their kindness, generosity-of-spirit and life wisdom is legendary. I personally was a beneficiary of their love and warmth and so dedicating this book in their memory is especially meaningful to me.

I am grateful to my many friends and members at the Iranian Jewish Center, Beth Hadassah Synagogue for their continued trust in me and providing me with a platform to serve our cherished community and secure a strong and healthy future for Sephardic Jewry.

Thank you to the leaders and supporters of the Maimonides Heritage Center who believe in our vision to amplify the voice and teachings of HaRambam. An especially heartfelt thank you to Mr. Joshua Setton, chairman and founding supporter of the Maimonides Heritage Center for his kindness and vision. May Hashem bless him with continued strength, *Lehagdil Torah U'Lehadira*, to grow and beautify the legacy of Torah.

A final shoutout to my family!

YAMIN LEVY, 2023

Table of Contents

Lost Enlightenment an Introduction	1
HaRambam's Introduction to the Mishneh Torah	19
Rabbenu Saadia Gaon bar Yoseph	32
Rav Sherira bar Hanina Gaon and Rabbi Hai bar Sherira Gaon	56
Rabbi Shemuel ben Hofni HaKohen Gaon	65
Rabbi Moshe nen Hanokh and Rabbi Hanokh ben Moshe	74
Hasdai Abu Yoseph ben Yitzchak ibn Shaprut	80
Rabbi Yona ibn Janah	90
Rabbi Shemuel ben Elkana ibn Nagrela HaNagid	98
Rabbenu Hananel ben Hushiel and Rabbenu Nissim ben Yaacov	108
Rabbenu Yitzchak ben Yaacov HaKihen Alfasi	111

Shelomo ibn Gabirol	117
Rabbi Bahya ben Yoseph ibn Pakuda	129
Rabbi Yoseph ben Meir ibn Migash HaLevi	148
Rabbi Avraham ben Meir ibn Ezra	151
Rabbenu Moshe ben Mimon, HaRambam	177
Yehuda ben Shaul ibn Tibbon and Shemuel ben Yehuda ibn Tibbon	247
Primary Sources	269
Selective Bibliography	271
Index	279

> The heavenly spheres and fortune's stars
> veered off course the day I was born;
> if I were a seller of candles,
> the sun would never go down.
>
> AVRAHAM IBN EZRA

Lost Enlightenment

I NAMED THIS BOOK *The Founding Fathers of Sephardic Jewry* because the various rabbis, sages, scholars, teachers, poets, mystics, philosophers, leaders, and translators who appear between the covers of this book are but a sampling of the original thinkers and scholars responsible for preserving and transmitting the rich Jewish heritage of Sephardic Jewry. Their legacy is the Jewish people's heritage.

There is an abundance of material about some of the personalities I chose to present here; about others there is very little. This study is not meant to be exhaustive; it is a historic and biographic taste of those responsible for transmitting and recording the Talmudic intellectual, spiritual, and esoteric culture of Rabbinic Judaism beginning with Rav Saadia Gaon of the late ninth century and ending with Andalusia's ambassadors and translators, Rabbis Yehuda ibn Tibbon and his son Shemuel ibn Tibbon who lived in the thirteenth century.

By writing a short biography of the intellectual, religious, and spiritual legacy of the sages who lived and led communities in Baghdad, North Africa, Southern Spain, and Egypt, I am in essence linking the close of the Talmud to the most enlightened period in Jewish history. The Talmud is the primary source of Jewish law, philosophy, biblical exegesis, and Jewish culture. As a literary work it has far-reaching socio-historical implications, as is evident from the fact that the Jewish communities that had been deprived of the study of Talmud did not survive the ravages of history.

Simply stated, the Talmud is the record of centuries of discussions expounding upon Jewish law and Jewish thought as it was understood and lived by the sages of the great Torah academies in the land of Israel and in Babylonia as early as the first century C.E. The Talmud developed in two distinct works: Talmud Yerushalmi, which was edited and produced in the Land of Israel and was completed around 350 C.E. Around that time the remaining Jewish communities in Israel had to flee due to the genocidal persecution of the newly empowered Byzantine Christians. The destruction of the then-vibrant Jewish communities in the land of Israel forced many of the Torah scholars to escape and emigrate to Babylonia, where the Jewish communities were flourishing. The Babylonian Talmud was completed towards the end of the sixth century. Because its editorial process outlasted that of the Yerushalmi Talmud and because of the authoritative stature of the scholars of Southwestern Asia at the time it became the definitive religious, cultural, and spiritual literary legacy of the Jewish people alongside the TaNaKH [the Bible].

Rabbi Yitzchak Alfasi, the great eleventh-century Talmudist and codifier of Jewish law, confirms that Jewish law will, in most cases rule in accordance to the opinions of the Babylonian Talmud over the Talmud Yerushalmi because the Babylonian Talmud assumes and takes into consideration the opinions discussed in the Talmud Yerushalmi that was edited earlier.

The Judaism that the Talmud (Babylonian Talmud was completed and closed in the early 6th century) envisioned is founded on Jewish law, study, and prayer through which the Jewish people fulfill their end of the covenant with God despite the loss of the Temple in Jerusalem and the rituals associated with animal sacrifices. The underlying core value of the Talmud is the need for Jewish survival and the continuing meaningfulness of Jewish religious practice. They put forth a culture and worldview that is essentially optimistic about improving the material world and humanity. Talmudic thought and the society they sought to create is based on reason, philosophical precision, and the proven sciences of the day. A society based on sound ethical principles that continually seeks to make the world a better place. Social status is earned based on knowledge and a strong work ethic. The sages of the Talmud showed great respect for knowledge that emerged from all places including non-Jewish sources. A careful reading of the history and biographies of the scholars recoded between the pages of this book shows how HaRambam the last of the Andalusian rabbinic scholars loyally recorded and preserved rabbinic Judaism.

Our book begins with Rav Saadia Gaon (882-942 C.E.), whose life history and literary legacy reflect his lifelong commitment to preserving and expounding an authentic Jewish religious tradition that is based on the rabbinic teachings as recorded in the Talmudic record. He regarded the tradition that he transmits as divinely inspired, linked to Moshe Rabbenu himself. Rav Saadia Gaon's teachings found their fullest expression in the intellectually open society of Southwestern Asia, North Africa, and Southern Spain where Jewish scholars flourished in all fields and disciplines.

Andalusia

Andalusia, at times referred to as Andalus is the southern region of Spain. The name Andalusia is derived from the Arabic word Al-Andalus, the etymology of which is debated by scholars. Andalusia is the place where the Sephardic Golden Age of Spain took place. This Golden Age of Spain refers to the Jewish scholarship and creative intellectual output that occurred in the southern, Muslim region of Spain during the Umayyad rule (711-1100 C.E.). The Northern region of

Spain was under the auspices of a monarch under the control of the Christian church; its Golden Age happened hundreds of years later.

The historical origins of the immigration of the Jews to Spain is the subject of numerous legends and folk tales spread by Jewish and Christian chroniclers. Historical evidence suggests that Jews have been in Spain since the destruction of the second Bet HaMikdash because of the Roman Empire's forced migrations. They first settled along the Mediterranean coast and gradually moved inland throughout the Iberian Peninsula.[1] For close to fifteen-hundred years, this region was considered the second homeland of the Jewish people until their expulsion in 1492.

The primary thrust of this short book is the substance of material I have been teaching for the better part of thirty years: Namely, that HaRambam did not, as some have flagrantly suggested, change or reinvent Judaism in the Middle Ages based on Greek and Arabic philosophy. This is not the place to call out the many scholars who have made such a claim. Such a belief is false and symptomatic of a European superiority complex.

The celebrated Maimonidean scholar Professor Isadore Twersky of Harvard notes how:

> The generations before the age of Maimonides had produced philosopher-scientists of great learning and dialectical skill as well as Talmudist-jurists of great erudition and versatility, many of them in Spain. There were even, as Rabbi Abraham ibn Daud reports with great pride and precision in Sefer HaKabbalah, philosophically trained Talmudists such as Rabbi Baruch ibn Albalia – or others such as Rabbi Bahya ibn Pakuda or Rabbi Joseph ibn Saddik . . . scholars well versed in both Greek science and rabbinic lore and thoroughly convinced of the need to maintain the peaceful coexistence of the two disciplines.[2]

---

[1] The earliest evidence of a Jewish presence in Spain is a trilingual inscription in Hebrew, Latin, and Greek on a child's sarcophagus found in Tarragona dating to the Roman period, now on display at the Sephardic Museum in Toledo, Spain. Also see Josephus 7:3, 3 and Mishna Baba Batra 3:2.

[2] Isadore Twersky, *Introduction to the Code of Maimonides*, page 356.

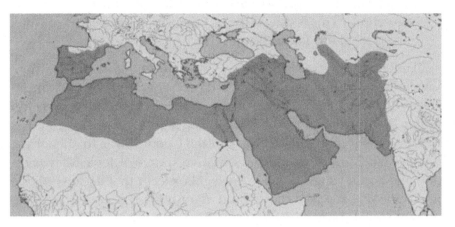

Umayyad Muslim Empire 800-1100 C.E.

HaRambam was primarily a transmitter of the traditions of the world of Andalusia. It is the Jewish heritage he inherited from his father, who, in turn, received it from his teachers who were the authentic link between the Talmud and the Middle Ages.[3] There is no doubt that HaRambam was indeed creative and innovative, and he was a first-rate educator, but he devoted his life and creative output to record the Jewish way of life, intellectual culture, and spiritual tradition as it was lived in Andalusia. This tradition is rooted in the rabbinic teachings as presented in the Talmud and through the filter of the Babylonian Geonim.

In his introduction to the *Mishneh Torah*, HaRambam follows in the footsteps of his predecessors who wrote similar histories as he details how the Torah was transmitted from one *Bet Din* [supreme court] to the next from the days of Moshe Rabbenu onward. When he arrives at the Babylonian Talmud he remarks:

> It is incumbent upon the entire house of Israel to comply with all that is contained in the Babylonian Talmud, and every city and every country is compelled to conform to all the customs adopted

---

[3] Gad Freudenthal, "Abraham Ibn Ezra and Judah Ibn Tibbon as Cultural Intermediaries," 52-81.

by the Talmudic sages to enforce their decrees and to follow their regulations. This is due to the fact that the entire people of Israel agreed to all the Talmudic precepts.[4]

HaRambam wrote this towards the end of the twelfth century, when the Babylonian academies and the Geonate were in advanced stages of decline. In the above quote, HaRambam ratifies two critical points that he gleaned from the *halakhic* legacy of the Geonim. His first point is to note that the task of the Geonim was to anchor the Babylonian Talmud as the authoritative source of Jewish law. Second and equally significant is the legal concept that because all the Jewish people adopted the Talmud as authoritative proves it is a legitimate legal source.

Political Landscape

At the beginning of the eighth century, about one hundred and fifty years after the close of the Talmud, the centers of Jewish learning were headed by *Rashei Yeshiva* [heads of the academies] known as "Geonim." When the Muslim Umayyad Caliphate made its capital Iraq, it enabled Babylonian Jewry to establish itself as a center of Jewish learning through its long-standing academies.[5]

Andalusia, in medieval Muslim Spain, was the westernmost frontier of the Muslim and Christian worlds. Its multiethnic inhabitants were rarely peaceful. This region was polluted with a militant culture and characterized by frequent friction. Tribal groups engaged in endless rivalries while the Christian monarchs in Northern Spain were animated by a desire to reconquer the Peninsula from the Muslims. And yet, paradoxically, Southern Spain was the only place in Europe where Jews, Muslims, and Christians lived side by side in relative harmony. Although often tenuous, the coexistence produced an extraordinary synergy and distinctive culture that manifested itself in art, poetry, architecture, music, science, philos-

---

[4] HaRambam, Introduction to *Mishneh Torah*.

[5] Robert Brody, *The Geonim of Babylonia*, pages 101 and 103.

ophy, and religion. This rich and intellectually open society was particularly suited for Jewish culture.

After the Muslim conquest of southern Spain (711-718 C.E.), waves of Arab tribes and Jewish refugees and merchants migrated across the Strait of Gibraltar from North Africa and the Middle East, looking for an opportunity to settle down and live in peace. They did not, however, find peace. Muslim rule was unstable, and conflicts were resolved with violence. And yet there was a culture of innovation and openness that pervaded the region. The Jewish merchants introduced a large number of luxury goods to the region, as well as the intellectual, religious, and spiritual culture of the Babylonian and Jerusalem Talmud from Bagdad, Israel, and the Yeshivoth from which they had emigrated.

For the Muslims, Andalusia was special: It was the only Muslim outpost on European soil. For the Jews, Andalusia was a unique opportunity: It was a multicultural, multilingual haven that valued linguistics, religious texts, philosophy, and the pursuit of science. For the first time since the destruction of the second Bet HaMikdash, Jews could do what they do best – research and innovate in all disciplines, particularly in the study of Torah, Talmud and Hebrew language.

Andalusia's multireligious and multiethnic human landscape was an anomaly in medieval Europe. Scholars disagree as to the nature of the region's mosaic, applying modern day definitions to a medieval reality. Modern forms of tolerance did not exist in Andalus. In fact, it was scarcely a place of tolerance typical of a modern-day pluralistic society. Medieval Europe, be it Muslim or Christian, begrudgingly tolerated Judaism. At its most hospitable times, Muslim Spain considered Judaism to be an autonomous religion but one inferior to Islam. They were defined as *dhimmis*, a non-Muslim protected class of people.

Despite the humiliating political, social, and economic status as well as the payments of added discriminatory taxes, the Jewish people nevertheless thrived. Memory of the persecution under the Visigoths made conditions for the Jews in Andalus seem benign; the option of living under Christian persecution and anti-intellectual dogma seemed a great deal worse. As *dhimmis*, Jews were free to practice their religion, administer their affairs, travel, do business, practice their professions, and be creative intellectually. In these conditions, the Jews of Andalusia found themselves on a stimulating trajectory of political, scientific, and religious influence. The social discrimination did not preclude cultural sharing. Jews were proficient in Arabic and even Latin, which made them very useful to their Muslim rulers.

Andalusia and its capital Cordoba were the epicenter of what is known as the Golden Age of Spain and the emergence of "Old Sepharad." It reintroduced to the world the Jewish personality that was stately, intellectual, devoutly religious, charitable, and pious. Innovations in Hebrew language, poetry, philosophy, mysticism, and Talmudic studies flourished in Andalus. Cities like Saragossa, Granada, Merida, and Lucena blossomed with Yeshivoth and a Jewish upper class of courtiers, physicians, economists, negotiators, and poets.

This period in Jewish history came to an end in the middle of the twelfth century with the invasion of the fundamentalist Almohads. Two of the most illustrious heirs of Andalus, Rabbi Moshe ben Maimon, also known as Maimonides or HaRambam, and Rabbi Avraham ibn Ezra, escaped the violence. Both sought to preserve the beautiful Jewish culture of Andalusia. Rabbi Avraham ibn Ezra went north to Christian Spain, France, and Britain. He wandered from city to city, from Jewish center to Jewish center, not finding a cultural space that welcomed his brand of Judaism and Jewish thought. He could not find a place in Europe that felt comfortable. For him living meant living like a Jew and the Judaism he was heir too was not compatible with the Judaism in Christian Europe. HaRambam went south, first to Morocco and then to Egypt. The Muslim lands afforded him a more welcoming environment for him to preserve and record the Jewish Andalusian tradition that was so dear to him.

The typical Andalusian Jewish scholar was modeled against the elite scholars of Baghdad.[6] Their educational curriculum and scholarly expertise included philosophy, physics, logic, math-

---

[6] Harry Austryn Wolfson, "The Classification of Sciences in Medieval Jewish Philosophy."

ematics, astronomy, ethics, metaphysics, and rhetoric. All these subjects were available in Arabic translations and expounded upon by Arabic scientists and philosophers. These subjects were made to seamlessly blend with Torah, Talmud, Midrash, *halakha*, and theology. Scrupulous observance of the *halakha* was always adorned by eloquent verbal and written skills. Their rulings and philosophies were accompanied by wit and beauty, characteristics inherited from their ancients. The Andalusian Jew was unapologetic about his pursuit of wealth. It freed one from distraction and removed the temptation to cheapen one's own status.[7] The rabbi never received a salary from the community for studying or teaching Torah. Such a practice was looked down upon.[8] Community service and charity were values that were taken seriously. A judge in the court of the autonomous Jewish community was expected to demonstrate irreproachable character, fairness, learning, and practiced humility. A communal leader or rabbi exemplified a demeanor that was above criticism from every point of view.[9]

Andalusia was a world where revelation, philosophy, and science were all valid sources of knowledge that could and had to be reconciled. Following in the footsteps legitimized by Rav Saadia Gaon, heir to the Babylonian Talmudic tradition, one learned to fashion a cohesive universe of discourse where philosophy and religion sought the same truth. When they clashed, the Jew always turned to revelation as the ultimate arbiter.

European thinkers lagged behind. It was not until the seventeenth century when the English thinker John Locke suggested that revealed religion could and should be able to coexist in a realm where reason could be freely exercised.[10] He accomplished this by acknowledging a realm of cognition that is "above reason" and then plunging back into

---

[7] See HaRambam's *Shemoneh Perakim [Eight Chapters]* chapter 6, where he explains why the *Nazir* was required to present a sin offering at the conclusion of his Nazarite vows.

[8] *MT Hilkhot Talmud Torah* 3:10-11.

[9] *MT Hilkhot De'ot* 5:1-5.

[10] For a well-researched history of Europe's resistance to higher education and philosophy see George Makari's *Soul Machine*.

the vast realm of science, philosophy, and social economic life. What was then considered a breakthrough in religion and philosophy was common knowledge to the Jews of Southwestern Asia, Central Asia, and Andalusia from as early as the ninth century.

The Andalusian Legacy

In his introduction to the *Mishneh Torah*, HaRambam makes an unexpected comment regarding the authentic transmission of Jewish law. After listing forty generations of rabbinical courts that were links in the chain of transmission of Jewish law and tradition from the time Moshe Rabbenu received the Torah directly from God until the close of the Talmud, HaRambam adds that each rabbinical court in the chain heard the Torah from God:

> Thus, the source of all these sages' knowledge is God, the Lord of Israel.[11]

Could it be that HaRambam is telling us each of the sages in his lengthy list were prophets like Moshe Rabbenu? Earlier he wrote that only Moshe Rabbenu received the Torah directly from God. So, which is it? The answer lies in the nature and quality of the transmission. It was not only knowledge and facts that were passed from one generation to the next but also a culture. With that short statement he is introducing his readers to a way of thinking, a perspective about the nature of Torah. Despite the numerous generations of transmission, interpretation, development, application, and innovation, the Torah that the Jewish people are heir to is the same Torah that was revealed to Moshe Rabbenu at Sinai directly from God. It is as if each and every one of the sages in the chain of transmission were recipients of the Torah directly from God. Each supreme court of Israel carried the weight of history and destiny of the Jewish people.

The transmission of a culture is the process through which the cultural elements – beliefs, attitudes, values, and behavioral scripts

[11] HaRambam, Introduction to *Mishneh Torah*.

– are passed on and taught to the subsequent generations. The primary role of cultural transmission is to provide a consistent and stable framework that ensures or at least enhances the chances of survival of the said group. Humans are unique in that they acquire and transmit knowledge, belief, and culture not only through practice but also through language.

> One of the most important functions of language is its role in the construction of reality. Language is not simply a tool for communication; it is also a guide to what Edward Sapir terms social reality. Language has a semantic system, or a meaning potential which enables the transmission of cultural values. Therefore, while a child is learning language, other significant learning is taking place through the medium of language. The child is simultaneously learning the meaning associated with the culture, realized linguistically by the lexica-grammatical system of language.[12]

Professor José Faur makes an insightful observation comparing two biblical texts. Man, writes Faur, is born into a culture and not "between two stones" as the Torah describes the birth of children in Egypt in the Book of Shemoth.[13] Culture is transmitted by family and society. In the Israelite society, children are born on the patriarch's knees:

> Joseph saw children of a third generation born to Ephraim; also, the sons of Machir the son of Menasheh were born on Joseph's knees.[14]

Culture is transmitted from parents to children and teachers to students, in other words from society as a whole to the next generation. The transmission of a culture involves communicating values, outlooks and perspectives that are not easily expressed in words or lessons. It's a way of life and living.

For HaRambam, language is what distinguishes the human

[12] See Linda Thompson, "Learning Language," 76-96.
[13] Shemoth 1:16
[14] Bereshit 50:23.

being from all other created creatures and what most identifies the human being with the Divine.[15] He devoted a significant amount of attention in many of his writings to the philosophical problems and conceptual confusions that arise due to language. Being aware of the beliefs and attitudes that language can unconsciously and subtly impart is what distinguished the Andalusian schools of thought from their European counterparts. Language influences culture. This is one of the reasons the Jews of Andalus took the study of languages and philology very seriously.[16]

Judaism and the teaching of the rabbinic sages were transmitted through three distinct but linked disciplines: The study of Torah and the biblical text, which we will call *mikra*; the interpretation of the biblical text, which we will call *midrash:* and the legal, legislative process of Jewish law, which we will call *hora'a*.

Mikra involves fluency of the biblical text. In Hebrew this is called *Shinun HaMikra*.[17] The goal was to have an effortless fluency with the biblical text. Often the Talmud will only quote the first few words of a verse and the student would have to complete the verse by heart. The study of Mikra also involved mastery of the Hebrew language. The earliest Geonim were themselves masters of biblical grammar, philology and syntax. They viewed themselves as transmitters of the biblical text and were obsessed with precision. Mastery of the biblical text also involved the study of theology and fundamentals of philosophy. One had to understand why a text would use anthropomorphic descriptions of God and what belief in God is. The goal of the second discipline in the educational process, *midrash*, was to generate meaning from the biblical text that spoke to cultural, psychological, and religious matters relevant to their demographic at that time and place. *Midrash* was not meant be an objective, scientific interpretation of the biblical text. *Midrash*

---

[15] See Guide 1:1.

[16] See ibn Ezra on the study of language and grammar in *Rabbi Abraham Ibn Ezra: Yesod Morah VeSod Torah* (Hebrew), edited by Joseph Cohen and Uriel Simon, Chapter 1 page 16, (Bar Ilan University Press, 2007).

[17] As the biblical verse states *"Veshinantam Levanecha ..."*

is a way in which the rabbinic teachers transformed the Torah into a dynamic text that was lived and experienced. The third discipline, *hora'a*, is strictly legal. The members of the Jewish society needed to know how and when to observe their holy days, mitzvoth and life-cycle events. The goal to make Jewish law accessible to all members of society. Jewish law was based on the rules of *halakhic* legislation, the rabbis interpret and determine the laws and practices of Judaism and present them to the community through writing or orally.

The study of Jewish theology was regarded as relevant to all members of society. Unlike their Muslim counterparts who assumed the masses would have corporeal notions of God, the Jews of Andalus insisted on educating the masses correctly. In his *Decisive Treatise Determining the Connection between Religion and Philosophy*, Averroes states that "one should not expect ordinary people to think of God in incorporeal terms."[18] Averroes invokes a story in the Quran where Muhammad declares a woman to be a believer even though she had stated that God resides in heaven, implying a physical notion of God. For Averroes, asking ordinary people to have an elevated conception of God will bring them to unbelief, since "ordinary people can conceive only of a corporeal God."[19]

In Andalus, the most basic educational curriculum involved eliminating, in absolute terms, all conceptions of corporeality of God. Untying this knot[20] is the first step and applies to all members of the Jewish community, not only the philosophically inclined. Everyone can and should achieve some understanding of this basic principle of Judaism. HaRambam writes:

> The masses will no longer cast the knowledge of God behind their backs, but will exert themselves, to the limits of their power, to

---

[18] Averroes, *The Book of the Decisive Treatise Determining the Connection Between the Law and Wisdom*, translated by G.F. Hourani, (Brigham Young University Press, 2001), 59-60.

[19] Ibid.

[20] This is an expression used by Abraham Abulafia to describe how the student of mysticism must first purge the mind of false notions.

attain knowledge that will perfect them and bring them closer to their Creator.[21]

The teachers of Andalus did not expect everyone to be philosophers or intellectuals, but they did expect their entire community to be educated correctly. Unlike Averroes who believed that teaching people that God does not have a body will lead them to unbelief, the Jews of Andalus believed that *not* teaching them that God does *not* have a body will stifle their spiritual ambitions and lead them further *away* from God. Members of the community had to believe this principle on the basis of the authority of the scholars who preceded them.

> Just as it behooves one to bring up children in the belief, and to proclaim to the multitudes that God, may he be magnified and honored, is one and none but He is to be worshipped, so it behooves that they should be made to accept on traditional authority [*al derekh hakabalah*] the belief that God is not a body and that there is absolutely no likeness in any respect whatever between Him and the things created by Him.[22]

This most basic theological principle is not reserved for the scholar and intellectual. The expectation in Andalus was that everyone – man, woman, and child, educated or not – must understand that the most fundamental principle of theology. The alternative is unimaginable.

> Accordingly if we never in any way acquired an opinion by following traditional authority and were not correctly conducted toward something by means of parables, but were obliged to achieve a perfect representation by means of essential definitions and by pronouncing true only that which is meant to be pronounced true in virtue of a demonstration – which would be impossible after the above mentioned lengthy preliminary studies – this state of affairs would lead to all people dying without having known

---

[21] *Letters* (Hebrew), ed. by Shailat, 1:343; also Hartman, *Epistles of Maimonides*, 213.

[22] Guide 1:35; this is a theme that is consistent with all the scholars that emerge from Andalusia, see the works of Rav Saadia Gaon and Bahya ibn Pakuda.

fairs would lead to all people dying without having known whether there is a God for the world, or whether there is not, much less whether a proposition should be affirmed with regard to God or a defect denied. Nobody would ever be saved from this abyss except "one of a city or two of a family" (Yirmiyahu 3:14).[23]

In another passage HaRambam writes:

> I do not consider as an infidel one who cannot demonstrate that the corporeality of God should be negated. But I do consider as an infidel one who does not believe in its negation; and this is particularly true in view of the existence of the interpretations of Onkelos and Yonatan ben Uziel, may peace be on both of them, who cause their readers to keep away as far as possible from the corporeality of God.[24]

That even ordinary people must think of God in incorporeal terms is evident from HaRambam's *halakhic* works. For example, the third of the thirteen principles of faith, which he wrote for all especially the ordinary folk, states that God is incorporeal. The principle as it is stated in his commentary on the Mishna requires:

> The denial of corporeality to God, namely that we believe that the unitary being that we have mentioned, God, is neither a body, not power in a body, and that no corporeal actions such as motion, rest, and place belong to Him, either essentially or accidentally.[25]

For the Jews of Andalus, this was a matter of survival of the Jewish people. It is naïve to suggest that all the Jews of Andalusia were philosophers and scholars. They were not! And yet the expectation was that all Jews must embrace the most fundamental principles of

---

[23] Guide 1:34.

[24] Guide 1:36.

[25] *Haqdamot HaRambam la-Mishna*, ed. Y. Shailat, 141; in English see *Maimonides Reader*, edited I. Twersky, 418.

[26] For a more elaborate discussion on this issue and how it distinguished Andalusian Jewry from Ashkenaz Jewry see my book The Mysticism of Andalusia chapter on

The expositors of Andalusia not only understood the first verse of the Ten Commandments as a mitzvah to believe in God and to have faith in God, but they also understood the first commandment as being interrelated with the second commandment, the prohibition of worshiping graven images. For the scholars of Andalus, understanding the prohibition of commandments one and two together includes not only creating, bowing, or worshipping graven images, but also includes the prohibition of imagining God in corporeal ways. Thinking that God has some shape or physical form is strictly prohibited. For example, one who prays with great devotion and piety while imagining God sitting on a throne in heaven is not better than one who bows to an idol. A mental representation of God is as bad, if not worse, writes HaRambam, than bowing to an actual idol of wood.[27] The key to Andalusian philosophical and religious culture begins with silence. Applying positive language such as "God is" or describing a form to God is an exercise that ends in futility and is looked down upon.

> What then should be the state of him whose infidelity bears upon His essence, may He be exalted, and consists of believing Him to be different from what He really is? I mean to say that he does not believe that He exists; or believes that there are two gods, or that He is a body, or that He is subject to affections, or that he ascribes to God some deficiency or other. Such a man is undoubtedly more blameworthy than a worshipper of idols . . .[28]

The sages of Andalus were unequivocal about the obligation to purge one's mind and soul of any form of corporeality to God. This is a point HaRambam makes clear in the first chapter of the Guide, where he writes:

> Now with respect to that which ought to be said in order to refute the doctrine of corporeality of God and to establish His real unity – which can have no true reality unless one disproves His corporeality,

---

[27] *MT Yesodei HaTorah* 1:9; Guide 1:59.
[28] Guide 1:36.

you shall know the demonstration of all this from this treatise.[29]

In this book I link the philosophic, spiritual, legal, and religious tradition set forth by HaRambam back to Rabbi Saadia Gaon (882-942 C.E.) and trace it through the teachings of Rav Sherira Gaon (906-1006 C.E.) and his son Rav Hai Gaon (939-1038 C.E.), Rabbi Shemuel ben Hofni Gaon (997-1013 C.E.), Rabbi Moshe ben Hanokh (910-965 C.E.) and Rabbi Hanokh ben Moshe (945-1014 C.E.), Hasdai ibn Shaprut (915-970 or 990 C.E.), Rabbi Yona ibn Janah (990-1055 C.E.), Shemuel ibn Nagrella (993-1056 C.E.), Rabbenu Hananel (990-1050 C.E.), and Rabbenu Nissim (990-1062 C.E.), Rabbeinu Yitzchak Alfasi (1013-1103 C.E.), Shelomo ibn Gabirol (1022-1048 C.E.), Rabbenu Bahya ibn Pakuda (1050-1120 C.E.), Rabbenu Yoseph ibn Migash (1077-1141 C.E.), Rabbenu Avraham ibn Ezra (1089-1164 C.E.), Rabbenu Moshe ben Maimon (HaRambam, 1138-1204 C.E.), Yehudah ibn Tibbon (1120-1190 C.E.) and Shemuel ibn Tibbon (1150-1230 C.E.).

This lineage links HaRambam's worldview to the early *Rishonim*, the early medievalists of Andalusia, the Geonim, and, by direct association, to the rabbinic tradition of the Babylonian and Jerusalem Talmud.

The cultural, architectural, and intellectual wonders of Andalusia are prevalent themes in both the Judaic and Arabic literature that emerged from that region. The poets and writers could not overstate their high praise of their land's natural beauty and superiority of their native sons and daughters in all respects. Rabbi Abraham ibn Ezra laments in a mournful poem the loss of his belove Al-Andalus and the collective exile of his co-religionists:

> Calamity came upon Spain from the skies,
> And my eyes pour forth their stream of tears.
> I mourn like an owl for the town of Lucena,
> where exile dwelled, guiltless and strong,
> for a thousand and seventy years unchanged –

---

[29] Guide 1:1, 21.

until the day that she was expelled,
leaving her like a widow, forlorn,
deprived of scripture and books of the law . . .
I shave my head and bitterly keen
for Seville's martyrs and sons who were taken,
as daughters were forced into strangeness of faith
Cordoba ruined like the desolate sea . . .[30]

The Mystery of History

At the risk of sounding like a washed-up romantic I will nevertheless, as an orthodox religious leader ask: So, what happened to that culture of old Sepharad? That was a time when literature, religious poetry, linguistics, scientific inquiry, and philosophy were all part of one's religious and mystical ambitions. This was always the authentic culture of rabbinic Judaism. This is how the heirs to the Talmudic tradition understood rabbinic Judaism. How did modern day orthodox Judaism become so distant from this culture remains a mystery.

---

[30] Rabbi Abraham ibn Ezra, Yalkut, editor Israel Levin (New York, Keren Israel 1985) Page 35. English translation by Peter Cole, *The Dream of the Poem*, (Princeton University Press, NJ 2007) page 181-182

HaRambam's Introduction to the Mishneh Torah

HaRambam's introduction to his great code of Jewish law, the Mishneh Torah, speaks for itself. He had two goals in mind when he penned the words below. He wanted to make it abundantly clear that the rulings and teachings he will be presenting in his Mishneh Torah are ruling that are directly linked to Moshe Rabbenu and Ma'amad Har Sinai, the revelation at Sinai. He writes: "We can therefore conclude[31] that they all received [their teachings] from the Lord God of Israel." His second goal in writing this introduction is to reaffirm the absolute halakhic and legal authority of the Talmud.

The Talmud writes HaRambam was accepted by all of Israel, and it is therefore the final authority in all matters of Jewish law. All later codes and decisions are binding only insofar as they derive their rulings, ethics, values, and worldviews directly from the Talmud. As I wrote earlier in the previous chapter the rabbis of the Talmud sought to create a society based on law, reason, and an optimistic passion to make the world a better place. The authority of the Mishneh Torah and all of HaRambam's legal and philosophical output is therefore based on its direct link to the Babylonian and Jerusalem Talmud.

The Following are HaRambam's words:

Research of the thousands of Geniza Manuscripts

[31] Literally "we find."

Translated by Yamin Levy

> Therefore, I will not be ashamed—
> when I reflect on all Your commandments.
> Psalms 119:6

All the mitzvoth[32] that were given to Moshe at Sinai were given together with their interpretation, as it is written, "And I will give you the Tablets of Stone, and the Torah, and the mitzvah" (Shemoth 24:12). "Torah" is the Written Law and "mitzvah" is its interpretation: We were commanded to fulfill the Torah, according to the mitzvoth. And this mitzvah is what is called the Oral Law.[33]

The whole of the Law was written down by Moshe Our Teacher before he died, in his own hand. He gave a scroll of the Law to each tribe; and he put another scroll in the Ark for a witness, as it is written, "Take this book of the Law, and put it by the side of the Ark of the Covenant of the Lord your God, that it may be there as a witness" (Devarim 31:26).

The mitzvah, which is the interpretation of the Torah – he did not write it down, but taught it orally to the elders, to Yehoshua, and to all the rest of Israel, as it is written, "All this which I command you, that shall you will observe to do . . ." (Devarim 13:1). For this reason, it is called the Oral Law.

Although the Oral Law was not written down, Moshe Our Teacher taught all of it in his court to the seventy elders and Elazar,[34] Pinchas,[35] and Yehoshua;[36] all three received it from Moshe. And to his student Yehoshua, Moshe Our Teacher passed on the Oral Law and ordered him concerning it. And so throughout his life Yehoshua taught it orally.

---

[32] Usually translated as commandment.

[33] Oral law as opposed to the written law; in Hebrew, Torah SheBe'al Peh versus Torah SheBichtav.

[34] Elazar was Aharon's son and heir to the priesthood.

[35] Elazar's son.

[36] His trusted student and future leader of the Jewish people.

Many elders received it from Yehoshua, and Eli received it from the elders and from Pinchas; Shemuel received it from Eli and his court, and David received it from Shemuel and his court. Ahiyah the Shilonite was among those who had come out of Egypt and was a Levite and had heard it from Moshe,[37] but was young in Moshe's time, and he received it from David and his court.

Eliyahu received it from Ahiyah the Shilonite and his court, Elisha received it from Eliyahu and his court, Yehoyada the Priest received it from Elisha and his court, Zecharyahu received it from Yehoyada and his court, Hoshea received it from Zecharyah and his court, Amos received it from Hoshea and his court, Yeshayahu received it from Amos and his court, Michah received it from Yeshayah and his court, Yoel received it from Michah and his court, Nahum received it from Yoel and his court, Havaqquq received it from Nahum and his court, Tsefanyah received it from Havaqquq and his court, Yirmiyah received it from Tsefanyah and his court, Baruch son of Neriyah received it from Yirmiyah and his court, and Ezra and his court received it from Baruch and his court.

Ezra's court is called the Men of the Great Assembly, and they were Haggai, Zecharyah, and Mal'achi, and Daniel, Hananyah, Mishael, and Azaryah, and Nehemyah son of Hachalyah, and Mordechai, and Zerubavel; and many other sages were with them, numbering altogether one hundred twenty elders. The last of them was Shimon the Righteous, who was included among the one hundred twenty, and received the Oral Law from all of them; he was High Priest after Ezra.

Antignos of Socho and his court received it from Shimon the Righteous and his court, Yosef son of Yoezer of Tseredah and Yosef son of Yohanan of Jerusalem and their courts received it from Antignos and his court, Yehoshua son of Perahyah and Nittai the Arbelite and their court received it from

---

[37] As mentioned in I Kings chapter 11. He lived a very long time as recorded in TB Baba Batra 121b.

Yosef and their court, Yehudah son of Tabbai and Shimon son of Shatah and their court received it from Yehoshua and Nittai and their court. Shemayah and Avtalyon, righteous converts, and their court received it from Yehudah and Shimon and their court. Hillel and Shammai and their court received it from Shemayah and Avtalyon and their court, and Rabban Yohanan son of Zakkai and Rabban Shimon the son of Hillel received it from Hillel and his court.

Rabban Yohanan son of Zakkai had five students, and they were the greatest among the sages who received it from him. They were Ribbi Eliezer the Great, Ribbi Yehoshua, Ribbi Yose the Priest, Ribbi Shimon son of Netanel, and Ribbi Elazar son of Arach. Rabbi Akiva son of Yosef received it from Ribbi Eliezer the Great, and his father. Yosef (Rabbi Akiva's father) was a righteous convert.[38] Ribbi Yishmael and Ribbi Meir, the son of a righteous convert,[39] received it from Rabbi Akiva. Ribbi Meir and his colleagues also received it from Ribbi Yishmael.

Ribbi Meir's colleagues were Ribbi Yehudah, Ribbi Yose, Ribbi Shimon, Ribbi Nehemiah, Ribbi Elazar son of Shammua, Ribbi Yohanan the sandal maker, Shimon son of Azzai, and Ribbi Hanania son of Teradyon. Rabbi Akiva's colleagues also received it from Ribbi Eliezer the Great; and Ribbi Akiva's colleagues were Ribbi Tarfon, the teacher of Ribbi Yose the Galilean, Ribbi Shimon son of Elazar, and Ribbi Yohanan son of Nuri.

Rabban Gamliel the Elder received it from his father, Rabban Shimon son of Hillel; his son, Rabban Shimon, received it from him; his son, Rabban Gamliel, received it from him; and his son, Rabban Shimon, received it from him. Ribbi Yehudah son of Rabban Shimon is called Our Holy Teacher, and he received it from his father, and from Ribbi Elazar son of Shammua, and from Ribbi Shimon, his colleague.

---

[38] Yosef the father of the great Rabbi Akiva was a convert. HaRambam informs his readers of this fact to demonstrate that converts to Israel can produce great leaders and luminaries such as Rabbi Akiva.

[39] See note 26

Our Holy Teacher[40] wrote the Mishnah. From the time of Moshe until Our Holy Teacher, no one had written a work from which the Oral Law was publicly taught. Rather, in each generation, the head of the court or the prophet of the time wrote down for his private use notes on the traditions he had heard from his teachers, but he taught in public from memory.

Similarly, each individual wrote down, according to his ability, parts of the explanation of the Torah and of its laws that he had heard, as well as the new matters that developed in each generation, which had not been received by tradition, but had been deduced by applying the Thirteen Principles for Interpreting the Torah, and had been agreed upon by the Great Rabbinical Court. Such had always been done, until the time of Our Holy Teacher.[41]

He gathered together all the traditions, all the enactments, and all the explanations and interpretations that had been heard from Moshe Our Teacher or had been deduced by the courts of all the generations in all matters of the Torah; and he wrote the Book of the Mishnah from all of them. He taught it in public, and it became known to all Israel, and everyone wrote it down, and he taught it everywhere, so that the Oral Law would not be forgotten by Israel.

Why did Our Holy Teacher do so, rather than not leave the matter as it had been? Because he saw that the students were becoming fewer and fewer, calamities were continually happening, the wicked government[42] was extending its domain and increasing in power, and the Israelites were wandering and reaching remote places. He therefore wrote a work to serve as a handbook for all, so that it could be rapidly studied and would not be forgotten. Throughout his life, he and his court[43] con-

---

[40] Rabbi Yehudah HaNasi (135-217 C.E.).

[41] According to HaRambam these thirteen principles of interpretation were received by Moshe Rabbenu at Sinai. See Introduction to HaRambam's commentary on the Mishna.

[42] Of Rome.

tinued giving public instruction in the Mishna.

These are the greatest sages who were in Our Holy Teacher's court and who received their teaching from him: his sons Shimon and Gamliel, Ribbi Afes, Ribbi Hanania son of Hama, Ribbi Hiyya, Rav, Ribbi Yannai, bar Kappara, Shemuel, Ribbi Yohanan, and Ribbi Hoshaya. These were the greatest who received it from him, and besides them there were thousands and myriads of other sages.

Although these eleven received it from Our Holy Teacher and attended his house of study, Ribbi Yohanan was young at the time, and later was a student of Ribbi Yannai and received Torah from him. Rav also received it from Ribbi Yannai, and Shemuel received it from Ribbi Hanania son of Hama.

Rav wrote the Sifra and the Sifre to explain and expound the principles of the Mishna, and Ribbi Hiyya wrote the Tosefta to explain the text of the Mishnah. So too, Ribbi Hoshayah and bar Kappara wrote alternative oral traditions to explain the text of the Mishna. Ribbi Yohanan wrote the Jerusalem Talmud in the Land of Israel about three hundred years after the destruction of the Temple.

Among the greatest sages who received the tradition from Rav and Shemuel were Rav Huna, Rav Yehudah, Rav Nahman, and Rav Kahana; and among the greatest sages who received from Ribbi Yohanan were Rabbah the grandson of Hanah, Ribbi Ame, Ribbi Ase, Rav Dime, and Rav Avin.

Among the sages who received from Rav Huna and Rav Yehudah were Rabbah and Rav Yosef. And among the sages who received from Rabbah and Rav Yosef were Abaye and Rabba; both of them received from Rav Nahman as well. Among the sages who received from Rabba were Rav Ashe and Rabbina; and Mar son of Rav Ashe received from his father and from Rabbina.

Thus, from Rav Ashe back to Moshe Our Teacher, there

---

[43] Supreme court of Israel. This is why the Mishna is authoritative.

were forty generations of great men; that is to say:
(1) Rav Ashe, (2) from Rabba, (3) from Rabbah, (4) from Rav Huna, (5) from Ribbi Yohanan, Rav, and Shemuel, (6) from Our Holy Teacher, (7) from his father, Rabban Shimon, (8) from his father, Rabban Gamliel, (9) from his father, Rabban Shimon, (10) from his father, Rabban Gamliel the Elder, (11) from his father, Rabban Shimon, (12) from his father, Hillel, and Shammai, (13) from Shemayah and Avtalyon, (14) from Yehudah and Shimon, (15) from Yehoshua and Nittai, (16) from Yosef and Yosef, (17) from Antignos, (18) from Shimon the Righteous, (19) from Ezra, (20) from Baruch, (21) from Yirmiyah, (22) from Tsefanyah, (23) from Havakuk, (24) from Nahum, (25) from Yoel, (26) from Michah, (27) from Yeshayah, (28) from Amos, (29) from Hoshea, (30) from Zecharyah, (31) from Yehoyada, (32) from Elisha, (33) from Eliyahu, (34) from Ahiyah, (35) from David, (36) from Shemuel, (37) from Eli, (38) from Pinchas, (39) from Yehoshua, (40) from Moshe Our Teacher, who received it from the "mouth of Glory."[44]

We can therefore conclude[45] that they all received [their teachings] from the Lord God of Israel.[46]
All of the sages mentioned here were the great men of their generations. Some of them were heads of academies, some were exilarches, and some were members of great Sanhedrin. Besides them in every generation there were thousands and myriads who learned from them and with them.

Rabbina and Rav Ashe were the last of the [authoritative] sages of the Talmud; it was Rav Ashe who wrote the Babylo-

---

[44] God.

[45] Literally "we find."

[46] HaRambam makes this assertion based on the Mishna in Rosh Hashanah 2:9 where Rabbi Dosa ben Harkinas comforts Rabbi Yehoshua and tells him they must all follow the ruling of Rabban Gamliel the Head of the Sanhedrin because if they question his ruling they are in fact questioning the rulings of all previous courts of Israel.

nian Talmud in the Land of Babylon, about a hundred years after Ribbi Yohanan wrote the Jerusalem Talmud.

The subject matter of the two Talmuds is the interpretation of the text of the Mishna and explanation of its depths and the matters that developed in the various courts from the time of Our Holy Teacher until the writing of the Talmud. From the two Talmuds, and from the Tosefta, and from the Sifra and from the Sifre, and from the Toseftot – from them all – are to be found what is forbidden and what is permitted, what is unclean and what is clean, what is liable and what is exempt, and what is fit for use and what is unfit for use, according to the unbroken oral tradition from Moshe as received from Sinai.

From theses sources we also find the restrictive legislations enacted by the sages and prophets in each generation, to serve as a protecting fence around the Law, as learned from Moshe in the interpretation of "you shall keep My preventive measure" (Vayikra 18:30), which means take preventive measures to preserve My preventive measures.

From them are found the customs and affirmative legislations that were enacted or brought into use during the various generations, as the court of each generation saw fit. It is forbidden to deviate from them, as it is written, "You shall not turn aside from whatever they shall declare unto you, neither to the right nor to the left" (see Devarim 17:11).

Additionally, we find extraordinary interpretative judgments and rules that were not received from Moshe, but that the Great Rabbinical Court of its generation deduced by applying the principles for interpreting the Torah that the elders judged to be appropriate, and decided that such shall be the Law. All of this, from the time of Moshe to his own time, Rav Ashe wrote in the Talmud.

The Mishna sages wrote other works to interpret the words of the Torah: Ribbi Hoshayah, a student of Our Holy Teacher, wrote an explanation of the Book of Bereshit. Ribbi Yishmael wrote a commentary [on the Biblical text] from the beginning of the Book of Shemoth to the end of the Torah, which is called the Mechilta; and Rabbi Akiva also wrote a Mechilta. Other sages later wrote collections of sermonic materials on the Tanakh. All of these were written before the Babylonian Talmud.

Rabbina and Rav Ashe and their colleagues were then the last of the great sages of Israel who wrote down the Oral Law, enacted restrictive legislations, enacted affirmative legislations, and enacted binding customs; and their legislations and customs gained universal acceptance among the people of Israel in all of the places where they settled.

After the court of Rav Ashe, who wrote the Talmud in the time of his son and completed it – the people of Israel were scattered throughout the world most exceedingly and reached the most remote parts and distant isles. Armed struggle became prevalent in the world, and the public ways became clogged with armies. The study of the Torah declined, and the people of Israel ceased to gather in places of study in their multitudes and myriads as they had before.

Rather a few individuals gathered. They were the remnant whom the Lord calls in each city and in each town, and occupied themselves with the Torah, understood all the works of the sages, and knew from them what the correct way of the Law is.

The enacted legislations or enacted customs of the courts that were established in any town after the time of the Talmud for the town's residents or for several towns' residents. This did not gain the acceptance of all Israel, because of the remoteness of their settlements. The difficulties of travel, and because the members of the court of any particular town were just individuals, and the Great Rabbinical Court of seventy members had ceased to exist several years before the writing of the Talmud.[47]

Therefore, a town's residents are not forced to observe the

---

[47] Only the Sanhedrin, the great rabbinical court of seventy-one, can enact rules and customs authoritatively for all of Israel. The local courts described here had limited local authority but could not legislate for other communities.

customs of another town, nor is one court told to enact the restrictive legislations of another court in its town. So too, if one of the Geonim understood that the correct way of the Law was such and such, and it became clear to another court afterwards that this was not the correct way of the Law written in the Talmud, the earlier court is not to be obeyed, but rather what seems more correct, whether earlier or later.

These matters apply to rulings, enactments, and customs that arose after the Talmud was written. But whatever is in the Babylonian Talmud is binding on all of the people of Israel;[48] and every city and town is forced to observe all the customs observed by the Talmud's sages and to enact their restrictive legislations and to observe their positive legislations.

All those matters in the Talmud received the assent of all of Israel, and those sages who enacted the positive and negative legislations, enacted binding customs, ruled the rulings, and found that a certain understanding of the Law was correct constituted all of Israel's sages, or most of them, and it was they who received the traditions of the Oral Law concerning the fundamentals of the whole Law in unbroken succession back to Moshe Our Teacher.

All the sages who arose after the writing of the Talmud, who studied it deeply, and who became famous for their wisdom are called the Geonim. All those Geonim who arose in the Land of Israel, in the Land of Babylon, in Spain, and in France, taught the way of the Talmud, clarified its obscurities, and explained its various topics, for its way is exceedingly profound. Furthermore, it is written in Aramaic mixed with other languages for that language had been clearly understood by all in Babylon, at the time when it was written. However in other places as well as in Babylon in the time of the Geonim, no one understood that language until he was taught it.

Many questions were asked of each Gaon of the time by the people of various cities, to comment on difficult matters in the

---

[48] Because it was ratified by the Sanhedrin.

Talmud, and they answered according to their wisdom. Those who had asked the questions collected the answers and made them into books for study. The Geonim in every generation also wrote works to explain the Talmud. Some of them commented on a few particular laws, some of them commented on particular chapters that presented difficulties in their time, and some of them commented on Tractates or Orders.

They also wrote collections of settled laws as to what is forbidden and permitted, who is liable and exempt, according to the needs of the time, so that they could be easily learned by one who is not able to fathom the depths of the Talmud. That is the work of the Lord that all the Geonim of Israel did, from the time the Talmud was written to the present day, which is 1108 years from the Destruction of the Temple [which is 4937 years from Creation, or 1177 C.E.].

In our time, severe troubles come one after another, and all are in distress. The wisdom of our sages has disappeared, and the understanding of our discerning men is hidden. Thus, the commentaries, the responses to questions, and the settled laws that the Geonim wrote, which had once seemed clear, have in our times become hard to understand, so that only a few properly understand them. And one hardly needs to mention the Talmud itself – the Babylonian Talmud, the Jerusalem Talmud, the Sifra, the Sifre, and the Toseftot – which all require a broad mind, a wise soul, and considerable time, before one can correctly know from them what is forbidden or permitted and the other rules of the Torah.

For this reason, I, **Moshe son of Rabbi Mimon the Sephardi**, found that the current situation is unbearable; and so, relying on the help of the Rock blessed be He, I intently studied all these books, for I saw fit to write what can be determined from all of these works in regard to what is forbidden and permitted, unclean and clean, and the other rules of the Torah: Everything in clear language and terse style, so that the whole Oral Law would become thoroughly known to all, without bringing prob-

A page from HaRambam's handwritten Commentary on the Mishna circa 1160

lems and solutions or differences of view, but rather clear, convincing, and correct statements in accordance with the law drawn from all of these works and commentaries that have appeared from the time of Our Holy Teacher to the present.

This is so that all the rules should be accessible to the small and to the great in the rules of each and every commandment and in the rules of the legislations of the sages and prophets: in short, so that a person should need no other work in the world in the rules of any of the Laws of Israel, but that this work would collect the entire Oral Law, including the positive legislations, the customs, and the negative legislations enacted from the time of Moshe Our Teacher until the writing of the Talmud, as the Geonim interpreted it for us in all of the works of commentary they wrote after the Talmud. Thus, I have called this work the Mishneh Torah [the Complete Restatement of the (Oral) Law], for a person reads the Written Law first and then reads this work, and knows from it the entire Oral Law, without needing to read any other book between them.[49]

I have seen fit to divide this work into groups of laws according to topics, and I divide the groups into chapters dealing with the same topic. I divide each chapter into paragraphs, so that they may be learned by heart.[50]

Among the groups in the various topics, some groups include the detailed laws relating to a single biblical mitzvah when the mitzvah comes with many oral traditions that make up a single topic, and other groups include the detailed laws of many biblical mitzvoth, when all the mitzvoth are on one topic. The organization of this work is according to topics, and is not according to the counting of mitzvoth, as will be clear to one who reads it.

The number of Torah mitzvoth that are obligatory for all generations is 613. Of those, 248 of them are positive commandments, whose mnemonic is the number of parts in the human body while 365 of them are negative commandments, whose mnemonic is the number of days in the solar year.

---

[49] This comment stirred significant controversy.
[50] Fourteen volumes, one thousand chapters.

> If this life's joy only ends in mourning
> and its respite gives way to failure and pain,
> and a person's existence is passing shadow
> suddenly shattered and crushed like an urn,
> What can we hope for apart from the Lord?
> All that we do without him is vain.
>
> — SHELOMO IBN GABIROL

Rabbenu[1] Saadia Gaon bar[2] Yoseph
(882-942 C.E.)

Rabbenu Saadia: The Scholar Who Saved Judaism

RABBI SAADIA GAON BAR YOSEPH can be regarded as the father of the Golden Age of Torah study and Jewish scholarship. His greatness is reflected not only in his many writings that cover a broad spectrum of scholarship, but also in the impact he had on all of Jewry in his lifetime and in future generations.

It was not by chance or by nepotism that Rabbenu Saadia Gaon rose to the helm of the Geonic leadership. In fact, he was very much an outsider, but he exemplified everything the rabbinic sages of the Talmud envisioned in a Torah scholar, communal leader, and national ambassador. He had mastered the entire corpus of Talmudic law and understood how to apply Talmudic law and legal principles into practice. He mastered both Hebrew and Aramaic languages, as well as

---

[1] Rabbenu means Our Rabbi. This is an illustrious way of referring to a rabbinic sage.

[2] Sephardic Jews have traditionally used the Aramaic Bar instead of Ben when writing or stating their patronymic name followed by their father's name.

Arabic. He was an expert grammarian, philologist, mathematician, and scientist. He was also a disciplined philosopher familiar with all the Greek and Muslim writers of his day. He was a man of uncompromising integrity who defended his principles and the honor of Torah. Rav Saadia recognized that wisdom and truth is gleaned from many places. He was the perfect embodiment of the kind of leader the Jewish world needed in transitioning from the world of the Geonim, whose primary task was to anchor the Talmud as the only source of Jewish law and tradition for Jewish continuity, and the world of the emerging *Rishonim*, medievalists who would put Jewish study and Jewish culture in motion.

Under the leadership of Rabbenu Saadia Gaon (hereon Rav Saadia), the Jewish world went from a series of scattered *batei midrash* [study houses] and various communities to a unified, single entity that required constant attention. The Geonim who preceded him administered a relatively closed world and focused their spiritual responsibilities within their own academies. Their sense of obligation towards the more distant Jewish communities was rather passive. Being that the Babylonian Geonate and Southwest Asian Yeshivoth were the most immediate link to the close of the Talmud, it was assumed that they would function as the central authority of the scattered Jewish communities in the diaspora and in Israel. All questions regarding religious and communal matters of governance were decided by the Geonim or the heads of the Babylonian Yeshivoth. The expectation was that the Jewish communities would, in return, financially support these institutions and their endeavors. The relationship between the Babylonian Geonate and the various other Jewish communities could be characterized as more reactive than proactive – that was until Rav Saadia assumed the leadership role of Gaon.

Since his early youth, Rav Saadia saw himself as responsible for the welfare of all Jews, not only those within (and immediately beyond) his geographic purview, but of future generations as well. He expresses this mission in his *Sefer HaGalui*, where he writes:

> God does not leave His nation in any generation without a scholar who instructs and enlightens His people, so that he may counsel

and instruct them so that they improve their condition . . . I am aware regarding myself of the grace that God has bestowed upon me to lead His nation.[3]

This attitude was evident long before Rav Saadia assumed any official leadership position. By the age of twenty, this precocious young man had undertaken the task of bringing about a revival of the Hebrew language by writing the Agron [Ha'Agron]. Ha'Agron, also known by its Judeo-Arabic name *Azul Alsha'ar Al-Aarabni* [The Rudiments of Hebrew Poetry], was his first book published. The word Agron means "thesaurus" according to Rav Saadia.[4] It is a Hebrew-language reference book for poets and *paytanim* [song writers] arranged alphabetically.

In his introduction to Ha'Agron, in beautiful biblical Hebrew Rav Saadia outlines a historical survey of the Hebrew language and the reasons for writing the book. He constantly refers to the Hebrew language as the holy tongue of the Jewish people, "the language of God, angels, and the language of primordial man before the construction of the Tower of Babel which led to the dispersion of nations and languages as recounted in the Torah."[5] Thereafter, writes Rav Saadia, the Hebrew language became the unique heritage of the decedents of Ever, who is identified in the Torah as the progenitor of Avraham, Yitzchak, and Yaakov. Rav Saadia continues by noting how the Jewish people preserved their Hebrew language, despite their many wanderings described in the Torah and in the books of the prophets, until they finally returned to the land of Israel under the leadership of Ezra and Nehemiah. Like Nehemiah the prophet, who worked hard at reviving the Hebrew language (as described in Nehemiah 13:24), the young Rav Saadia saw himself as the one in his generation tasked to revive the Hebrew language.

---

[3] Abraham E. Harkavy, *Fugitive Remnants of the Egron*, 154-155.

[4] In modern day Hebrew, *agron* means database.

[5] Nehemiah Allony, *The Egron: The Book of the Principles of Hebrew Poetry by Rav Sa'adyah Gaon* (Jerusalem 1969), 23. Note the various spellings for Sa'adyah and for Egron. I prefer Saadia and Agron.

HaAgron, of the Holy Tongue, which God chose from all eternity, in which His holy angels ever sanctify Him in their song, and therewith all beings worship Him on High. The whole earth was one language and one speech from the day when God created Adam and conferred wisdom upon him [. . .] until the band of the tempest generation [Tower of Babel] and the land was divided into various languages according to the number of peoples but the Holy Tongue remained in the mouths of the descendants of Ever alone. Because they were truthful in the sight of God and from them issued our forefathers Avraham, Yitzchak, and Yaakov [. . .] Generation after generation it has been our heritage from the time we dwelled in the land of our inheritance given to us through the tender mercies of our Holy One. It was the language used by our kings, the songs of our Levites, the music of our priests, the visions of our prophets until the people of Jerusalem were exiled to Babylonia in the days of Zidkiahu when we began to abandon the Holy Tongue and speak alien languages . . . In the days of Nehemiah, the governor and all his men saw that the people were speaking the language of Ashdod and he was angered and rebuked them and contended with them. And afterwards we were exiled through all the gates of the land and the islands of the sea – there was no nation our outcasts did not reach and in their midst we raised our children to speak foreign languages. [. . .] So it behooves us and all the nation of our Lord, us and our children and our wives and our servants, to enquire and understand and investigate it always, so that it may never depart from us again, for through the Holy Tongue we understand the laws of our Torah, of our Rock which are our very life [. . .] for eternity.

And in the year 902, from the day that vision and prophecy were sealed, [I, Saadia] the collector wrote this book to serve as a source of wisdom for all the people of God and for all those who know the law and the tradition. [. . .] The people of our God will converse in it, in their going out and coming in, in all their occupations, and in their bedrooms and with their children. Never again will the Holy Tongue leave their minds or depart from their hearts, for through it they will know the Torah of God.[6]

We see how the young budding scholar was deeply troubled by the state of the Hebrew language in his generation and took it upon himself to rectify the problem.

Pathway to Leadership

The amount of biographical material about Rav Saadia's life is significantly more than any other Jewish figure of the first millennium. This is indeed a testament to the impression and influence he had on the Jewish people during his lifetime. The historian and Talmudic scholar Professor Robert Brody writes:

> True, much of his life remains unknown, yet compared to our knowledge of his contemporaries, even the most prominent among them, and considering the fact that no organized archives have survived from his day – if indeed any such existed – the amount of information that has come down to us about his life is truly impressive, almost astounding.[7]

Born in 882 C.E. in an Egyptian village called Fayyum, Rav Saadia is often referred to as "the Fayyumite" or as "Al-Dilasi," which is where his parents came from. Rav Saadia traced his ancestry back to Yehudah the son of Yaakov, making him eligible to be king of Israel if the Messiah had arrived. As a young man in Egypt, he focused on his studies, corresponded with the then-renowned theologian Isaac Israeli, and published Ha'Agron. In his late twenties he traveled to Israel, Syria, and Babylonia. In Israel he spent time with the Tiberian Masoretes and schools of Hebrew grammar.

Rav Saadia's scholarship and linguistic abilities were first noticed

---

[6] Allony, *Egron*, 156-159. At a later time in his career Rabbi Saadia writes that he wrote the Agron because he saw how concerned the Muslim leaders were about preserving their Arabic language and he felt the Jews should be as concerned about preserving their Hebrew language. See Allony, 150-153.

[7] Robert Brody, *Sa'adya Gaon*, 25.

when he stepped into the "great Jewish calendar dispute" of 921-923 C.E.[8] While it is evident that he had already achieved a degree of prominence prior to this dispute, his ability to understand both the Palestinian perspective and the Babylonian perspective and make a strong case for the Babylonian position catapulted him into eminence and notoriety. In response to the dispute, he wrote a book called *Sefer Hamo'adim*, in which he took upon himself the role of official spokesperson for the Babylonian scholars. Although the Palestinian rabbis did not accept the proclamations of the Babylonian Rabbinate, the Babylonian position eventually won due in large measure to Rav Saadia's influence.

In 928 C.E. Rav Saadia was appointed Gaon, the title of leadership of the academy of Sura in Babylon, one of the two most famous institutions of Talmudic studies.[9] What makes this appointment quite extraordinary is the fact that Rav Saadia was not raised and educated among the Babylonian schools of Talmudic study. While Rav Saadia's scholarship, literary accomplishment, and proven leadership skills made him a natural candidate for the position, his appointment was a divergence from the accepted tradition of appointing one of their own. The leaders of the academies of Babylonia always selected from amongst their own families of scholars with longstanding relationships with the central academies. Their interests lay exclusively in elucidating the Babylonian Talmud and practical Jewish law [*halakha*]. They had limited knowledge and exposure to communities outside of their own and had no contact with the surrounding Muslim and Christian cultures. In fact, the then exilarch [*reish geluta*] of the Jewish community wrote to one of his leading community members, Nisim

---

[8] In the years 921/922, the Jewish leaders of Palestine, Israel and Babylonia disagreed on how to calculate the Jewish calendar. This led to confusion about when to celebrate the Jewish holy days and for two years Jews in the Near East celebrated their holy days on different dates. This was indeed a major controversy but was forgotten until the late 19th century rediscovery of the Cairo Geniza. Research continues to be done on the nature, scope and aftermath of the controversy.

[9] Prior to Rav Saadia's appointment there was serious thought of closing the doors of the academy of Sura. Due to a variety of circumstances, it had dwindled in size by the early years of the tenth century.

al-Nahrwani, who had advised him to appoint a significantly less impressive candidate for the position of Gaon for:

> Although he [Saadia] is a great man of prodigious wisdom, he fears no one in the world and looks with favor upon no one in the world.[10]

Because he saw himself as the defender of Jewish values and Jewish thought, he never shied away from using his forceful and assertive personality to engage in intra-Jewish polemics. Indeed, Rav Saadia was a fierce leader who was not to be intimidated and was not afraid to stand by his principles. When Rav Saadia refused to endorse one of the exilarch's rulings, a dispute broke out between the two leaders. The community was divided into two factions. The exilarch tried to depose Rav Saadia and Rav Saadia tried to depose the exilarch. Eventually a prominent leader, Bishar ben Aharon, intervened and Rav Saadia and the exilarch were reconciled. Rav Saadia was universally recognized as Gaon and leader of the Babylonian community until he died in 942 C.E.

Robert Brody characterizes Rav Saadia Gaon's career as a communal leader as follows:

> Although the new symbiosis that Saadia created between his roles as defender of traditional Judaism and as head of the academy left a definite mark on the remaining century of Geonic life, no other Gaon, or medieval Jew, for that matter, ever burned with such a sense of mission.[11]

Intellectual Approach

Under Rav Saadia Gaon's leadership, radical intellectual changes took place in the world of the curricula of the Babylonian Geonim, securing a strong Jewish future. Rav Saadia's early exposure to a broad selec-

---

[10] Adolf Neubauer, *Mediaeval Jewish Chronicles and Chronological Notes,* quoted by Brody page 28.
[11] Brody, 31.

tion of intellectual pursuits such as philology, poetry, and philosophy was the impetus to an expanded curriculum of study in academies of Babylon.

Even in areas where the Babylonian academies boasted expertise, Rav Saadia's creative and broad approach expanded their intellectual reach. He successfully introduced the Babylonian scholars to the Talmud Yerushalmi that was edited in Israel at the time, as well as the Palestinian aggadic materials that were unfamiliar to the school of Babylonia. His use of the Talmud Yerushalmi in his *halakhic* works was revolutionary and influenced his successors such as ibn Migash, Alfasi, and HaRambam.

While his predecessors limited their *halakhic* output of responses to questions asked by individuals or communities, Rav Saadia innovated the genre of *halakhic* monographs on various topics. This innovation is not something that can be taken for granted. The Geonim were accustomed to writing responses only to a question or query, whether *halakhic* questions or relating to understanding the Talmud. They had no intention of making the Talmud available to all.[12] Avraham Grossman put forth the idea that the Geonim were elitists who sought to maintain authority by withholding knowledge. He notes:

> Writing a commentary on the sources is by its very nature an activity that speaks of democratization. In other words: rendering the source accessible to the masses.[13]

By choosing who receives a response, the Geonim were safeguarding their status as teachers and authorities of the Talmud – and by withholding the knowledge they possessed (by not writing commentaries and monographs), they perpetuated the knowledge gaps that assured their dominance and compelled communities to turn to them for information. This is what makes Rav Saadia's innovation so dramatic and remarkable: He sought to educate the masses. His

---

[12] This is one of the issues HaRambam had against the Geonate of Babylon. See HaRambam's commentary on Pirkei Avot 4:7

[13] Avraham Grossman, "The Relationship Between the Social Structure and Spiritual Activity of Jewish Communities in the Geonic Period," 266.

monographs were independent documents of Torah study. This innovation was later adopted by some of his successors and led to a fundamental change in the nature and expounding of rabbinic *halakhic* literature.

Rav Saadia ventured into disciplines that were known but not generally cultivated by the scholars of Babylon academies, such as philosophy and biblical exegesis. He is considered the first rabbinic authority to commit to writing works on Jewish philosophy and wrote a commentary on the Torah and on sections of the Neviim and Ketuvim.

Preserving the Authority of the Sages

Rav Saadia Gaon found intellectual and spiritual comfort in the idea that Judaism is a tradition with core values, knowledge, and beliefs handed down by previous schools of scholars and transmitted from one generation to the next. Embracing this concept is especially true with regards to the observance of mitzvoth that are not easily understood or logical. In general, argues Rav Saadia, there are three sources of knowledge universally recognized by people:

1. One's senses
2. One's intuitive intellectual perception
3. One's ability to make logical inferences

To this list he added a fourth source of knowledge:

4. The knowledge transmitted by our prophets and authentic sages through the ages.

Without the fourth source of knowledge, the Torah could not be understood. He lists several examples to illustrate his point. There are Biblical commandments that require clarification, such as the mitzvah of building a sukkah or wearing *tefillin*, that would not make any sense without the rabbinic tradition that dates back to the times of Moshe Rabbenu. With regards to the mitzvah of Sukkah all the Torah says "and you shall dwell in sukkoth for seven days . . ." If not for the tradition, the ancient tradition, passed on from rabbinic authority to rabbinic authroity we would not know what a sukkah is, how it is built and what criteria makes it valid for fulfilling the mitzvah. The same is true of Tefillin and many other biblical commandments.

Furthermore, Rav Saadia notes the Torah speaks of sizes and measurements most of which we would not know if it were not for the details that are provided by the tradition of the sages. Similarly, the commandment to observe the Shabbath requires belief in the tradition that has been passed down and preserved by the sages of the Talmud. The Torah prohibits work; the sages identify the kind of work that is prohibited or permitted. Additionally, commandments such as prayer that are not included in the Torah must be observed by authority of the rabbinic sages of the past. Finally, Rav Saadia notes that the Jewish people's core beliefs about the messianic era and the world-to-come are all based on our belief in the rabbinic tradition that has been preserved through the ages from the time of Moshe Rabbenu.

Halakha [Jewish law] and Jewish religious, spiritual philosophy are transmitted through an unbroken chain that was initially transmitted orally through the prophets and later committed to writing. For Rav Saadia, the sages of the Talmud were not innovators but rather steadfast guardians of an ancient tradition. Even laws that appeared necessary based on historical circumstances, he argues, were in fact ancient laws that were preserved by the prophets and unveiled at their appropriate times.

> And at the completion of a thousand years . . . from the days of Moses, the man of God, at the end of the remaining prophets in the days of Media, when prophecy was sealed in the fortieth year after the construction of the second Bet HaMikdash with few people, when our forefathers saw that the multitude had been dispersed throughout the land and feared lest the speech be forgotten they gathered all the teachings thereof which had been transmitted from

ancient times . . . and called them Mishna. There remained the knowledge which they hoped would be reserved with their occupation of the land of Israel since it belonged to the branches of the law. But we continued to go astray and deviated and were exiled again . . . and fearing lest they be forgotten, the sages gathered them as well and called them Talmud, 500 years after the first time.[14]

For Rav Saadia, the knowledge and wisdom contained in the Talmud is the unbroken link between his generation and the tradition of Moshe Rabbenu. The veracity of its authenticity is a basic understanding of the history of the people of Israel. Some two hundred years later, HaRambam makes the same point but in much greater detail when he lists every Sanhedrin in the chain of transmission from Moshe Rabbenu until the close of the Talmud.[15]

Rav Saadia saw himself as the next link in the historical lineage of the Jewish people and as a preserver of the ancient tradition. He took this role very seriously and wrote a chronological history of the Jewish people in Arabic for his generation's edification. His goal was to reach and educate the masses, not just the students at the Yeshiva. Despite his generally conservative tendencies when it came to placing Jewish law in a historical context, he remained open to embracing the best of the surrounding cultures and never hesitated to admit that there is much that can be learned from scholars and teachers who are not Jewish.

Rav Saadia was driven by one truth only – that the pursuit of knowledge in this world is a means of revealing man's ultimate purpose on earth, which is the love and service of God.

His Philosophical Writings

Rav Saadia is best known for his exquisite work on Jewish philosophy called *Emunot VeDe'ot* [Beliefs and Opinions] which was published in 933 C.E. He is also known for his running commentary of the Ta-

---

[14] Solomon Schechter, *Saadya: Geniza Fragments*, 5.

[15] Introduction to *Mishneh Torah*.

NaKH. Two years earlier, in 931 C.E., he published a commentary on an early esoteric text called *Sefer Yesira* [the Book of Creation].[16]

Rav Saadia argues that *Sefer Yesira* was written by early scholars of Israel based on an ancient oral tradition, as a poetic interpretation of a mystical experience that defies description. In other words it is not an esoteric text but rather a description of an esoteric experience.

Sefer Yesira

His commentary on *Sefer Yesira* is Rav Saadia's attempt to respond to the early proto-kabbalists and mythical-magical interpreters of *Sefer Yesira*. In his commentary, Rav Saadia defends a more rationalist, esoteric tradition and argues that those who see Jewish mysticism as a series of magical, mythical, and irrational string of ideas are misguided and must be silenced.

In his commentary to *Sefer Yesira*, Rav Saadia alludes to the numerous difficulties involved in understanding the creation of the world. Based on a rabbinic teaching that God looked into the Torah and created the world, Rav Saadia notes that God used its letters and numbers, per *Sefer Yesira*, after having created the four elements of fire, air, water, and earth. For him the study of creation is a worthwhile discipline as he writes:

> For although they [the sages] have described this as inaccessible and profound, one must not neglect its study, as philosophy corresponds to what occurred as a result of the acts of the Creator, may he be magnified and exalted, of whom it is said: "He reveals deep things from the darkness, and brings death's shadow to light" (Iyov 12:22), and it behooves them too, to enquire into this as far as they are capable.[17]

---

[16] *Sefer Yesira* itself is shrouded in enigma. Its premise is that God created the world with the twenty-two letters of the Hebrew Alphabet and introduces the idea of *sefirot*, referred to as the ten *sefirot* of "nothingness." The book is full of numerical allusions and references to the human body and corporeality of God.

[17] Yosef Kafikh, *Sefer Yetzirah*.

Rav Saadia argues that the *Sefer Yesira* expresses esoteric and philosophical concepts in non-philosophical terms. He therefore explains that the ten names of God mentioned in *Sefer Yesira* relate to Aristotle's ten categories of existing things. Rav Saadia further links the concept of God's ten names, Aristotle's ten categories and the Ten Commandments that were given at Mount Sinai. This approach is in line with Rav Saadia's goal to bridge the gap between Jewish tradition and the contemporary theories of philosophy of his day.

Emunot VeDe'ot

Two years after the publication of his commentary on *Sefer Yesira*, Rav Saadia published his groundbreaking work called *Emunot VeDe'ot*.[18] The primary goal of this work was to demonstrate that one can indeed believe in the absolute, divinely revealed truths of the Torah alongside the rational truths of the philosophy of his day.

Rav Saadia argues that the study of philosophy is important for two reasons: It deepens one's understanding of the truths transmitted by Torah and the prophets, and it prepares the student to respond to those who seek to introduce doubt in the faith. Both reasons are necessary because the prophetic truths of the Torah are the anchor for all seekers.

One cannot and should not be content solely with the conclusions of prophetic tradition, argues Rav Saadia. God expects us to engage in theoretical speculation, personal study and creative research and not rely only on revelation. He quotes the verse in Yeshayahu as a rhetorical question asking the seeker to engage in speculation:

> Do you not know, have you not heard, has it not been told to you from the beginning? Do you not understand the foundations of the earth?[19]

---

[18] The book is also called *Kit b al-Am n t wa l-I tiq d t Emunot VeDe'ot*, translated by Rabbi Yosef Kafikh as *HaNivchar Be'Emunot VeDe'ot* [The Most Important Elements of Faith and Beliefs, but popularly known as simply Beliefs and Opinions]

[19] Yeshayahu 40:21

Emunot VeDe'ot is divided into ten chapters and an introduction. Each chapter presents a central core principle of Judaism together with an unbiased, rational analysis and defense of that principle. Rav Saadia devotes the first two chapters to refuting all dualistic concepts of God and denying the possibility of corporeality of God. The rest of the book is devoted to the relationship between God and mankind and the purpose of mankind's existence.

He covers the following topics:

1. Unity of God
2. Revelation
3. Divine justice
4. Reward and punishment
5. The soul and death
6. Resurrection of the dead
7. Messianic redemption
8. Life after death
9. The best way to live life
10. Correct and incorrect beliefs

The belief in the absolute unity of God is foundational in early post-Talmudic thought, which was the basis of making it a primary concern for Andalusian Sephardic thought. It is based on the premise that God created the world from nothing, as Rav Saadia writes:

> Our exalted Lord has made it clear to us that all things are created and that He created them ex nihilo, as it is written, "In the beginning God created the heavens and the earth," (Bereshit 1:1) and so forth and it is written, "I am the Lord that creates all things that stretch forth the heavens alone." (Yeshayahu 44:24)[20]

In his discussion about the significance of the mitzvoth, Rav Saadia distinguishes between rational and irrational commandments – what he called *mitzvoth sichliot* [rational commandments] and *mitzvot shimiot* [irrational commandments]. Rational commandments are those mitzvoth that can be deduced by moral intuition but have been

---

[20] Saadia Gaon, *Emunot DeVe'ot*, Kafikh edition (Jerusalem: Sura Press, 1969), 40.

formalized by the Torah, such as the prohibition to commit murder, steal, or bear false testimony, and the requirement to honor one's parents. The non-rational commandments would not be initiated by moral necessity, such as *para aduma* [the service of the red heifer] or *sha'atnez* [combining threads of wool and linen]. God includes them in the Torah to further benefit the one who observes them and thereby refines the individual's relationship with God. He adds, that while counter intuitive, even the non-rational commandments have reasons that benefit mankind.

In these chapters Rav Saadia discusses the nature of prophetic revelation and how the prophet knows that his or her vision is authentic. He writes the prophet can never, under any circumstances, add a mitzvah or negate a mitzvah. If the prophet attempts to change any part of Torah, he is deemed to be a false prophet.

> Because it is clear that the Creator, may He be exalted and magnified, was alone in primordial existence, the creation of the world was an act of goodness and generous kindness on His part ... and His goodness and beneficence are attested in scripture as well as the verse says: "The Lord is good to all and His tender mercies are over all His works" (Tehillim 145:9). And the first of these kindnesses to His creatures is that He brought them into being, that is He created them when they were not in existence, as He said to the chosen ones among them, "Everyone that is called by My name and whom I have created for my glory" (Yeshayahu 43:7). And then He gave them the means through which to attain perfect joy and absolute bliss, as it is written, "You make me to know the path of life; Your presence is fullness of joy, In Your right-hand bliss forever more" (Tehillim 16:2).
>
> Human intelligence reflects upon this and says: He could have given them perfect bliss and eternal happiness without commanding or prohibiting them, and it would even seem as if this kindness of His would have been a greater benefit to them in this way ... And I would say in clarification of this matter just the opposite – making their observance of the commandments the means of attaining eternal goodness is the greatest kindness, as it

stands to reason that one who receives benefit for a deed which he has performed is rewarded twice as much as one who receives a benefit gratuitously.[21]

The Soul and Resurrection

Rav Saadia writes[22] the human soul is created by God and individualized for each person. Rav Saadia does not distinguish between Jew and gentile. All human beings have a "pure soul as pure as the celestial spheres" but it needs a body in order to perform good deeds, grow closer to God, and earn reward in the world-to-come. The soul animates the body, but the human being makes choices that affect the soul. When the physical body dies the soul continues to exist until the time of its resurrection.

Rav Saadia vigorously rejects the idea that there is such a thing as the transmigration of souls. This ancient Egyptian and Greek idea posited that after death the soul of the person migrates to the body of another human or animal. This notion was popular among the Karites and uneducated masses in the Jewish community at the time. The proponents of these ideas were referred to by Rav Saadia as "so-called Jews." This doctrine, writes Rav Saadia, is foreign to Judaism and must be absolutely rejected.

Rav Saadia believed the resurrection of the dead will take place in the messianic era and in the world-to-come. Based on his reading of various biblical passages, he argues that only the children of Israel will enjoy the resurrection of the dead during the messianic era. The resurrection of the rest of humanity will occur in the world-to-come.

The last chapters of *Emunot VeDe'ot* are devoted to the messianic era and the spiritual redemption of the people of Israel. The belief in both these principles are based on the prophetic words in the TaNaKH and on logic. Divine reward is not only given to individuals but also to the nation as a whole.

---

[21] Ibid Kafikh translation, 119.
[22] Ibid, 193-2003

And this nation has already been visited with great and prolonged suffering, and there is no doubt that some of these have been punishments, and some are set as tests, and for each of these two conditions there is a finite span of time and when they come to an end He will of necessity stop punishing those who are deserving and reward those who have been tested.[23]

Redemption is inevitable, according to Rav Saadia. God has a predetermined time when the messianic age will occur, whether or not the Jewish people repent. He engages in calculating the time of redemption based on the verses in the Book of Daniel and describes the various stages of redemption.

It has been shown . . . that the heavens and the earth and all that lies between them were created solely for the sake of man, and this is why God placed man at the center of creation and gave his soul an exalted degree of wisdom and intelligence, and also gave it [the soul] commandments and admonitions so that it might attain eternal life . . . And the souls of created beings that I have known are never tranquil and serene in this world, even if they reach the highest station and this is not due to the nature of the soul, but to its knowledge of a greater world than that of earthly delights, for which it longs and aspires.[24]

Rav Saadia the Biblical Exegete

Rav Saadia is not only the father of Jewish philosophy but also the trailblazer in the genre of biblical exegesis. There is no evidence that the Babylonian sages before Rav Saadia engaged in a systematic commentary of the TaNaKH. As mentioned earlier, Rav Saadia authored the first Hebrew-Arabic dictionary called HaAgron. He wrote two commentaries on the Torah: *Perush HaKatzar* [the short commentary] and *Perush Ha'Arokh* [the long commentary]. The *Perush HaKatzar* is

[23] Ibid, 237-245.
[24] Ibid, 323-324.

essentially an Arabic translation of the Torah with minor comments, while *Perush Ha'Arokh* is a more elaborate commentary on the Torah with linguistics, grammar, *halakha*, and philosophy. Rav Saadia goes out of his way to identify places, nations, objects, and animals based on the geography and science of his times. His commentary is meant to be clear, concise, and logical, based on as precise a literal reading as possible of the TaNaKH.[25]

In his introduction to his shorter commentary, Rav Saadia describes why he wrote the *Perush*:

> My only motivation for composing this work is the request of one of my students, who asked for a book dedicated to the simple meaning of the Torah, without integrating any element of linguistic flourishes, metaphors, synonyms or antonyms . . . . I note that what I have been asked to do has merit so that the reader will understand and comprehend the issues of the Torah – the narrative, the command, the reward in sequence.[26]

In addition to his two commentaries on the Torah Rav Saadia wrote commentaries on the books of Yeshayahu, Tehillim, Mishleh, and Iyov. He assigned names to each of his works.[27] Rav Saadia's ground-breaking commentaries influenced all subsequent commentaries on the TaNaKH.

His goal was to minimize ambiguity. One of the primary goals of Rav Saadia's commentary is to avoid misleading readers into thinking that God can be described in physical terms. For example, when the Torah says that "God went up," he translates it as "and the glory of God went up." Rav Saadia writes that staying clear of describing God in physical terms is a tradition that "has been

---

[25] See *The Mysticism of Andalusia: Exploring HaRambam's Mystical Tradition*, (MHC Press, NY/NJ 2023) Part 2 chapter 3 pages 176- 192

[26] Introduction to Rabbi Saadia Gaon's *Perush HaKatzar*.

[27] The commentary on Yeshayahu is called *The Book of Seeking Perfection of Divine Service as Revealed to the Prophet Yeshayahu*. His commentary on the book of Tehillim is called the *Book of Praise*, while his commentary on the book of Mishle is called the *Book in Search of Wisdom* and on Iyov it's called the *Book of Theodicy*.

handed down by the great scholars of our nations who are trustworthy in matters of faith."[28]

He translates the text in the way it was meant to be understood by the original readers of TaNaKH. For example, when the Torah says, "Hava was the mother of all living things," he makes sure that the reader understands that the Torah means that she is "the mother of all speaking things," to reflect the meaning as the mother of human beings. Rav Saadia was also very concerned about problematic moral issues that may arise when the text is not translated correctly. For example, the Torah says, "God brought plagues upon Pharoah on account of Sarai, Avram's wife" (Bereshit 12:17). He translates this to mean that God informed Pharoah that plagues will befall him if he does not return Sarai to Avram. Rav Saadia was concerned that the Torah should not give the impression that God would punish Pharaoh for a mistake he unknowingly made.

He was not apologetic about adding a letter or even a word for clarity. For example, he translates the words of God to Adam in Bereshit 2:17 where the Torah states, "But of the Tree of Knowledge of good and evil you shall not eat of it, for on the day that you eat of it, you shall surely die." In his short commentary Rav Saadia translates the verse as "Adam will deserve to die" since he does not die after he eats from the Tree of Knowledge.

Rav Saadia was committed to understanding the literal meaning of the biblical text. The only times he would deviate from the *peshat* [literal meaning] of the text was when:

1. One's sensory perception of the world refutes the *peshat*.
2. The intellect or philosophical truth refutes the *peshat*.
3. Verses contradict each other.
4. Rabbinic tradition refutes the *peshat*.
5. **In Pursuit of *Peshat***
6. One of the big misconceptions in the study of TaNaKH is the notion that the pursuit of *peshat* is the pursuit of the simple reading of the text. The study of *peshat* is what distinguishes

---

[28] *Emunot VeDe'ot* 1:9, Kafikh translation.

the Andalusian biblical scholars from the European exegetes. *Peshat* seeks to understand the text in the way the Jewish people who first received the Torah understood it. Being that the Torah was originally given in biblical Hebrew, nothing can or should replace the study of Torah in its original language. Every translation will be an interpretation of sort.

7. A *peshat* approach restricts the meaning of the text to its historical, linguistic, theological, and legal contexts. The text is read and studied in accordance with the grammar and syntax of biblical Hebrew, as well as references and allusions that would have had meaning to the original recipients of the Torah. It is the language and linguistic nuances that would have been familiar to the Israelite people some three thousand years ago that the student of *peshat* must master. The most important commentary on the Torah in pursuit of *peshat* is the Torah itself and the *TaNaKH*. Words, terms, and expressions are defined by the manner they are used throughout the biblical period.

8. Talmudic sages as well as many of the medieval commentaries repeated the idea that when studying Torah, the biblical verse should always be read in its *peshat* – *ein mikra yotzeh midei peshuta*[29] [the biblical text should not deviate from its *peshat*]. The assumption among the Geonim and the Andalusian medieval commentators is that God's word finds its fullest expression in the *peshat*, and therefore the student of TaNaKh must initially pursue and master the *peshat* meaning of the text. Rabbi Saadia Gaon set an important precedent when he stated that the pursuit of *peshat* takes precedence over the Midrashic understanding of a text.[30]

His Poetry

Like many of the Hebrew linguists of Babylonia and the Iberian Peninsula, Rav Saadia was a soulful poet, yet he remained an intellec-

---

[29] TB Shabbath 63a, Yevamoth 11b.
[30] *Otzar HaGeonim Berakhot*, 91-92

tually sound and philosophically precise poet. He avoided poetic imagery that may lead his readers to believe that God has a body or that the soul transmigrates. One of his most remarkable poems lists the six hundred and thirteen commandments. While he did not originate the genre of putting all the six hundred and thirteen commandments into poetic form, he alludes to all the mitzvoth by grouping them as branches of the Ten Commandments. For example, in the passage below he includes in the prohibition of the third of the Ten Commandments [not to take God's name in vain] all mitzvoth associated with speech and language:

> You shall not take in vain the greatness of the Name,
> mightier and more hallowed than any god
> Lest you defile and pronounce it, defile it in dismay
> In saying what you will and will not do, fail not to execute
>   your speech
> I counsel you: keep the King's command,
> and that regard in the oath of God (Kohelet 8:2)
> Make speech virtuous, pursue justice, from bribery desist
> Lest you commit iniquity and pervert the law,
> for I will search you out from hair to fingertips,
> My seers have found me said, be not respecters of persons,
>   commands our exalted Lord
> That respects not the person of princes, not regards the rich man
>   more than the poor.[31]

Another beautiful poem called *Barchi Nafshi* [My Soul Blesses the Lord] is an expansion of the first four verses of Tehillim 104:

> Bless You, great and strong One, and render glory and praise
>   forever.
> To the great and strong One exalted on high forever.
> Bless you created being with an end to your allotted days, and
>   by time encumbered,
> The Creator of all creation, without end and years without
>   number

---

[31] Simcha Assaf, *Misifrut Hageonim, Rav Sa'adia Gaon Siddur* (Jerusalem, 1933), 199.

Bless you O lady who rules the body but who none may rule or restrict
The Almighty who rules alone . . . to gather and sift
Bless You who rises above all works of men while they study You
He who rises above the earth and the sphere of heavens that with His word came to be.
Bless You who fills the body and by whom its greed is stilled
He who fills heaven and earth and cannot be contained even by many such as they.[32]

Rav Saadia's poetry was characterized by its exacting meter, philosophic themes and content, allusions to rabbinic writings, and his command of the biblical text. He loved writing long and running poetry that one senses could go on forever.

Sefer HaGalui

Later in his life Rav Saadia revisited the dispute between him and David ben Zakai, the exilarch who had appointed him Gaon. He felt that despite his illustrious career as Gaon and *halakhic* authority, his reputation had been damaged by the controversy and so he decided to write what he called an open letter to the entire Jewish world. In Hebrew the book is called *Sefer HaGalui* [the Open Book]. The *Sefer HaGalui* was written in a highly elevated Hebrew style – written in verses with biblical cantillation marks. Opponents of Rav Saadia leveled harsh criticism of the book and so he responded by writing a second edition in Judeo-Arabic.

The second edition not only covers his perspective of the controversy with David ben Zakai but also includes other subjects that he considered relevant to his greater goal of preserving Jewish faith and thought. The book is divided into seven sections. In the introduction, before describing the nature of the controversy and responding to his detractors, he describes the importance of wisdom and the qualities

[32] Menachem Zulay, *Sa'adia*, 111-112.

Handwritten letter dated 922 about the calendar controversy

of those who have earned it and those who have not. Interestingly, Rav Saadia defends a section in the book where he praises himself. He gives two reasons: He felt it was important to list his accomplishments so that his detractors realize who they are criticizing. His second reason is that it is important for readers who did not know him to learn who he was.

Final Thoughts on Rabbi Saadia Gaon bar Yoseph

As Rav Saadia wrote, every generation is sent their leader to preserve their tradition and inspire subsequent generations. There is no doubt that he was his generation's leader. Rav Saadia's extraordinary intellect, his forceful personality, uncompromising integrity, and deep-felt passion for Torah, for the Jewish people, and for God left a mark on subsequent generations of Jewish scholarship, especially the Jewish rabbinic scholars of South Western Asia, Central Asia and Andalusia. His literary contributions, his philosophical writings, and his *halakhic* works represent a significant leap forward from the traditional scholarly activities of those who preceded him. He elevated the platform of Jewish studies by engaging in biblical exegesis, philosophic discourse, theology, and polemics. He defended rabbinic Judaism with great vigor against internal and external critics placing the Babylonian Talmud at the center of Jewish law, Jewish thought, and Jewish culture.

All subsequent Jewish literary output must be measured against Rav Saadia's influence.

> What's familiar is sometimes distanced,
> and the distanced sometimes brought near—
> and the cavalier rider in fetlock-deep water
> who falls finds it up to his ears.
>
> SHEMUEL IBN NAGRELA

The Last Geonim

Rabbi Sherira bar Hanina Gaon
(906-1006 C.E.)
and his son
Rabbi Hai bar Sherira Gaon
(939-1038 C.E.)

BOTH RABBI SHERIRA GAON and his son Rabbi Hai Gaon were blessed with unusual longevity. They both lived into their late nineties. According to some records Rabbi Sherira Gaon died in his hundredth year of life. The medieval historian Rabbi Avraham ibn Daud writes:

> Rabbi Sherira Gaon lived a very long life, in fact for about one hundred years. When he saw that his life was prolonged and that his son Rabbi Hai was worthy of being head of the academy, he stepped down in favor of his son.[1]

Rabbi Sherira Gaon was the descendent of prominent families on both his mother's and father's sides of the family. He writes that he is a descendent of exilarches, but his grandfather Rabbi Yehuda gave up the exilarchic status in favor of the Geonate because he felt the ex-

---

[1] Abraham ibn Daud, *Sefer Ha-Qabbalah, The Book of Tradition*, translation and annotated by Gerson D. Cohen, 58 (Philadelphia: JPS Press, 1967).

ilarches were not executing their responsibilities ethically.[2]

Rav Sherira Gaon was the son of Rabbi Hanina and the grandson of Rabbi Yehuda, both Geonim who lived during the golden age of the Geonate. They headed the Academy of Pumpedita, near modern day Falluja, Iraq. Jewish history remembers them as two of the most illustrious Geonim.

Rav Sherira Gaon also enjoyed his share of fame and notoriety. He is most famous for the short book called *Iggeret Rav Sherira Gaon* [Epistle of Rav Sherira Gaon], which is a comprehensive historical record of the composition of the Talmud. Rav Hai Gaon literary legacy is comprised of his many monographs and responsa on *halakhic* issues.

Both Sherira Gaon and his son Hai were victims of the Caliph's anti-Jewish policies and spent one year in prison and had their properties confiscated in 997-998 C.E. This experience did not deter either of them from continuing their communal service on behalf of the Jewish people. Shortly after their experience with the law, Rav Sherira appointed his son to the position of Gaon. His installation was greeted with great enthusiasm by Jewish communities throughout the diaspora, including the Jews of Andalusia. On the Shabbath following Rav Hai's appointment, the Jews of Babylon read the Torah portion that describes Moshe Rabbenu appointing Yehoshua as his successor and the prophetic portion where King David appoints Solomon as his successor. Ibn Daud writes about Rav Hai:

> Of the Geonim before him there was none like him, and he was the last of the geonim. Among the geonim Rav Hai was what Moses had been among the prophets. He was of the house of King David, of the royal line, of the descendants of Zerubbabel the son of Shealtiel and the princes of the exilarch who came after him. I have seen his seal affixed to documents which he issued, and a lion was engraved in it just as there had been a lion engraved on the pennant of the kings of Judah.[3]

---

[2] *Igeret Rav Sherira Gaon*, edited by Benjamin Lewin, 92-93 (Jerusalem: Makor, 1972).

[3] Daud, *Sefer Ha-Qabbalah*, translated by Cohen, 59.

Rav Hai Gaon ascended to the post as head of the Academy of Pumpedita in the year 968 C.E. Many of his responsa have been preserved. His primary literary activity was limited to Talmudic topics written in Hebrew, Aramaic, or Arabic depending on his correspondent. He was very exacting in his rulings and often included elaborate clarifications of his thinking. For example, he notes how the term mitzvah is equivocal and used in different ways throughout the Talmud. The sages of the Talmud sometimes use the term to refer to a commandment that may not be broken, while at other times they use it more loosely, when referring to a practice that is highly recommended by the sages but may be disregarded without fear of punishment.[4]

Rav Sherira Gaon was known to be a first-rate mystic but was vehemently against those texts and teachers who were careless about ascribing corporeality to God.[5] Although he studied and commented on aggadah, he was opposed to all forms of magic, superstitions, and sorcery.[6]

Iggeret Rav Sherira Gaon [Epistle of Sherira Gaon]

Despite being referred to as an epistle, *Iggeret Rav Sherira Gaon* [Epistle of Rabbi Sherira Gaon] is really a short book and is quite remarkable. It is considered one of, if not, the most important historical works produced by the Geonim of Babylonia. It addresses several questions about the literary history of the Mishna and the nature and history of both the Talmud Bavli and Talmud Yerushalmi. The book is a response to the questioner, Rabbi Nissim ben Yaacov ibn Shahin on behalf of the scholars of Qayrawan [present day Tunisia], who also wanted to know the nature and history of the close of the Talmud and the post Talmudic schools that preceded the Geonim. Professor Robert Brody notes how "the nature of the questions reflect the intellectual

---

[4] *Teshubot Ge'one Mizrah u-Ma'arab*, no. 141 in Bet Talmud volume iv. 351.

[5] *Shaare Teshuva*, No. 122.

[6] Introduction to *Megillat Setarim*.

breadth and curiosity which characterized the scholarly community of Qayrawan."[7]

Rav Sherira Gaon begins this letter/book by describing the origins of the Babylonian Talmud, "We have seen fit to explain the roots of the matter, and how the leadership of Israel was organized previously."[8] This letter is one of the first of its kind in terms of recording the history of the Talmudic sages. As was mentioned earlier, Rav Saadia found it necessary to create a chronology of rabbinic scholars to affirm the legitimate legacy of the oral law.[9] Simlarly Rav Sherira Gaon clearly and lucidly lays out the history of Jewish law through the rabbis of Sura and Pumpedita. He sheds light on obscure periods in Jewish history, especially the period of the *Savora'im*, of which we know very little other than what is written in his letter/book. Unlike Rav Saadia's presentation his historical account also includes periods of persecution.

In a parallel letter also written to the scholars of Qayrawan, Rav Sherira explains the various titles used by the sages of the Talmud such as "Rabban," "Rabbi," "Rav," and "Mar," and why some sages had no titles at all.

Although Rav Sherira used various sources in composing the letter and outlined the literary history of the Mishna, Tosefta, and Talmud, his primary source is the Talmud itself. His command of the material is remarkable. He also made use of various non-Talmudic historical sources, both written and oral. He often speaks of knowledge that is well known to everyone.

In a letter to the Jewish community of Fostat, Rabbi Sherira Gaon writes:

And if you are greatly learned then undoubtedly there are ques-

---

[7] Robert Brody, "Epistle of Sherira Gaon" in *Rabbinic Texts and the History of Late Roman Palestine*, edited by Martin Goodman and Philip Alexander (London: British Academy of Scholarship, 2011).

[8] Ibid.

[9] This exercise was fully developed by HaRambam (1138-1204 C.E.) in his introduction to the *Mishneh Torah*, about 150 years after Rav Sherira Gaon lived.

tions and doubts among you . . . You should know that the Torah is not taught other than by an authentic rabbi.[10]

For Rav Sherira Gaon, Torah is exclusively transmitted according to the hierarchical relationship between teacher and student – rabbi and disciple. In another letter Rav Sherira makes a bold statement that the Babylonian academies of Torah function as a surrogate for the Sanhedrin [supreme court] of Israel.[11]

> Since even though Torah study flourishes in other places, the four cubits of *halakha* are here. And the Academy replaces the Sanhedrin, and its heads are in place of Moshe Rabbenu and the rulings of the Sanhedrin are here and hence issued.[12]

Rav Hai Gaon

The name Hai is pronounced Hay and is a derivation of the name Hayyim or Hiyya, which means life. Rav Hai Gaon, as was mentioned earlier, is a fourth generation Gaon in a lineage of Geonim. With such lineage and having been steeped in the traditions and politics of the Babylonian Academies, Rav Hai assumed his post with an aura of command and authority. Marrying the daughter of Rabbi Shemuel ben Hofni, Gaon of Sura, further ratified his uncontested legitimacy and authority.

From a young age Rav Hai helped his father write *halakhic* rulings, deal with communal issues, and train students. He was appointed *Av Bet Din* [the head of the court] by his father in 985 C.E. He assumed the position of Gaon some fifteen years later. He was instrumental in helping his father reestablish the Academy of Pumpedita as a center of Torah learning and authority in the Jewish world.

---

[10] Cited by Moshe Gil, *In the Kingdom of Ishmael* (Tel Aviv: Tel Aviv University Press, 1997), 2:77.

[11] HaRambam categorically rejected this premise.

[12] Ibid, 73.

During his tenure, unlike previous generations, the Academy was financially solvent, and no political controversies are reported. This gave Rav Hai the opportunity to devote his efforts and skills to the needs of the Academy, to study, to the dissemination of Torah responsa, and to fostering close relationships with communities beyond the borders of Babylonia. He developed especially close ties with the communities of North Africa, Egypt, and Spain. He even managed to maintain close relations with the generally hostile community in Israel. Under his leadership, the Academy of Pumpedita thrived and recruited thousands of students from all over Iraq and the many communities mentioned above under its religious spiritual influence, in addition to Italy and Israel. Rabbi Shemuel HaNagid (993-1056 C.E.) of Southern Spain poetically noted how Rav Hai would heap attention and care upon his students as if they were the son he himself did not have.

He was a prolific writer of numerous responsa on various religious issues that have, thankfully, been preserved. Despite his longevity we have very little biographical information about Rav Hai's life. It is not surprising, however, that his activity as the head of the Academy and as a Jewish religious leader can be depicted with fairly accurate detail. History has preserved a portrait of Rav Hai through his religious, spiritual, and communal leadership and impact. His literary and halakhic output was extensive and relevant. His impact especially on the early North African and Spanish schools is evidenced by the fact that whenever they wrote "the Gaon" they were referring to Rav Hai Gaon.[13]

Rav Hai's legacy and religious influence is measured by the vast number of responsa he published to questions asked of him by rabbis and leaders of countless communities. The questions he dealt with covered a wide range of topics including all aspects of Jewish religious and civil law, requests for clarifications on Talmudic texts, and advice on communal appointments and administrative disputes. There are close to fourteen hundred responsa penned by Rav Hai Gaon. He is quoted by most post-Geonic scholars, especially those of North Africa and Spain.

---

[13] Tsvi Groner, *The Legal Methodology of Rav Hai Gaon*, 124-126.

His most important *halakhic* contributions, however, are in the form of monographs. His most famous monograph is the Treatise on Purchase and Sale, originally written in Arabic and later translated into Hebrew as *HaMekach VeHaMemkar*. A second important *halakhic* monograph is on the laws of oaths; he organizes and explains the many legal details and aspects of the laws of courtroom oaths. Rav Hai also wrote commentaries on portions of many Talmudic tractates.

Rav Hai saw himself as the final arbiter on many communal practices and customs. He was asked by the community of Qayrawan to explain and justify the customs associated with the blowing of the shofar on Rosh Hashanah, in particular the tradition where the community sits during the first blowing and stands during the blowing while reciting the Amida of Musaf. The also asked for clarification about the number of notes blown on the Shofar during Rosh Hashanah. The questioners were curious as to whether these were innovations of the rabbis of the Talmud. Rav Hai responded:

> The practice by which we fulfill our obligation, and the will of our Creator is established and certain in our hands. That which we do is a legacy which has been deposited, transmitted, and received in tradition from our fathers to sons, for continuous generations in Israel from the days of the prophets until present time. Namely that we blow the shofar while sitting, according to *minhag* [custom], and then while standing during the reading of the Musaf Amida where we again blow three notes three times. This is the current law and it is obvious and widespread throughout all of Israel. Since this is the established practice in our hands and the law transmitted to Moshe at Sinai is that the obligation is thus fulfilled, all differences therein have vanished.[14]

He continues with a courageous and innovative legal principle:

> How do we know at all that we are commanded to blow the shofar on this day? Moreover, regarding the essence of the written law, how are we to know that it is indeed the law of Moshe, that which

[14] Rav Hai, Teshuvot 117.

he wrote through Divine revelation, if not through the mouths of the community of Israel? Behold then, it is these very same mouths which testify as to the veracity of the law of Moshe, which testify equally that by our actions we fulfilled our obligations and that thus it has been transmitted to them by tradition from the mouths of the prophets, as the law transmitted to Moshe at Sinai. Indeed, it is the words of the multitude which stand to prove the authenticity of each Mishna and Gemara. Greater than any other proof is to go out among the people and see how they act "go out and see the custom of the folk" (TB Berakhot 45a). Herein lies the essence of authority. Only afterwards do we examine all that has been discussed in the Mishna or Gemara about the issue. All conclusions derived from them which are compatible with how we are minded are perfectly fine, but if there is anything which is not quite in keeping with our understanding – and cannot be clearly proven – it cannot uproot roots! It is incumbent that we look upon that root not on account of any specific need concerning the performance of the commandment. Behold that root furnishes itself with the greatest proof of its authenticity, the fact that it has been perpetuated, just as a law transmitted to Moshe at Sinai.

Rav Hai establishes the authority of tradition by virtue of it being a tradition that has been passed on from generation to generation. The very fact that this is the way we have been doing something as important as the shofar is authoritative enough to make it binding. Similar responsa deal with the common practice of how to fulfill the mitzvah of lulav and the practice of drinking four cups of wine at the seder night.

Like most Jewish scholars in that region, Rav Hai was highly educated in linguistics, sciences, mathematics, and philosophy. In a letter to Rabbi Shemuel HaNagid, Rav Hai writes that he permits children to be educated in Arabic and arithmetic, but he was against teaching children philosophy. He is known to have criticized his own father-in-law Rabbi Shemuel ben Hofni for studying "the books of the non-Jews."

He wrote numerous *piyyutim*, many of which express profound bitterness for being in exile from Eretz Yisrael. Like his father, Rav Hai was a celebrated mystic who believed that God performed signs in his day and that prophecy was alive and well. He, like his father and all the scholars of his day, opposed all forms of magic, superstitions, and sorcery. He vehemently opposed those who used God's names and charms to change the course of nature. He opposed all forms of anthropomorphism and ascribing corporeality to God. He taught that all forms of anthropomorphism in aggadic literature must be interpreted metaphorically.

Rav Hai maintained his physical and mental abilities into his late nineties. There is evidence that at the age of ninety-nine, a few months before he passed away, he replied to a query with remarkable sharpness. Ibn Daud writes how Rav Hai was regarded by later generations as the supreme authority in *halakha*:

> He more than all the Geonim propagated the Torah in Israel . . . both in the east and in the west . . . no one among his predecessors can be compared to him . . . he was the last of the Geonim.

He was eulogized most famously by Shemuel HaNagid, who said, "During his lifetime he acquired the choicest wisdom, and though he left no children, he has, in every land, both east and west, children whom he reared in Torah."[15] Solomon ibn Gabirol composed four elegies in his memory.[16]

Following the death of Rav Hai Gaon in 1038 C.E., the Torah scholars of the diaspora ceased directing their questions to the Academies of Babylon. The rise of new centers of Jewish learning began to establish themselves. About one hundred twenty years after Rav Hai's death ibn Daud wrote that the death of Rav Hai triggered the decline of the Geonate.[17]

---

[15] Shemuel HaNagid, *Ben Tehillim* 11.

[16] *Shire Shelomo ben Yehudah Ibn Gabirol*, volume 1, edited by Bialik and Ravnitzky, 88-90 (Hostaat Dvir Publishers, 1924).

[17] Ibn Daud, *Sefer HaQabalah*, translated by Cohen, 93-94.

> Therefore, I'll praise the name of the Lord
> so long as his breath in me lives
>
> SHELOMO IBN GABIROL

Rabbi Shemuel Ben Hofni HaKohen Gaon
(Unknown-1034 C.E.)

R ABBI SHEMUEL BEN HOFNI GAON (hereon RSbHG) was also a descendant of Geonic royalty and destined for great things, like his son-in-law Rav Hai Gaon. As is true of most of the personalities of this period in Jewish history, very little is known about RSbHG's personal life and upbringing.

We do not know when Shemuel was born to Rabbi Hofni, a judge and Talmudic scholar. His grandfather Kohen Zedek ben Yoseph Gaon was a scion of Talmudic scholars and one of the most powerful early Geonim of his generation. His family members were prominent leaders in one of the ruling factions of the famous Yeshiva in Pumpedita, in competition with the Sherira Gaon family until RSbHG married his daughter to Rav Hai Gaon. In a letter written in 985 C.E. by the Hofni family to potential supporters, the competitive nature of the rival families comes to light:

> Please write to us with your questions and doubts concerning the TaNaKH, Mishna or Talmud, for then you will receive their solutions as your heart desires, so that you will enjoy and discuss the

matters. In this way you will recognize our ability and the difference between us and others – and you will appreciate our strength in God's Torah.[1]

In response to this letter Rav Sherira Gaon appointed his son Hai as *Av Bet Din* [head of the Jewish judiciary], thereby making it clear to the Hofni family that their son Shemuel had little or no chance of attaining a leadership position in the Pumpedita Yeshiva.

Having little chance of assuming the leadership of the Pumpedita Yeshiva, RSbHG was appointed head of the Sura Yeshiva. Marrying his daughter to Hai Gaon significantly reduced the tension between the families and institutions.

As head of the Sura Academy, RSbHG innovated the genre of writing commentaries on Talmudic tractates. He did so, because he believed it was important to make the Talmud available to as many students as possible.

Prolific Author

In the tradition of Rav Saadia, RSbHG's most important contribution to Talmudic studies is his monumental work on methodology called the *Introduction to the Study of the Mishna and Talmud*. This work has one hundred forty-five chapters explaining the technical knowledge necessary for studying Talmudic law. The first fifteen chapters deal with the nature of tradition in general and the character of Tana'itic and Amora'ic traditions in particular. Unfortunately, much of this work did not survive. We have evidence of the popularity of this work by the many times it is quoted and referenced in later books and in letters.

Avraham ibn Daud writes that RSbHG "wrote many books."[2] This may indeed be an understatement. RSbHG was the most prolific

---

[1] This letter is published in Assaf, *Letters*, 146-152. Reprinted by David E. Sklare in *Samuel Ben Hofni Gaon and his Cultural World*, 6.

[2] *Sefer Ha-Qabalah*, 44.

writer of the Geonim. He wrote and published over sixty-five books.[3] All his books were written in Judeo-Arabic and referenced in many of RSbHG's later works and by others including Rabbi Abraham ibn Ezra. He is extensively quoted by Rabbi Abraham ben HaRambam (1186-1237) in his commentary on the Torah. There are forty-three known *halakhic* monographs penned by RSbHG. Much research has yet to be done on these monographs. We have fourteen of RSbHG's responsa and there are about a dozen letters scattered in museums and libraries. Unfortunately, most of RSbHG's works have not survived history and are known to us from medieval book lists.

RSbHG wrote a commentary on the second half of the book of Bereshit, on the entire book of Bemidbar, and on the first half of the book of Devarim. He saw himself as a student of Rav Saadia Gaon, which explains the strange order of his publications. He finished the works that Rav Saadia did not complete. This conclusion is confirmed by a comment made by Rabbi Yoseph Rosh ha-Seder ben Yaacov (12th century Egypt), who wrote a commentary on the weekly and holiday Haftarot[4] and references this point numerous times. Like Rav Saadia Gaon, RSbHG's commentary on the Torah was based on new standards of philological precision and on literary analysis that distinguished between literal and figurative language.

This is what we know with certainty about his intellectual pursuits and his religious spiritual worldview. Like his predecessor and mentor Rav Saadia Gaon, RSbHG understood that the Talmud, while authoritative, is made up of various genre of material. *Halakha* is determined by legal principles and must be observed. Midrash and aggadah, while sacred, are not meant to be studied literally. As early as 985 C.E. he wrote the following regarding Midrash:

> Our early predecessors, the holy Geonim, were accustomed to compose their letters with appeasing and persuasive words from the aggadot in order to appease and persuade you to make dona-

---

[3] List can be found in Assaf, "Book Lists," 280.

[4] See Moshe Gil, "The Babylonian Yeshivoth and the Maghrib in the Early Middle Ages," in *Proceedings of the Academy for Jewish Research*, Volume 57 (1990-1991), 82-83.

tions. I however have forged a new path, writing *halakhoth* and traditions. These are the finely sifted flour, whereas the aggadot are the waste.[5]

While this was the general attitude of the Geonim, the strong words of RSbHG are remarkable. As a teacher who wanted to impress upon his students the rabbinic tradition, he felt the need to use strong words. He repeats this idea in his works on Jewish thought and theology:

> One of the scholars of aggadot has said that Pharaoh's astrologers told him: "You will be destroyed by a man whose death will be caused by water." They were referring to the story of Moshe Rabbenu and the waters of Meribah. Because of this Pharaoh ordered every male child to be thrown into the Nile. We believe however that only the Master of the Universe knows the hidden things. He is unique in His knowledge and only He knows such things, along with those individuals whom He informs such as his prophets and messengers. Therefore we know the falsehood of anyone who claims knowledge of such things in a different fashion (without being a prophet) . . . . It is not appropriate for us to believe the truth of something only because one of the early authorities said it when there are proofs that it is false. Rather it is necessary to examine the matter rationally. If there is a proof that it should be accepted, then we will accept it as true. If there is an indication that it could possibly be true, then we will consider it to be possible – and if shown to be impossible, then we will consider it impossible.[6]

The Geonim were consistently concerned about any text that describes God corporeally and made sure to interpret all anthropomorphic descriptions metaphorically. When it came to esoteric material, RSbHG was more radical than his son-in-law Rav Hai Gaon.

---

[5] Assaf, *Tekufah*, 283.

[6] David Sklare, page 41 concerning the aggadah; see Sota 12b; Sanhedrin 101b; and Shemoth Rabbah 1:18.

When Rav Hai was asked to explain the esoteric passages in Talmud Hagiga he responded by saying:

> Know that our path has never been to cover over something and to explicate it not in accordance with the opinion of the person who said it, as others are wont to do. Therefore, we will explain to you the view of the Tana, the content of what he intended and the truth of what he thought. We will not guarantee that the Tana's words represent an authentic tradition. There are certainly many *Mishnayot* which are not authentic traditions, and yet we explain them according to the opinion who taught them. [7]

Rav Hai takes a neutral position regarding the passages in the Talmud tractate Hagiga. He places this section of the Talmud in the context of *Heikhalot* literature and goes on to explain the experience of the four who entered the *Pardes* and the ascent through the heavenly palaces described in the *Heikhalot* as inner meditative experiences. He then likens these experiences to that of the prophets.

RSbHG vigorously objects to Rav Hai's understanding of these passages. He rejects the linkage between these passages and prophetic experiences and declares all these passages as not authentic.[8] Rav Hai apologetically links his father-in-law's views to the fact that he reads many non-Jewish books.

Treatise on the Commandments

RSbHG applied scientific methodology in the way he divided and categorized the commandments. He does not, however, explain how he determined which of the commandments made it to the list of six hundred and thirteen, as did HaRambam about one hundred years later. The commandments are all a grace and gift of God. They are for the benefit of those who observe them, as he writes, "The aspect of

---

[7] *Otzar HaGe'onim* Hagigah, 13-15.
[8] Ibid.

goodness for all the revealed commandments is that they are a grace for the rational commandments."[9]

The wide range and variety of the commandments address variety of adherents in the community and man's constant physical and spiritual growth. Man/ woman writes RSbHG matures and changes with the passage of time and the practice of mitzvoth is designed for that process in a person's life.

> God may know that the character of some people is such that they, by themselves, will adhere to the rationally known laws and therefore have no need for the revealed commandments, or conversely, God may know that for some people the revealed laws would not provide assistance in helping them adhere to the rational laws. In such cases, it is not necessary for God to impose the revealed laws upon them. The matter here is as we have described – that is if it will not render Divine assistance for someone because he has no need for it, God will not impose it on him.
>
> For this reason, the laws vary. There are some laws which obligate non-priestly Israelites but do not obligate priests, some which obligate priests but not the Levites, some which obligate Levites but not priests, some which obligate women but not men, as well as those which obligate men and not women, and some laws which obligate everyone but only at certain times. This being the case, and since gentiles who can have obligations imposed upon them are indeed bound by all of the rational laws, it is reasonable that God may know that either all or just some of the revealed commandments would not benefit the gentiles, and that it would not therefore be necessary to impose the revealed commandments on them.[10]

RSbHG's book on the commandments was most certainly influenced by Rav Saadia Gaon's work on the commandments, which RSbHG references in detail in his introduction. There are however significant differences in content and in purpose. He wrote this book

---

[9] RSbHG *Treatise on the Commandments*, line 1060.

[10] Ibid, chapter 7.

with two goals in mind: He wanted to classify the commandments in a scientific and rational manner, and he wanted to "refute the attacks made against the commandments and remove all doubts."[11]

For RSbHG placed supreme value in intention [*kavanah*] of the person performing the commandments. *Kavanah* determines whether the commandment was correctly performed. Performing a mitzvah without appropriate intent and understanding is an empty ritual. He illustrates this position by using the fast of Yom Kippur as an example:

> When this fast is performed by someone who is capable of it and who has *kavanah* [intent] to perform the service of God, it becomes a legally valid fast. But if he performs it out of fear of someone, or out of embarrassment, then it is not a legally valid fast.[12]

He continues by suggesting that all mitzvoth must be performed with sincere *kavanah*:

> If one fasts, prays, or gives charity only for the sake of appearance or for the good reputation or some similar reason, he does not merit reward. Rather he is like someone who has prayed and not performed his obligation in that he will merit punishment instead of reward.[13]

The observance of the commandments is a means to spiritual awakening and proximity to God. *Kavanah* is a critical aspect of all mitzvoth, elevating their performance to an optimal level. Observance of the Jewish holidays is no exception. The goal is to transmit the inner world of Judaism along with the external performances and restrictions. It is true, he writes, that Judaism emphasizes the deed regardless of *kavanah* or motive,[14] but this does not mean that there is no

---

[11] Sklare, 178.

[12] Ibid, chapters 18 and 19.

[13] Ibid.

[14] The matter of whether or not *mitzvoth zerihot kavana*, commandments require intent is debated in the Talmud. See TB Berahot 13a. See also Yoseph Karo SA OH 60:4. Many early medieval commentators such as Rabbenu Hananel on Berahot 13a Rav Sherira Gaon, Rav Yitzchak Giyat and others ruled mitzvoth do not require intent.

room for the heart and soul. Judaism has survived precisely because the receivers and transmitters of our heritage and tradition understood that without the heart, all religious practices become a "spiritual wasteland." Service of God involves the body, mind, and heart. One is commanded writes RSbHG "to love God with heart, soul, and resources." RSbHG's prooftext is the Mishna in Zevachim:

> All sacrifices not made for their own sake are acceptable, but they are not considered as fulfilling the obligation of the owner except for the Pascal sacrifice and the sin offering.[15]

Knowledge of God

Knowledge of God, writes RSbHG, can only be achieved through rational scientific demonstration.[16] He wrote a book called *Treatise on Divine Names and Attributes*. This is a first of its kind in terms of a work dedicated to theology. With this work he demonstrated a strong handle on contemporary philosophical material and made himself available to respond to matters other than *halakha*. Indeed, people and communities directed questions to him on matters of ethics, philosophy, and theology.[17]

RSbHG was firmly rooted in traditional Jewish life, as prescribed by the rabbis of the Talmud where one is fully committed to *halakha* and *minhag*. He also understood that the rabbis of the Talmud sought to construct a worldview that emphasized the centrality of reason as an ordering principle in God's governance of the world. Revelation, prophecy, and miracles were to be understood through rational

---

There are some mitzvoth, however, that all agree require intent such as the sounding of the Shofar. See Rif Rosh Hashanah 7a.

[15] TB Mishna Zevachim 1:1.

[16] For the source and reaction of other Geonim to RSbHG's position see David Sklare, 58.

[17] Sklare, 95.

lenses. He had little tolerance for magic, superstitions, and sorcery. RSbHG was in good company on this philosophy. He followed the teachings of Saadia Gaon, Zemakh Zedek ben Itzchak, Rav Hai Gaon, Rav Sherira Gaon as well as some non-Babylonian scholars such as Elhanan ben Shermariah (1026 C.E. in Fostat), Nissim ben Yaacov (tenth century in Quarywan). HaRambam would later commit to writing this religious spiritual world-view throughout his many writings.

RSbHG addressed the question of how one is to treat a convert to Judaism. Like most Geonim, he felt the act of conversion was considered redundant – similar to the fulfillment of a vow taken by a Jew. Torah is universal and God's word is beneficial to all people. The convert must be welcomed and loved like a biological Jew.[18]

RSbHG is described as a humble servant of the community. Nowhere is he ever mentioned as being pompous or arrogant. He had a rare quality among scholars in that he would admit when he was wrong on *halakhic* matters. In one instance he writes how he reviewed what the author of *Halakhot Ketanot* had written, which differed from his positions but which he found to be sound and correct. As a result, he retracted what he had previously ruled and brought more proofs for the newly adopted position.[19] Rav Hai Gaon praises his father-in-law RSbHG for his humility and reports similar qualities.

---

[18] See HaRambam's Letter to Ovadia the Convert in English in Isadore Twersky's *A Maimonides Reader* (New York: Behrman House Publishers, 1972), 475.

[19] Sklare, 40.

> Let man remember throughout his life
> he's on his way toward death:
> each day he travels only a little
> so thinks he's always at rest—
> like someone sitting at ease on a ship
> while the wind sweeps it over the depths.
>
> MOSHE IBN EZRA

Rabbi Moshe ben Hanokh
(910-965 C.E.)

Rabbi Hanokh ben Moshe
(945-1014 C.E.)

GREAT SCHOLARS from the centers of Torah study in Babylonia would often travel to the Maghreb, Egypt, and Spain to raise much needed funds to support the Yeshivoth of Sura and Pumpedita. In *Sefer Ha-Qabbalah*, the medieval Jewish historian Avraham ibn Daud tells the fascinating story of the four captives which, from a historical perspective, answers the great mystery of how such a high level of the study of Talmud made its way to the shores of Southern Spain.

Ibn Daud records that four great Torah scholars set out together on a one such fundraising trip: Rabbi Moshe, the father of the future Torah scholar Rabbi Hanokh ben Moshe, Rabbi Hushiel, the father of the future Rabbenu Hananel, and Rabbi Shemariah ben Elkanah. The fourth name is lost to history and time.

While traveling around the Italian coast their ship was captured by the Moorish Spanish pirate ibn Rumahis.[1] "The sages," writes ibn

---

[1] The vulgar pirate became infatuated with Rabbi Moshe's beautiful and timid wife. Foreseeing the inevitable, she asked her husband whether those who die at sea in the vast ocean will be resurrected in the end of days. The great rabbi responded by

Daud, "did not tell a soul about themselves, their status as scholars or their wisdom."[2] They understood that if the pirates learned that they were prominent Torah scholars, their ransom price would escalate and place a significant burden on the Jewish communities that would pay their ransom.

As is expected of any faithful Jewish community, the mitzvah of *pidyon shevu'im* [ransoming the captives] was immediately undertaken and they were each ransomed for a servant's price by Jewish communities across the region. The Jewish community of Egypt ransomed Rabbi Shemariah in Alexandria, where he became the head of the academy of Fostat. Rabbi Hushiel was ransomed by the community of Qayrawan, where he became the head of the academy and whose son became the famous Rabbenu Hananel. The ship was then taken to Cordoba, where the Jewish community ransomed Rabbi Moshe ben Hanokh and his young son Hanokh.

Even after arriving at the Jewish community, Rabbi Moshe did not divulge who he was because it is forbidden for a Torah scholar to use his Torah knowledge for any form of personal gain. This was the way of the Jews of Babylonia, and this was a core value of the Jews of Andalusia. Some two hundred years later HaRambam codified this law and wrote discussed it at length in his commentary on Pirke Avot. He begins this important essay by reporting his hesitancy, knowing that many people will object to his words:

> After I decided not to speak about this testament because it is clear and since, according to my opinion, my words will not please most of the great Torah sages – and perhaps any of them – I went back on my decision and I will speak about it, without paying attention to the earlier or contemporary [rabbis].[3]

HaRambam then continues to berate those who seek honor and

---

quoting the verse in Tehillim, "The Lord said, 'I will bring them back from Bashan, I will bring them back from the depths of the sea.'" When she heard these words, she threw herself overboard and drowned in the sea.

[2] Ibn Daud, *Sefer Ha-Qabbalah*, 64.

[3] HaRambam's Commentary on Pirkei Avot 4:5, Kafikh edition.

take money because of their Torah knowledge. He explains in passionate and graphic terms the essence of this core value, and after a lengthy discourse he writes:

> And they said,[4] "A Torah scholar that proliferates his meal in every place, etc." And they [also] said, "It is forbidden for a Torah scholar to benefit from any meal that is not [pertinent] to a commandment." And why should I write at length about this matter? Instead, I will mention a story which elucidates it in the Gemara.[5] And it is said that a [certain] man had a vineyard in which thieves would enter. And each time he would see them on each day he [would] find his fruit lessening progressively. And he did not have a doubt that one of the thieves put his eye upon it. And [so], he was pained by this all the days of the harvest until he harvested what [was left for him to] harvest. And he put them out to dry until they dried and he gathered in the raisins. And the way of people when they gather dried fruit is that a few individual figs or grapes would fall. And it is permissible to eat them because they are ownerless, and the owners already left them for their finders due to their small quantity.
>
> Rabbi Tarfon came to that vineyard by chance, and he sat and took from the raisins that fell and ate them. And the owner of the field thought that this was the thief that stole from him the whole year – and he did not recognize [Rabbi Tarfon] but had heard of him. And [so] he immediately took him and overpowered him and placed him in a sack and placed him on his back to throw him into the river. And when Rabbi Tarfon saw this, he yelled out and said, "Woe to Tarfon, for this man is killing him." And when the owner of the vineyard heard, he left him and ran away, knowing that he had sinned a great sin.
>
> But Rabbi Tarfon was distressed from that day onwards all of his days and he mourned about that which happened to him, as

---

[4] Pesachim 49a.

[5] Nedarim 62a.

he saved himself through the honor of the Torah, while he was very rich and could have said, "Leave me and I will give you such and such gold coins." And he could have given them to him and he did not need to inform him that that he was Rabbi Tarfon. And [that way] he would have saved himself with his money and not with Torah. And they said, "All the days of that righteous man, he was distressed over this matter, saying, 'Woe is me, for I made use of the crown of Torah'" – as anyone who use the crown of Torah does not have a share in the world-to-come and is uprooted from the world. And they said about this, "It was since Rabbi Tarfon was very rich, and he should have appeased him with money."

And so [too, the story that] Rebbi (Rabbi Yehuda Hanasi) opened his storehouses in a year of drought and said, "Anyone who wants to come and take his sustenance, let him come and sustain himself, but only if he is a Torah scholar." And Rabbi Yonatan ben Amram came and stood in front of him and he did not recognize him; he said, "Rebbi, sustain me." He said [back] to him, "Have you read [scripture]?" "No." "Have you studied mishnah?" "No." "[If so], with (in the merit of) what should I sustain you?" He said, "Sustain me like a dog or a raven" – meaning to say, even though there is no wisdom in me, just like God, may He be blessed, sustains the impure animal and the impure bird – as an ignoramus is no less than them. And he gave him. But afterwards he regretted [it], since he had seduced him with his words and he said, "Woe to me, since I benefited an ignoramus from my possessions." And the listeners of what happened to him said to him, "Maybe it was Yonatan ben Amram, your student, who does not want to benefit through the honor of Torah, when he could avoid it – and even with a ruse." And he investigated and found that it was so. And these two stories will silence anyone who disagrees about this matter. The things that the Torah did, however, permit to the Torah scholar are that they should give their money to a man to do business according to his choice and the profit will be all for them, if he wants. And one who does this has a great reward for it – and this is "the one who puts merchandise into the 'pocket' of a Torah scholar." And [also] that their merchandise be sold before all [other] merchandise, and that [things] be purchased for them at the beginning of the market [session]. These are rules that God, may He be blessed, established, [just] like He established the gifts for the priest and the tithes for the Levite – according to that which has been received by tradition. As these two actions are done by some businessmen towards each other by way of honor and even though there is no wisdom [to be honored] – a Torah scholar is worthwhile to be like an honored ignoramus. And the Torah eased the rules upon Torah scholars [regarding] taxes and quartering troops and [taxes] specific to each person, and that is called the poll tax – the community pays it for them. And so [too] with [revenue for] the building of walls and similar to them. And even if a Torah scholar is endowed with money, he is not obligated in anything of all this. And Rabbi Yosef Halevi, may his memory be blessed, already instructed a man in a certain place who had gardens and orchards and was obligated to pay thousands of gold coins [in taxes] on their account – and he said that he would be exempted from giving anything on their account from all that we have mentioned, since he was a Torah scholar. And [this is so] although even a poor man in Israel would give this tax. And this is a law of the Torah, [just] like the Torah exempted the priests from the half shekel [that even the poor had to pay] – as we have elucidated in its place – and that which is similar to it.[6]

Like Rabbi Tarfon or Rabbi Yonatan ben Amram in the two Talmudic stories retold by HaRambam, Rabbi Moshe refused to better his situation in the Jewish community of Cordova by revealing that he was a Torah scholar. Instead, he was hired as the floor sweeper and cleaner of the Yeshiva, a task he performed diligently and with pride.

One day Rabbi Moshe overheard Rabbi Nathan, the head of the

---

[6] HaRambam Commentary on Pirke Avot, Chapter 4 Mishnah 5; also see his rulings in *MT Hilkhot Talmud Torah* 3:3-6

community, struggling to explain a difficult Talmudic passage. Rabbi Moshe, in his dusty clothing and with his broom in hand, raised his head and in perfect rabbinical Aramaic explained the entire Talmudic passage by heart with clarity and confidence. Astonished, all those who were present realized that they had a giant Torah scholar in their midst. Rabbi Nathan humbly and with great integrity immediately resigned, ceding his position to Rabbi Moshe ben Hanokh.

The wealthy community of Cordova named him their head rabbi and a Yeshiva was created for him to train students. The Yeshiva of Cordova attracted the finest students and became a center of Talmudic law and Torah study.

Rabbi Moshe ben Hanoh went on to train many students, most famously his own son Rabbi Hanokh ben Moshe. Rabbi Hanokh left no written works although there is some correspondence between him and Rav Hai Gaon. He died of injuries while falling from the *bima* in the synagogue of Cordova on Simchat Torah. His most famous student was Shemuel HaNagid.

> Six slaves the weekdays are; I share
> With them a round of toil and care,
> Yet light the burdens seem, I bear
> For your sweet sake, Sabbath, my love!
>
> YEHUDA HaLEVI

Hasdai, Abu Yoseph ben Yitzchak ibn Shaprut
(915-970 or 990 C.E.)

THE MID-TENTH CENTURY was a particularly good period for the Jewish people, Jewish culture, and the study of Torah in Andalusia. One of the most visible and memorable personalities of the period was Hasdai ibn Shaprut from Jaen, an important city in eastern Andalusia. Hasdai's father Yitzchak ben Ezra left the city of his forebears and moved his family to Cordova, the capital city of Muslim Spain. Yitzchak ibn Shaprut was a wealthy man known for his charitable work and piety. In Cordova he established a synagogue and generously supported the study of Torah and its scholars.

Around 915 C.E. Yitzchak ibn Shaprut and his wife brought a son into the world and named him Hasdai. The etymological origin of the name is hesed [kindness], while the name refers to the kindnesses of God as in *Hasdei Hashem*. Young Hasdai received the most outstanding education available at the time. In addition to being taught Hebrew and Arabic, he was also taught Latin, a language spoken by Christians and known by few in Muslim Spain. He received a first-rate Torah and Talmud education as well as an education in sciences, mathematics, and logic. As Hasdai matured he pursued the study of medicine, to which he devoted all his intellectual energies. He grew into a young man who was beloved by all:

> He knew how to get along with people, was pleasant to everyone, and won their trust. He actually took people's hearts captive. He was very bright and each word he uttered was measured and properly reasoned out. He was also ambitious and had already decided to succeed and become famous.[1]

By the 940s C.E. Hasdai had made a name for himself as a distinguished practitioner of medicine. His cures, treatments, advice, and drugs were successful, and his practice was oversubscribed. It is reported that he successfully rediscovered a secret drug that could heal all kinds of ailments. It is no surprise that his notoriety reached the highest levels of the palace and as a young man was summoned to the royal court of Abd-al Rahman III.

The multi-talented Hasdai rose quickly through the ranks of government as he navigated the difficult and dangerous politics of the royal court skillfully and wisely. His calm demeanor and pleasant ways made a good impression on all those who met him. When the opportunities presented themselves, he consistently made strong impressions on the Caliph especially when they discussed matter of government, economy, and security. It was not long before Abd-al Rahman III appointed Hasdai to an administrative position. His first position was the administration of taxes and customs and head of the Jewish population in the kingdom. Among the Jews he was referred to as the Nasi [the prince].[2] As a result of his acquired influence and power he was able to defend individuals and entire Jewish communities against harm and against those who hated Jews. Despite the general tolerance of the time, Jews were always an easy target for tax collectors and corrupt government officials.

As a young man he already earned the reputation of being generous to the needy. He never discriminated between Jew and Arab

---
[1] Eliyahu Ashtor, *The Jews of Moslem Spain*, 160.
[2] Ibn Daud, *Sefer Ha-Qabbalah*, 42, 49.

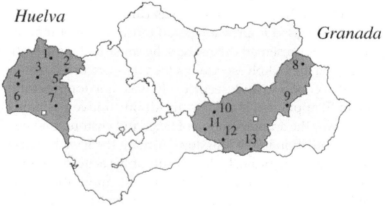

when it came to helping the poor. He was known as Abu Yoseph throughout Cordova and her surroundings.

The foresight of Hasdai's father to teach his son Latin paid off early on in the young man's career. Latin was the language of the Christian kingdoms of the North of Spain. The Caliph called upon

Hasdai at first as a translator. The Caliph and his advisors soon realized that Hasdai was an excellent negotiator who remained calm even under difficult situations. They recognized his broad knowledge and ability to think clearly and rapidly. His most useful skill was his verbal ability to express his thoughts and persuade all parties to trust and move forward. As Cordova was becoming a center for diplomatic activity, Hasdai's negotiating skills were in high demand. In the late 940s the diplomatic ties between the Byzantine Empire and the Omayyad Kingdom of Spain were renewed and Hasdai was indispensable.

Despite his onerous diplomatic and medical responsibilities, Hasdai devoted any spare moments to the study of Torah, Talmud, literature, and philosophy. He showed great concern for the welfare of the Jewish communities throughout the diaspora and used the power given to him for the good of the Jewish people and the advancement of Torah and Jewish culture. Hasdai did all he could to revive and restore communities. We know that he maintained correspondence with the communities in Israel and assisted them financially. He regularly sent emissaries to Jewish communities in order to have firsthand reports of their wellbeing.

Leaders of the Jewish community in Italy wrote to Hasdai, describing the oppression and religious discrimination they experienced. The letter describes how the church banned all religious books and banned scholars from studying them and teaching them. The church searched for the Jewish leaders and rabbis and forced conversion upon them. The letter described how Rabbi Isaiah ben Menachem (we know nothing about this rabbi) committed suicide instead of being arrested and forced to convert.

Hasdai ibn Shaprut heard about a Jewish kingdom in Khazar which fascinated him. He was eager to make contact with them. In 947 C.E., Hasdai carefully questioned a visiting envoy from the Byzantine emperor about the Jewish empire of Khazar and realized that what he had heard about the Khazar kingdom was not false. He sought to correspond with the Jewish king by sending a letter with two Jewish emissaries of the Slavic king who came to Cordova on a diplomatic mission. The letter was written in Hebrew and addressed to the Jewish king. In that letter he describes himself as "belonging to the exiled Jews of Jerusalem, in Spain."[3]

> I, Hasdai, son of Isaac, may his memory be blessed, son of Ezra, may his memory be blessed, belonging to the exile of Jews of Jerusalem in Spain, a servant of my lord the king, bow to the earth before him and prostrate myself towards the abode of your majesty. From a distant land I rejoice in your tranquility and magnificence and stretch forth my hands to God in heaven that He may prolong your reign in Israel.
>
> But who am I? and what is my life that I should dare to write a letter to my lord the king? I rely however on the integrity and uprightness of my object. How indeed can an idea be expressed in fair words by those who have wandered after the glory of the kingdom has departed, who have long suffered afflictions and calamities? We are indeed the remnant of captive Israelites . . . dwelling peacefully in the land of our sojourning for our God has not forsaken us nor has His shadow departed us.

His writer Menachem ben Saruk (10th century, Cordoba) continued with a beautiful description of Andalusia as a sacred land, a treasure house of nature and a place of repose:

> The land is rich, abounding in rivers, springs, and aqueducts; a land of corn and oil and wine, of fruits and all manner of delicacies, pleasure gardens and orchards, fruitful trees of every kind including the leaves of the tree upon which the silkworm feeds of which we have great abundance. In the mountains and the woods of our country cochineal is gathered in great quantity; there are also mountains covered by crocus and with veins of silver, gold, copper, iron, tin, led, sulphur, porphyry marble, and crystal. Merchants congregate in it and traffickers from the ends of the earth, from Egypt and neighboring counties, bringing spices, precious stones, magnificent wares for kings and princes

---

[3] Franz Kobler,' *Letters of Jews Through the Ages*, 98.

and the desirable things of Egypt. Our king has collected such large treasure of silver, gold, and precious valuables such as no king has ever amassed.

Despite the long distance that separated Hasdai and the king of Khazar, it seems that the king did respond. The scholar Solomon Schechter discovered a number of letters in the Cairo Geniza which make it apparent that there was correspondence between Jews of Khazar and Cordova. There are two versions of the king's reply to Hasdai. In both versions the king himself describes angelic visions which prompted his ancestor King Bulan to convert to Judaism and believe in one God.

As it turns out, at the time of this correspondence the Jewish kingdom of Khazar was on the threshold of disaster. The Russian and Byzantine rulers destroyed the proud Jewish kingdom of the Khazars and devastated their lands, including their capital. Thereafter, their fortunes waned until their fate became unknown and lost to history. The curiosity and exchange between Hasdai and the king of Khazar is the only historical record of a Jewish kingdom which might have otherwise remained unknown to history.[4]

This was a time of significant migration of the Jewish people from North Africa, Babylon, and Israel making their way to Southern Spain. The Jews brought with them crafts and artisanship that helped make Cordova and her surrounding cities centers of economic growth. Living conditions flourished, as did Jewish culture. Significant investments were made in expanding Torah study, Hebrew language, and Talmudic law. As was the practice of Geonic Judaism, the Jewish scholars of Andalus made use of the immense library of Cordova that housed over 400,000 books including the writings of Muslim scholars, translations of all the primary Greek philosophers, and books on mathematics, logic, geometry, optics, rhetoric, calligraphy,

---

[4] In *The Story of the Jews*, 265, Simon Schama writes how coins that date back to the mid-ninth century were discovered in Crimea and Viking Scandinavia bearing the words "Moses is the Messenger of God" on one side and "Land of Khazar on the other side."

metrics, medicine, philosophy, and religion. All these disciplines were then applied to the advancement and better understanding of the Bible, Talmud, and Midrash. It was in this environment where the Sephardic Jews of Andalusia thrived and flourished.

The Umayyads[5] of Cordoba had successfully transferred much of the imperial, artistic, cultural, and intellectual tradition of Baghdad. Jewish merchants not only brought the luxury goods of the East to Spain, but they also brought with them the intellectual achievements of the Talmudic academies of Baghdad. Geonic prayer rituals, philosophic outlooks, mysticism, and religious culture arrived in Andalusia in all its richness.

Andalusia became the most direct link in Europe to the Rabbinic tradition of the Talmud.[6] The Jews of Andalus began to feel like they found a home culturally, intellectually, and religiously. Jews were engaged in the latest research in medicine, pharmacology, philosophy, philology, astronomy, and mathematics. This period saw Jewish scientists build astrolabes to calculate latitudes, improving astronomical tables and navigational instruments. The famous exegete and poet Rabbi Abraham ibn Ezra wrote three books on arithmetic and number theory, accurately describing the reception of Indian numbers in the Islamic East.

The famous Yeshiva of Lucena was created in the image of the illustrious academies of Babylon. Its influence and prestige are very much attributed to the scholars who visited it, taught there, and learned there, such as Moshe ibn Ezra of Granada the disciple of Itzchak ibn Gayyat. Yehuda HaLevi, the famous poet and philosopher who was born in Tudela as well as Abraham ibn Ezra, Shemuel ibn Nagrela, Rabbi Itzchak ben Yaacob al-Fasi, Rabbi Meir Yoseph ibn Migash were all later products of the Yeshiva in Lucena.[7] This was in large

---

[5] The Umayyad Caliphate of Cordoba was an Iberian state ruled by the Umayyad dynasty that also dominated North Africa. This period is characterized by an expansion of trade, art, and culture. See Simon Barton, *A History of Spain* (London: Palgrave Macmillan, 2004).

[6] ibn Daud, *Sefer Ha-Qabbalah*.

[7] *Sefer Ha-Qabbalah*, 87-88.

gash were all later products of the Yeshiva in Lucena.[7] This was in large measure thanks to the efforts and influence of Hasdai ibn Shaprut. A poet of that period wrote about Hasdai ibn Shaprut the following:

For the Torah sages
He provided light and aid
His wealth went to Sura
Whence came the books
To teach the laws
As sweet honey
And righteous statutes
Clear and just[8]

Hasdai was known to send subordinates to towns the Jews had left to collect the remaining books and libraries and deliver them to the cities where the Jews moved to. He didn't limit his search for books or manuscripts alone. He was always on the lookout for Torah scholars who could serve as teachers and mentors for the communities in Spain. These efforts were very successful. A Judeo-Spanish poet wrote about Hasdai that "he strengthened the pillars of wisdom and gathered to him men of knowledge from Israel to Babylon."[9]

While Southern Spain was becoming a center for Jewish learning, the religious spiritual center in Babylonia was struggling to remain relevant. Even the once firm ties between Southern Spanish and Babylonian Jewry grew weaker. The communities of Andalusia stopped relying on the Babylonian scholars for answers regarding Jewish law, Talmud, and Torah. They had their own renown scholars who were local and able to answer all their questions.

Hasdai's own home became a gathering place for both Jewish and Arab writers, poets, and linguists. He supported them materially and encouraged them to persist in their work. One poet wrote:

That prince sectored to life those who were dying of folly with the dew

---

[8] Ashtor, page 229.

[9] Rabbi Moshe ibn Ezra, *Sefer Shirat Israel*, translated into Hebrew from the original Arabic by Benzion Halper, 63-64, (Leipzig, Germany: Avraham Yosef Stiebel, , 1924).

Attracting the hearts of the dispersed nation with the cords of his generosity
And making a proclamation: Whoever is for the Lord, let him come to me[10]
And I will provide for all his needs
And every gaon and rabbi were gathered unto him
From the lands of Edom and Arabia, from the East and from the West
Complainers have since learned
And princes have welcomed men of song
For his kindness has made the tongues of the dumb to break out in song
Opening hearts grow obdurate
So that they gathered about him with sweet songs
Bright as the stars on high[11]

[10] An allusion to Moshe Rabbenu, Shemoth 33:25.

[11] Yehuda Ben Shelomo Haziri, *The Book of Tahkemoni: Jewish Tales from Medieval Spain*, translated by David Simha Segal, 180 (Liverpool: Liverpool University Press, 2003).

Hasdai was the financial and material patron of the famous grammarian and poet Menachem ben Saruk who wrote an essential biblical lexicon that was used by many of the medieval commentators of the TaNaKH. When Hasdai's father died, Menachem ben Saruk wrote a series of laments that were recited during the seven days of mourning.

It was difficult for the Muslims in Cordova to be reconciled with the fact that the Caliph had exalted a Jew and bestowed upon him so much honor. Despite the fact that the masses as well as all upcoming noblemen despised followers of other faiths, especially the Jews in their midst, Hasdai ibn Shaprut went from one successful endeavor to the next.

Hasdai ibn Shaprut's legacy is one of a proud Jew who rose to the highest realms of society. He was a statesman, a negotiator, and an ambassador of his Muslim emperor. He represented an ideal of the of Andalusian Jew. Hasdai was a first-rate Torah scholar, linguist, and intellectual who used his skills to better the world around him, sustain peace between societies, and benefit his people, Jewish culture, and the advancement of Torah study.

> My knowledge goes forth to point out the way
> To pave straight its road.
> Lo everyone who goes astray in the field of Torah,
> Come and follow its path
> The unclean and the fool shall not pass over it;
> It shall be called Way of Holiness
>
> HaRambam

Rabbi Yona ibn Janah
(990-1055 C.E.)

RABBI YONA IBN JANAH was renown not only in the Jewish world but also in many Muslim circles. Among the Muslims he was known as Abu al-Walid Marwan ibn Janah. The name Yona was given to him later in life based on the translation of the Arabic ibn Janah, which means "the winged." His Arabic first name is Marwan, which is how Rabbi Avraham ibn Ezra always refers to him.

He was born in Cordova, Spain and supported himself as a physician to the Jewish, Muslim and Christian communities of his city. He wrote numerous works on medicines and the healing efficacy of certain herbs and drugs. His reputation as a first-rate medical practitioner reached far beyond the borders of Cordova. People came from as far as Zaragoza to consult with him and seek his medical advice. He is mentioned is mentioned in a number of medieval Muslim medical diaries. He was married and we know that had at least one son.

Ibn Janah devoted his intellectual creative output to the study of TaNaKH and in particular, the Hebrew language. He wrote a book titled *Kitab al-Anqih*. Also known as *Sefer Hadikduk* in Hebrew. It is a first of its kind. He wrote the first complete reference guide on the rules and details of Hebrew grammar. Additionally he wrote an extensive dictionary for biblical Hebrew. He contributions to Hebrew language are considered to be the most influential works in Hebrew grammar ever written.

Rabbi Yona ibn Janah (hereon ibn Janah) studied in the Yeshiva of Lucena. His teachers included Rabbi Isaac ibn Gikatilla and Rabbi Isaac ibn Mar Shaul. He studied Arabic, Aramaic, and Hebrew language. He received an intensive education in Talmud, Midrash, and Biblical exegesis. In addition to his religious studies, he mastered the sciences of the day: mathematics, logic, and philosophy. When he was twenty-two, he returned to Cordova and practiced medicine until he had to leave the city due to the instability of the caliphate atrocities committed by Berber tribal leaders. He moved to Zaragoza where he spent the last years of his life. In Zaragoza he was known to Solomon ibn Gabirol and to Shemuel HaNagid.

Ibn Janah was significantly influenced by the works of Yehuda ben David Hayyuj (10th century, Fez, Morocco and Cordoba, Spain). The early grammarians such as Menachem ben Saruk and Rav Saadia Gaon proposed that Hebrew words can have letter roots of any length. Hayyuj argued that this was incorrect and Hebrew words must have three-letter roots. Ibn Janah strongly supported this thesis and improved upon it.

An unintended and unfortunate consequence of ibn Janah's admiration for Hayyuj's work and his desire to improve on the master's research was the reaction of Hayyuj's students. They interpreted ibn Janah's scholarship as a criticism of Hayyuj and as presumptuous. The famous Shemuel ibn Nagrela was one of Hayyuj's most staunch defenders. What was supposed to have been a wonderful meeting of the minds tore the Andalusian scholarly community apart. As a result of misunderstanding and poorly reported lessons Shemuel ibn Nagrela launched an campaign against ibn Janah.

Ibn Janah died around 1055 C.E. His works quickly became very popular and inspired significant interest in the study of TaNaKH, Hebrew language, and philology. His works were translated by Yehuda ibn Tibbon (12th century, Granda, Spain and Marseille, France), who made them accessible to European scholars. The Encyclopedia Britannica refers to ibn Janah as "perhaps the most important medieval Hebrew grammarian and lexicographer" and adds that his works "clarified the meaning of many words" and contained the "origin of various corrections by modern textual critics."

Sefer HaDikduk

Sefer HaDikduk was originally named *Kitab al-Anqih*. It is divided into two sections: *Sefer HaRikma* which deals with Hebrew grammar and *Sefer HaShorashim* which is a Hebrew dictionary based on the three letter roots of words.

The goal of *Sefer HaRikma* is to examine the biblical text and formulate grammatical rules that are tied to its language and its form of expression. These rules are indispensable in understanding the message of TaNaKH. He brings numerous examples from within TaNaKH illustrating the rules' applicability and shows how the Rabbinic sages applied the same rules in Midrash and *Halakha*. He gives three reasons for writing his book and for the need-to-know Hebrew grammar:

1. You cannot be a good Jew without knowing the Hebrew language. Liturgy and Torah study are meaningless without comprehension. He insists that a translation, no matter how precise it may be, will always be inferior to the original Hebrew.

2. Language is the basis of all knowledge. Without an in-depth understanding of language, knowledge and culture cannot be acquired. As he writes:

    Because the work of linguistics is a tool for everything expounded and a preface for everything researched, the effort of the linguist is to reach its end and to stand on all its is-

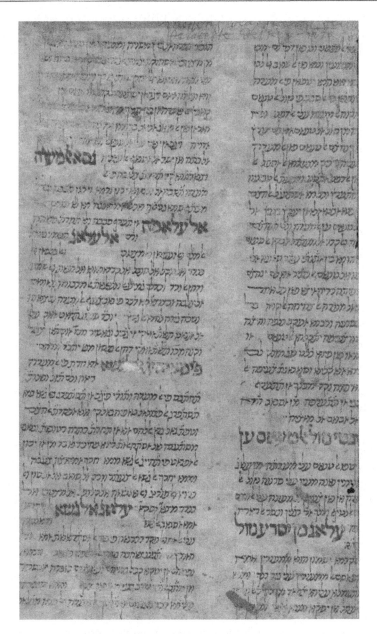

A page from Ibn Janah's Kitab al-Anqih

sues, and the desire to reach the edge and to know what is complete from it and what is not complete, the full and the deficient, and the true language and the langue of transfer ... as we will find it of the abridged and the deficient, it will be the lack of understanding of the researched and the abridgment of knowledge of that which is sought.[1]

3. One cannot understand the Torah and live as a good Jew without knowing the Hebrew language. He writes:

> The reward the Creator, may He be praised, the good in everything man will acquire for himself in this world ... reaching this will not be complete unless one understands what is written in the prophetic books and the fulfillment of their mitzvoth and their admonitions. It will not be feasible to understand anything written in these books except by the wisdom of the language so that the obligation of man's toil to pursue this wisdom and strengthening to acquire it and improve it and be precise in its uses ...[2]

Ibn Janah bemoans how tragic it is that, unlike their Muslim counterparts, Jews do not know Hebrew language well:

> And I have seen that the people among whom we live exert themselves to attain the wisdom of their language ... but the speakers of our language in our generation have already cast this wisdom behind their backs, and they have set this issue outside their interests. In fact they treat it lightly, considering it superfluous and pointless. As a result they remain bereft of its felicities and empty of its beauty, indeed they have divested themselves of its ornaments. We have come to a point of individual expression and personal speech, but we do not pay attention to this, and we are not exacting about it, as if language has no order to be restored and no boundary to be demarcated. Instead, they have sought from the language whatever is easy for them to expropriate and ex-

---

[1] Introduction to *Sefer HaRikma* Hebrew Edition (PublishYourSefer.com, December 2007).
[2] Ibid.

pound. They pay no heed to its roots, nor do they care about its branches.[3]

Ibn Janah divided *Sefer HaRikma* into forty-six chapters each of which he calls gates, each dealing with an independent topic. The examples ibn Janah uses to explain his points are the strength of this work. For instance, in *Sefer HaRikma* ibn Janah notes how the letter *lamed* changes the meaning of a noun. He says:

> The letter *lamed* indicates exchange or substitution as if saying "in place of." For example, the *lamed* used in the verse "and the bricks were as stone [*le-aven*] for them and the asphalt was as mortar [*la-chomer*]." (Bereshit 11:3)[4]

In other words, the *lamed* at the beginning of the noun transforms the meaning of the verse. The builders transformed their bricks into stones for construction and their asphalt into mortar. The transformative *lamed* is significant especially when it comes to ibn Janah's understanding of the binding of Yitzchak. God tells Avraham to bring "him [Yitzchak] up as a burnt offering [*le-ola*]."[5] According to ibn Janah, God never intended that Avraham sacrifice Yitzchak but rather bring him up to the mountain at the time of his bringing a sacrifice. The fact that Avraham understood it as a request to sacrifice Yitzchak merited him great reward – but based on a careful reading of the text and with precise Hebrew grammar one sees that that was never God's intent. God never changed His mind because He never commanded Avraham to sacrifice Yitzchak. With this comment ibn Janah is responding to the philosophic claim that God's word in not immutable and that God can change His mind, a notion that was rejected by Andalusian Jewry.[6]

> This is it, and may the Lord God grant you success in it, for in my mind, it is a pleasing matter, fine and wonderous, though no one

---

[3] Ibid.
[4] *Sefer HaRikma* chapter 6.
[5] Bereshit 22:2.
[6] See HaRambam's Thirteen Principles of Faith Principle #9.

else seems to have apprehended it ... but this will negate the confusion of one who demands that we accept the Torah's mutability.[7]

Sefer HaShorashim is similarly essential to the study of TaNaKH. He explains the goal of the book:

> This book, which we have called *Sefer HaShorashim*, contains most of the Hebrew roots that we find in the TaNaKH, and we will explain their definitions as well as their connotations, as proves necessary.[8]

Ibn Janah lists all the root words in alphabetical order, citing various conjugations in which the root appears and offering different meanings for the root. He is the first grammarian to recognized the relationship between semitic languages, often using Arabic or Aramaic to draw conclusions about the definition or etymology of a word.

Not all of ibn Janah's theories were welcomed and accepted. Rabbi Avraham Ibn Ezra (12th century, Andalusia Spain) opposed one of ibn Janah's innovative theories where he states that biblical words can be substituted by other words that share a similar meaning. For Rabbi Abraham ibn Ezra the divine nature of the Torah precluded such a suggestion. And Yet while Ibn Janah also believed in the divinity of the Torah but insisted the meaning of the text is the goal and not the text itself.

Another point of contention in ibn Janah's teaching has to do with the nature of rabbinic interpretations. At times ibn Janah insists that the *peshat* meaning of the text is contrary to the way the rabbis ruled. For example, regarding the captive woman taken from the battlefield the Torah says, "You shall bring her into your home, and she shall shave her head and [*ve'asta*] let her nails grow." Ibn Janah says she should actually cut her nails and be disgusting to him. Cutting her

---

[7] *Sefer HaRikma* chapter 6.

[8] Introduction to *Sefer HaShorashim, The Book of Hebrew Roots* edited by Adolf Neubauer (Kloof Books, Amsterdam).

nails is parallel to her shaving her head. This is not consistent with the way the Talmud rules[9] – namely that she must shave her head and let her nails grow.

His Legacy

For Rabbi Yona ibn Janah, the study and interpretation of TaNaKH represents both the most fundamental element of Judaism and the ultimate application of the study of Hebrew language and grammar.[10] His pursuit of precise translations, innovative grammatical insights, and persistent linguistic excellence laid the foundation for biblical exegetes throughout the ages. Thanks to Shemuel ibn Tibbon's translations, ibn Janah's works reached the schools of Southern France that had a particular interest in Hebrew grammar. Tragically, the fine art of excellence in Hebrew grammar and philology has been ignored in Lithuanian and Chassidic circles and has not had a place in the Yeshiva curriculum.

---

[9]TB Yevamot 38b.

> There isn't a bird in the air, or a tree in the
> Forest, or a flower in the meadow,
> or an animal in the mountain, a fish in the waters,
> an herb in the field, that tacitly as a working clock
> is not indicating that hand that made them and the wisdom
> that designed them.
>
> ISAAC CARDOSO

Shemuel ben Elkana ibn Nagrela HaNagid
(993-1056 C.E.)

SHEMUEL HaNagid is celebrated in Jewish history as the foremost Hebrew poet of the Jewish people and has assumed almost mythic status in Jewish history. His accomplishments are so stunning that many people think of them as legends – but they are not. He really was quite remarkable. He earned a reputation as a first-rate doctor and a master of the sciences of astronomy. He was an authority in Jewish law and a genuine Talmudic scholar as well as a master Hebrew and Arabic linguist who wrote countless poems. He was also a renown biblical scholar and wrote a commentary on the TaNaKH. In addition to his intellectual and rabbinic legacy he was very active politically. He was prime minister of the kingdom of Granada and commander-in-chief of her military. The Muslim records of the kingdom's military exploits describe him a valiant soldier who brave and wisely led his soldiers to war.

Shemuel HaNagid received much praise from Muslim scholars and historians for the many battles he fought and the many powerful Muslim rulers he defeated. Norman Roth collected these testimonies,

Street in Jerusalem named after Shemuel Ibn Nagrela HaNagid

and they provide extremely important information about Shemuel HaNagid, known by his Arabic contemporaries as Abu Ibrahim Isma'il ibn Yusuf ibn Ghazzal, that is not found in Jewish sources. The Muslim scholars especially admired his proficiency in both Arabic and Hebrew languages as well as his skills in sciences and the healing arts. His expertise in astronomy is also attested to by the fact that he accurately predicted two eclipses.

Moshe ibn Ezra (Granada, 1060-1138 C.E.) praised Shemuel HaNagid effusively, acknowledging his poetic skills, halakhic authority, and leadership abilities. Rabbi Avraham ibn Daud writes about him:

> He achieved great good for Israel in Spain, the Maghreb, Ifriqiyya [Tunisia], Egypt, Sicily, indeed as far as the academy in Babylonia and the Holy City . . . Moreover he retained scribes who would make copies of the Mishna and Talmud which he would present to students who were unable to purchase copies for themselves in the academies of Spain as well as of other counties we mentioned.[1]

His curiosity for knowledge had no bounds. As the son of a

---

[1] Shemuel HaNagid, *Hilkhot HaNagid*, edited by Mordecai Margalioth.

wealthy businessman in Cordoba, Shemuel HaNagid received a first-rate education as was expected of the Jews in Andalus. He was taught Hebrew, Arabic, and Latin. He studied Torah and Talmud with the preeminent scholars of Cordova such as Rabbenu Hanokh and his son Rabbi Moshe ben Hanokh. He also learned science, medicine, geometry, logic, and astronomy. Independently he studied the Koran as well as Bible commentaries of the church fathers. His education included hearing the stories about Hasdai ibn Shaprut and the many Jewish leaders who rose to positions of power and influence. There is no doubt that he was inspired and ambitious.

Shemuel HaNagid was most famous not only for his Talmudic scholarship but he was recognized as a *halakhic* authority as well. He headed his own Yeshiva in Granada that attracted many of the finest students. He wrote a book on Jewish law called *Hilkhot HaNagid*, of which only fragments have survived the passage of time.[2] He also wrote a commentary on the Talmud that is quoted by many early medieval scholars. He is cited several times by Nachmanides and his students. He also wrote a commentary on the TaNaKH cited by Abraham ibn Ezra and David Kimhi.

Ibn Nagrela got involved in business before his twenties, but his blissful youthful years came to a halt when he had to flee the city of Cordova during the savage Berber uprisings of 1013 C.E. He left behind his family and an exquisite quality of life. We know this from a long poem he composed as a young man after returning from a business trip that almost ended calamitously. While fleeing Cordova he wrote:

On leaving Cordoba:

Spirit splits in its asking, and soul in its wanting is balked;

> and the body, fattened, is vital
> and full —
> its precious being uneasy...

---

[2] Shemuel HaNagid, *Hilkhot HaNagid*, edited by Mordecai Margalioth.

But the modest man
walks on the earth with his
thought drawn toward sky.

What good is the pulse of man's flesh
and its favors
when the mind is in pain?

And the friends who fray me,
their fine physiques
and slender thinking, thinking it's ease or gain
that drives me, pitching from place to place,
my hair wild, my eyes
charcoaled with night —
and not a one speaks wisely,
their souls blunted, or blurred,
goat-footed thinkers.

Should someone unguilty hold back from
longing toward heights like the moon?
Should he wait,
weaving its light across him
like a man stretching taut his tent skin,
until he acts and they hear of his action,
as he adds and then adds like the sea
to his fame?

By God and God's faithful —
and I keep my oaths —
I'll climb cliffs and descend to the innermost pit,
and sew the edge of desert to desert,
and split the sea and every gorge,
and sail in mountainous ascent,
until the word "forever" makes sense to me,

and my enemies fear me,
and my friends in that fear
find solace;

then free men will turn
their faces toward mine,
as I face theirs, and soul will save us,
as it trips our obstructors.

The beds of our friendship are rich with it,
planted by the river of affection, and fixed like a seal in wax,
like graven gold in the windowed dome of the temple.

May YAH be with you as you love, and your soul which He loves be delivered, and the God of sentence
send aegis,

beyond both the sun and the moon.[3]

    Shemuel HaNagid made his way to Granada with a number of other refugees. In search of other scholars who shared similar intellectual pursuits, he met Ali ben Ahmed ibn Hazm, a young Muslim philosopher who would later devote his intellectual abilities to denigrating and disparaging Judaism. On numerous occasions Shemuel HaNagid entertained ibn Hazm by responding to him in writing or in public debates, but nothing positive came of that effort. As Shemuel HaNagid grew in fame, ibn Hazm intensified his attacks on Judaism and on Shemuel HaNagid. Ibn Hazm wrote an encyclopedia on the history and beliefs of different religions, referencing his debates and discussions with Shemuel HaNagid. He writes that Shemuel HaNagid wrote a book attacking the Quran but, curiously, he could not find a copy of it. He nevertheless wrote a refutation of this unwritten book's alleged criticisms of the Quran, which he claims are based on earlier debates with the Jewish writer.

---

[3] English Translation by Peter Cole published in *Selected Poems by Shemuel Hanagid*.

It was not long before word got out that Shemuel HaNagid was a young man of many talents and broad erudition as well as an excellent Arabic stylist. He became known to the stewards of the Muslim officials, and he was asked to write official letters on behalf of the Caliph. Shemuel's quiet but confident manner of speaking made good impressions on the right people, and he was asked to work in the royal court. He initially functioned as a tax collector in some districts of the Granada principality. With his professional and financial accomplishments on a growth trajectory, he married and in the year 1035 C.E. he had a son and named him Yoseph.

Early on in his political career the Jewish community asked him to intervene on behalf of a Dayan in Malaga who was falsely accused by the Muslim authorities. Shemuel HaNagid sed his influence and writing skills and sent a letter to the officials of Malaga. The Dayan was cleared of all charges and released. Ibn Nagrela had the Dayan and his family brought to Granada where he worked for the Nagid. Throughout his life Shemuel intervened on behalf of Jews and continued to use his influence and power to protect them against corrupt government officials.

Shemuel HaNagid was able to navigate the politics of the royal court and enemies on the battlefield but there are two opponents that he could not eliminate from leaving a stain on his legacy. The first is the aforementioned ibn Hazm, whom he had known in Cordoba. The far more serious conflict erupted within the scholarly Jewish community. Shemuel HaNagid attacked a young linguist and possibly the finest Hebrew grammarian of the time, Yona ibn Janah from Zaragoza, for his theories and the poet's dislike of Yehudah Hayyuj. Ibn Janah replied in a book, from which we learn that the debate focused on technicalities of the Hebrew language and verb forms. This dispute between scholars divided the communities between those who supported the new generation and those who supported the older grammarian.

Shemuel HaNagid did everything in his powers and with his own resources to support the study of Torah and especially talented scholars. He made his large library in Granada available to all students and scholars. He sent money and resources to the Yeshivoth of Babylonia that bestowed upon him the honorary title of *rosh haseder* [honorary head of the academy]. He financially supported the study houses in Israel and in Qayrawan, and he befriended one of the greatest Talmudic scholars of the period there, Rabbi Nissim ben Yaacov Gaon. Shemuel HaNagid wrote at least three poems about the great rabbi and the rabbi's daughter who later married Shemuel's son Yoseph. In his later years Shemuel HaNagid befriended the young up-and-coming scholar and poet, Solomon ibn Gabirol, who left Zaragoza to meet and study with the great teacher.

Shemuel HaNagid continued to succeed in his political endeavors. When the opportunity presented itself and he had access to the king, he demonstrated his efficiency and diligence in financial matters. This earned him another promotion as minister of finance, which he served with great success. The Muslim ruler of neighboring Almeria piously objected to the appointment of a Jew to such a high government post and used this a pretext for declaring war on Granada.

The very clever Caliph appointed Shemuel HaNagid commander-in-chief of the military and made him responsible for the state's security. This pious Jew who was a Talmudic scholar and community leader with a growing family was forced to lead troops in battle against various enemies of the state, including Christian mercenaries. About war he wrote:

> War is at first like a beautiful girl
> With whom all men long to play,
> But in the end like a repulsive hag
> whose suitors all weep and ache.[4]

Shemuel HaNagid's military career is legendary. The enemy forces that he faced were substantial. Over a period of nineteen years, he never lost a battle. He no doubt recognized that in spite of the apparent support of the Muslim ruler of Granada, if he lost even one battle he would soon be removed from office and even executed.

---

[4] *The Penguin Book of Hebrew Verse*, edited by T. Carmi, 291 (New York: Viking Press, 1981).

Shemuel HaNagid wrote poems about each of his battles expressing pride in victories, gratitude and praise to God, and his desire to be home with his wife and children, particularly on Shabbath and holy days. From the battlefields he also wrote poems as well as biblical commentaries and Talmudic interpretations for his son Yoseph.

> When God came to his rescue, he spoke this song
> The great victory took place on Friday the first of Elul, in the year 4798
> Then Av – the month of ancient woe – departed and
> Elul arrived speeding good fortune.
> Ibn Abbas pitched his tents on the mountain side,
> And we pitched ours in the pass
> Taking no heed of his army, as though it were a passing caravan
> Then he drew near and with many words tried to incite my men against me.
> But when my adversary saw that my company spoke with my voice, as one man
> He uncovered spears, swords, and lances, and prepared his weapons for battle.
>
> ———
>
> My enemy rose – and the Rock rose against him
> How can any creature rise up against his creator? . . . [5]

Shemuel HaNagid's most difficult enemy in battle was the king of Seville, whom he fought from 1039-1056 C.E. In 1039 C.E. He won a major victory against the combined armies of Seville and Carmona, where the son of the king of Seville was killed. Shemuel's troops finally defeated the king of Seville in a decisive battle, the horrors of which Shemuel HaNagid describes graphically in a series of poems.

> The sun came out the earth rocked on its pillars as if it were drunk
> The horses lunged back and forth, like vipers darting out of their nests

[5] Ibid, 286.

> The hurled spears were like bolts of lightning, filling the air with light
> Arrows pelted us like raindrops, as if our shields were sieves
> Their strung bows were like serpents, spewing forth the stinging bee[6] . . .

In 1049 C.E., when Shemuel HaNagid was in his late fifties, while he was fighting yet another war, his wife bore him a second son who he named Elyasaf. Both his sons received the finest education Southern Spain could provide. He children learned Hebrew, Arabic, and Latin, as well as all the secular and religious subjects with the finest of teachers. His son Yoseph edited his father's poems and added headings to them. Shemuel HaNagid also had a daughter who received an education equal to her brothers'. There is evidence that she authored several Arabic poems found in an Andalusian collection.[7]

Shemuel ibn Nagrella had predicted that he would die at a relatively young age, at home and peacefully and indeed that is how he passed away in 1056 at the age of 64 years old. Yoseph assumed his father's position, but he did not inherit his father's political savvy and generosity. He made enemies quickly and was assassinated during the Jewish massacre in the city of Granada in the year 1066.[8]

The general consensus is that as a poet Shemuel HaNagid was exceptionally talented and unequaled both in terms of the amount of poetry he produced and the quality of his compositions. He named his three volumes of his poetry after the biblical books in *Ketuvim*. His religious poetry is called *Ben Tehillim*, his rhymed poetry is called *Ben Mishle*, and his more pessimistic and didactic poetry is called *Ben Kohelet*. Probably not coincidentally, all three biblical books are ascribed to King David the warrior, philosopher king poet.

His poetry is characterized by a style that is beautiful and easy to read. He is the first Hebrew poet to successfully adapt Arabic meter while adding several more meters. He even created several new He-

---

[6] Ibid, 287.

[7] John Bellamy, in *Journal of the American Oriental Society* 103 (1983), 423-424.

[8] Carmi, 285.

brew words that eventually made it into the Hebrew language. He wrote on a range of topics such as love, friendship, battle, war, family, science, death, and God. He was also known to write satire, especially about incompetent rabbis. Unlike ibn Gabirol and Yehudah Halevi, Shemuel HaNagid's poetry did achieve wide recognition during his lifetime.

About life, living in the moment, and death, Shemuel ibn Nagrela HaNagid wrote:

The Moment
She said: Rejoice for God has brought you to your fiftieth year
   in the world!
But she had no inkling that, for my part there is no difference at
   all
Between my own days which have gone by and the distant days
   of Noah
In the rumored past. I have nothing in the world but the hour in
   which I am; it pauses for a moment, and then, like a cloud
   moves on.[9]

---

[9] Carmi, 285.

> The enlightened will shine like the radiance of the sky
> And those who lead many to righteousness,
> Like the stars forever and ever
>
> DANIEL 12:3

Rabbenu Hananel ben Hushiel
(990-1050 C.E.)

Rabbenu Nissim ben Yaacov
(990-1062 C.E.)

RABBENU HANANEL AND RABBENU NISSIM represent the generation of new Torah leadership after the Geonic period. Rabbenu Hananel and Rabbenu Nissim had countless students, some of whom came from Spain, Israel, and even Babylonia. So widespread was their teachings that they are often referred to as "Ge'onim."[1]

Both Rabbenu Hananel and Rabbenu Nissim were the most outstanding students of Rabbi Hushiel (the father of Rabbenu Hananel) and they jointly succeeded Rabbi Hushiel as head of the famous Yeshiva of Qayrawan. In the tradition of their teachers, both these rabbis studied and applied the Jerusalem Talmud to their rulings. They each contributed a great deal to the spread of Torah and Talmudic studies throughout central Asia, the Iberian Peninsula, and Europe. It is interesting how the Tosafists of France and Germany assumed they

---

[1] Solomon Judah Lieb Rapaport, "Toldot Rabbenu Nissim ben Yaacov," in *Bikkure Ha'Ittim*.

were from Italy and referred to Rabbenu Hananel and Rabbenu Nissim as "the Rabbis from Rome" (or Hananel of Rome).

Rabbenu Hananel and Rabbenu Nissim followed the method of Rav Saadia Gaon in defending the Torah's use of anthropomorphism as a means of helping the uneducated better understand God. However, they were both very much against the use of corporeality or anthropomorphic language in the classroom and in other writings. Neither of these rabbis entertained any interest in mythical and magical aggadot: All miracles and fantastic aggadot were interpreted symbolically. They rejected all forms of magic, superstitions, and sorcery within Judaism.

Very little is known of these scholars' personal lives. Rabbenu Hananel was a very successful businessman and did not accept payment for rabbinic duties, per the tradition of the Jews of old Sepharad. Rabbenu Hananel had nine daughters, each of whom received a very generous dowry and then inherited his wealth.[2] Unlike his colleague Rabbenu Hananel, Rabbenu Nissim was not successful in business. Rabbenu Nissim's daughter married Yoseph, the son of the wealthy and famous Shemuel HaNagid, who helped support his father-in-law.

Rabbenu Hananel and Rabbenu Nissim both knew Arabic and Greek, as reflected in many of their explanations of Arabic and Greek words. While Rabbenu Nissim wrote in Arabic, Rabbenu Hananel wrote all his works in Hebrew.

Rabbenu Hananel's commentary on the Talmud helps elucidate the text and preserves correct versions of ancient manuscripts. Rabbenu Hananel is cited by many biblical exegetes and his responsa are mentioned in later rabbinic texts. He is most famous for his commentary on the Talmud utilizing Rabbi Yitzchak Alfasi's *Halakhot Rabbati*, even though Alfasi was his student. He wrote a commentary on the Torah that can be read as a polemic against the Kararites. Karaism was a Jewish sectarian movement that originated in the early 8th century. Their founders and later exponents believed in the prophecy of Moshe Rabbenu and in the divine nature of Jewish law but rejected the entire corpus of rabbinic Judaism and the oral law. This movement

---

[2] Ibn Daud, 91.

was very influential in the Jewish communities of Central Asia, South Central Asia and in Southern Spain and many rabbis like Rabbenu Hananel felt it necessary to respond in writing to their teachings.

His commentary on Yechezkel has been edited and published in a work called *Migdal Hananel*. He also authored a siddur and numerous *pizmonim* [religious songs]. Later European rabbis, such as Mordechai ben Hillel HaKohen (thirteenth century Talmudic scholar) writes in his commentary on Tractate Ketubot and in his commentary on Tractate Shevuoth that *Sefer HaMikzo'ot* [Book on Ritual Law] was authored by Rabbenu Hananel.

Rabbenu Nissim gained a great deal from his teacher Rabbi Hushiel, and he also learned very much from his correspondence with Rav Hai Gaon. Rabbenu Nissim acted as an intermediary between Rav Hai Gaon and Shemuel HaNagid, sending responsa and monographs to Southern Spain.

As mentioned earlier, Rabbenu Nissim authored several important works, all in Arabic. Rabbenu Nissim is most famous for his siddur, which is quoted by numerous rabbinic authorities. He wrote several *Viduyyim* [confessions] recited by Sephardic communities on Yom Kippur. He wrote an introduction to the Talmud called *Kitab Miftah Maghalik al-Talmud*, in Hebrew it is called the *Sefer HaMafte'ach* [the Key to Unlock the Talmud]. This work is much more than an introduction to the Talmud – it is also a kind of commentary. He quotes from a wide range of texts such as the Tosefta, Mehilta, Sifre, Sifra, old Midrashim, and Jerusalem Talmud. The second half of *Sefer HaMafte'ach* is divided into fifty sections, organizing laws of the Talmud that are found in unexpected places.

Also preserved is his book *Sefer HaMitzvoth*. Rabbi Avraham ibn Ezra quotes Rabbenu Nissim just once in his commentary of Shemoth 34:6, which leads some to believe that Rabbenu Nissim may have also written a lost commentary on Torah. He also wrote *Megillath Setarim* [Scroll of Secrets], which was published by his students after his death. It is a notebook of *halakhic* decisions, explanations, and midrashim that was intended for private use. Additionally he wrote a small book of about sixty religious and inspiring stories based on Talmudic and Mishnaic texts for a friend who lost a son.

> I am a man who when ... he finds no stratagem for
> teaching a demonstrated truth except by putting
> it in a manner appropriate for a single person but
> not for 10,000 ignoramuses, chooses to address
> the individual and disregard the outcry of the masses.
> HaRambam

Rabbenu Yitzchak ben Yaacov HaKohen Alfasi
(1013-1103 C.E.)

Known simply as Rabbenu Alfasi, or in the world of the Lithuanian Yeshivoth as The RIF, Rabbenu Yitzchak ben Yaacov HaKohen Alfasi was one of the preeminent Talmudic scholars of the early Middle Ages. Rabbenu Alfasi devoted his religious and intellectual pursuits exclusively to the study of Talmud. He was a student of Rabbenu Hananel (990-1050 C.E.) and Rabbenu Yaacov ben Nissim (990-1062 C.E.) of Qayrawan.

Rabbenu Alfasi was born in a North African Jewish village near Fez. After the death of his mentors around 1055 C.E., Rabbenu Alfasi assumed the position of head of the community. In 1088 C.E. he had to flee because of some unknown charges against him. He left North Africa and settled in Lucena, where he taught the rising scholars of Andalusia until his death. Rabbenu Alfasi served the Jewish community as a judge, rabbinical scholar, *poseq halakha*, and author of seminal works in Talmudic law. While in North Africa and in Lucena his presence attracted large numbers of students from throughout central Asia and Israel. His rulings on religious and civil matters were considered authoritative and carefully studied by following generations of rabbis and judges.

His *magnum opus* was his *Halakhot Rabbati*, referred to by some later medieval scholars such as Rabad of Posquieres (French twelfth century Talmudist) as "the little Talmud" because it summarizes the entire Talmud into law. He did this by first eliminating all tangential digressions and aggadic material that was not relevant to the *halakha*. He records the fundamental elements of the Talmudic deliberations by quoting them or paraphrasing them. His own *halakhic* ruling is, in most instances, appended at the end of each discussion. He undertook the arduous and difficult task of distinguishing between aggadah that was speculative or anecdotal versus aggadah that served as a basis for a legal ruling. For example, the Talmud in Tractate Berakhot records the following two statements:

> If a person prays for Divine favor on behalf of another when he himself is in need of the same thing, his need will be responded first... If a person complains to Heaven against his fellow instead of taking him to court, he himself will be punished first.

Of these two aggadic texts Rabbenu Alfasi included only the second because it relates to practical conduct that must be observed. He did not include the first because it is esoteric in nature, not binding *halakhically* and not provable.

His goal was to retain only the legal conclusions of the Talmud. He was a pioneer in collecting various Talmudic manuscripts and always stressing the importance of understanding the *halakha* based on correct versions of the Talmud text. He provides an abridged format of the *halakhic* discussions, occasionally identifying the correct edition of the Talmudic text, and adding a comment or criticism of post-Talmudic authorities.

> And this reason appears erroneously in all the versions... and Rabbi Hai was asked about this previously and he responded... yet his words have no basis in reason even though it is simple, he did not comprehend it and did not interpret it correctly... and

thus his interpretation is nullified ... and I sought the version of the academies and found the exact version and it is indeed clear and not difficult at all and that is the explanation of this chapter.[1]

Rabbenu Alfasi collected only the relevant and practical *halakhot* of the relevant Talmudic tractates such as Tractates: Berakhot, Shabbath, Eruvin, Pesachim, Ta'aniot, Bezah, Rosh Hashanah, Yoma, Sukkah, Megillah, Moed Kattan, Yevamoth, Ketuboth, Gittin, Kiddushin, Nedarim, Hullin, Baba Kama, Baba Mezia, Baba Batra, Sanhedrin, Makkoth, Shebu'oth, Niddah, and Avodah Zarah.

Rabbenu Alfasi is not the first to have tried to gather the *halakhot* of the Talmud into a concise, well-organized work. Scholars such as Shimon Kahira (author of *Halakhot Gedolot*), Yehudai Gaon (author of *Halakhot Peskot*), or Rav Hai Gaon (author of the *She'iltot*) all made valiant attempts, but they have all fallen short. HaRambam praises only Rabbenu Alfasi for his *halakhot*:

> The *halakhot* of our great teacher Rabbenu Yitzchak of blessed memory have surpassed all of their predecessors because there is included therein everything useful for the understanding of the decisions and laws at present in force; that is, in the time of the exile. The author clearly demonstrates the errors of those before him when his opinion deviates from theirs, and with the exception of a few *halakhot*, whose number at the very most does not amount to ten, his decisions are unassailable.[2]

Rabbenu Alfasi based his *halakhic* rulings on the Babylonian Talmud without ignoring the Jerusalem Talmud. He followed several rules, one of which was to always rule in accordance with the Babylonian Talmud when the Jerusalem Talmud drew a different conclusion:

> The Babylonian Talmud is more recent than the Jerusalem Talmud, and its authors knew the content of the Jerusalem Talmud

---

[1] Rabbi Yitzchak Alfasi on Sanhedrin 16b.

[2] HaRambam, Introduction to his commentary on the Mishna.

better than we do. Had they not been convinced that the passage from the Jerusalem Talmud cited in opposition to their opinion was untrustworthy, they would never have deviated from it.[3]

The above quote has led some who have claimed that Rabbenu Alfasi is not consistent and deviates, on numerous occasions, from the ruling of the Babylonian Talmud. These discrepancies are usually resolved with the use of variant texts or by alternative ways of interpreting a particular passage in the Babylonian Talmud. Rabbenu Alfasi was consistent and never waivers or suggests any doubt, always firmly asserting the correctness of his ruling. Like his predecessors, Rabbenu Alfasi had to consider the vast material found in both the Babylonian and Jerusalem Talmud as well as the extensive material produced by the Geonim before determining a ruling. He will often cite a range of views and in most cases indicates his own support or opposition to the views. He relied heavily of the views of Rav Hai Gaon and Rav Yehuda Gaon. While he mentions others by name, he routinely cites the general view of the rabbis by writing "some rabbis."

Rabbenu Alfasi's *Halakhot Rabbati* was reprinted and studied throughout the Southern Spanish, Northern Spanish, and European centers of Torah learning. He had his share of commentaries, critics, and advocates. His work spawned so much Torah learning and discussion. His chief critic was Rabbi Zerahiah HaLevi of Girona, Catalonia (1115-1186 C.E.), the author of the *Maor* [the Luminary]. He is often referred to as *Ba'al HaMa'or* [the author of the Luminary]. Nachmanides (Northern Spanish, Rabbi Moshe ben Nachman 1194-1270 C.E.) came to Rabbenu Alfasi's defense in a work called *Milhamot Hashem* [the Wars of the Lord]. Rabbi Avraham Ben David[4] also wrote a commentary where he both defends and criticizes Rabbenu Alfasi's rulings.

He died on a Tuesday, May 19th, 1103, C.E., which corresponds

---

[3] Rabbenu Alfasi, *Halakhot Eruvin*, end.

[4] Known as Ra'abad, of Southern France (1125-1198 C.E.).

19th century Pressburg edition of
Alfasi's Halakhot Rabbati

to the tenth day of Sivan. A monument was erected in his memory and the following words are inscribed:

> It was for that the mountains shook on the day of Sinai; for the angels of God approached you and wrote the Torah on the tablets of your heart; they set the finest of its crowns upon your head.

Rabbenu Alfasi's work displaced many *halakhic* works that preceded his, that were written in his own time, and even those that came later. His influence is evidenced by the fact that Alfasi continues to be one of the most influential halakhic authorities some four hundred years later, despite the appearance of other great works such as Ha-

Rambam's *Mishneh Torah* and Rabbenu Yaacov Ben HaRosh's *Sefer HaTurim*. When Rabbenu Yoseh Karo (sixteenth century) set out to establish a basis for what he had hoped would be a universal code of Jewish law, he writes:

> Since I concluded that the three pillars of instruction upon which the House of Israel rests are Rabbenu Alfasi, HaRambam, and Rabbenu Asher of blessed memory, I resolved that when two of them agree on any point I will determine the law in accordance to their view, except for those few instances when all or most of the other authorities disagree with that view and a contrary practice has therefore become widespread.

Remarkably, many of Rabbenu Alfasi's ruling have found their way into the authoritative corpus of Jewish law.

> A bundle of myrrh is my beloved to me;
> between my breasts he shall lie.
> A cluster of henna-flowers is my beloved to me,
> in the vineyards of Ein-Gedi
>
> SHIR HASHIRIM

Shelomo ibn Gabirol
(1022-1048 C.E.)

SHELOMO IBN GABIROL was an unusual savant whose Hebrew poetic art-form has no parallel in style, form, and depth. He is by far the most illustrious Jewish religious Hebrew poet and one of the "most creative geniuses of all time."[1] The late Jochanan Wijnhoven said it best:

> Solomon ibn Gabirol appeared in the literature of medieval Spain something like a meteor: a bright, rapid, and unexpected phenomenon that strikes, fascinates, and puzzles, but after its luminous trail dies out, it is quickly forgotten, or remains a riddle for those who wish to understand it. Solomon ibn Gabirol is perhaps the most puzzling figure in the intellectual history of Medieval Judaism; the scholarship which has tried to deal with him, and his influence is just as contradictory and enigmatic as the sources themselves.[2]

---

[1] Andrew Gluck, Introduction to *Keter Malkhut*.

[2] Jochanan Wijnhoven, "The Mysticism of Solomon Ibn Gabirol," 137-152.

We have his poetry and works on Jewish philosophy, but we know very little about the man and his life other than the fact that he died very young. The earliest biographical information we have of Shelomo ibn Gabirol (hereon ibn Gabirol) is from a Muslim source. Saeed al-Andalusi, the Qadi of Toledo (1029-1070 C.E.), wrote a book on the famous people who had made contributions in the disciplines of science and knowledge. One of the chapters in Saeed's book is devoted to the Jews and includes a section on ibn Gabirol.[3] Here Saeed tells us that ibn Gabirol died before his thirtieth birthday.

A slightly fuller account of ibn Gabirol is provided by the younger poet and author Rabbi Moshe ibn Ezra (1060-1139 C.E.), who wrote a book about the Jewish poets of Andalusia. In this book he devotes a good amount of attention to ibn Gabirol's life and legacy. There he writes that ibn Gabirol's full name was Abu Ayyub Sulayman ben Yahya ibn Gabirol Kurtabi. Sulayman is Arabic for Shelomo, and Yahya is Arabic for Yehuda; Kurtabi is Arabic for Cordova. Moshe ibn Ezra writes that ibn Gabirol was a profoundly serious and impassioned person who completely devoted himself to the development of moral qualities, philosophy, and poetry. Even in his youth he surpassed his older contemporaries in literary and poetic merit and earned himself an illustrious reputation. Rabbi Moshe ibn Ezra describes ibn Gabirol was a young man of an irritable disposition which sometimes led him to lose his temper. He adds that often ibn Gabirol might even use his sharp intelligence and wit to subject great men to insult and satire.

Ibn Gabirol's family originated in Cordova. He, however, was born in 1022 C.E. in Malaga where he received a first-rate Andalusian education. Ibn Gabirol, which is the poetic form of *Gavriel* or *gevurah* and means strength, often ends his poems with his name followed by *Ha-Malaki* [from Malaga] or *HaSefaradi* [the Spaniard]. Based on ibn Gabirol's poetry we can infer that his parents died at a young age, and he was left orphaned and impoverished until he was adopted by

---

[3] The *Tabaqat al-Umam*, of Said al-Andalusi of Toledo was first published in Beirut in 1911. The chapter on the Jews was translated into English by J. Frankel and published in *Jewish Quarterly Review*, New Series, xviii, 1927-28 on pages 45-54.

Yekutiel ben Yitzchak ibn Hasan, a wealthy Jewish patron of literature and culture. He was also supported by Shemuel HaNagid, who appreciated the young poet's talents. Ibn Gabirol dedicated numerous poems in honor of Yekutiel ben Yitzchak and in honor of Shemuel HaNagid's military victories.

Ibn Gabirol's faith was grounded in Judaism and an unrelenting pursuit of God and the mysteries of existence. The relationship between nature and the cosmos transported him to faraway places in his subconscious. He wrote tender and amorous songs expressing his impassioned quest for God and his personal relationship with God. It is evident from his poetry that he was an extremely sensitive and susceptible soul. His vulnerable nature was encumbered by life's traumas, physical suffering, solitude, poverty, and lack of human love. For Ibn Gabirol there is no such thing as personal suffering; rather, from his vantage point, there is a great cosmic-wound that spares no one.[4] The inner and outer lack of harmony in his life was sufferable by his deep-felt spiritual trajectory.[5] His awareness of the nature of human existence found expression in his intimate relationship with God. One gets the impression that his thoughts and his ability to express them in writing were his only companions in solitude.

Tragically, Ibn Gabirol's character and disposition did not make him many friends. He was misunderstood and seen as a social outcast. Many prominent members of the Andalusian intelligentsia while recognizing his literary gifts abandoned him to a life of loneliness. Even his relationship with Shemuel HaNagid "lacked the warmth of his friendship with Yekutiel."[6] This may have had something to do with ibn Gabirol's lack of enthusiasm for Shemuel HaNagid's poetry.

Despite his death at an early age, ibn Gabirol wrote many books (he claims to have written twenty) and over four hundred poems that

---

[4] In two autobiographical poems where he describes the death of his genuine friend and benefactor Yekutiel, ibn Gabirol invokes a cosmic suffering. See Haim Schirmann, *HaShira Ha'Ivrit BiSefarad* (Jerusalem: Mosad Bialik and Dvir, 1959), 202.

[5] See HaRambam's Guide of the Perplexed 3:22-23

[6] Solomon ibn Gabirol, *Introduction to The Kingly Crown: Keter Malkhut*, translated by Bernard Lewis (Notre Dame: University of Notre Dame Press, 2003), 5.

appear in published editions of his works. New ones continue to be discovered. Only three of his books have survived. The first is called *Kitab Islah Al-akhlag* (the Book for the Improvement of Moral Qualities or Improvement of the Qualities of the Soul), in Hebrew it is called *Tikkun HaNefesh*. It was translated into Hebrew by Yehuda ibn Tibbon. In clear, and precise language he offers practical guidance on issues relating to ethics, education, and a classification of good and evil character traits. In this work he tries linking ethics with physiology and with behavioral conditioning, an idea that was prevalent in Andalusia.[7] The general theory is that good actions and consistent good habits leads to the improvement of the soul, allowing for access to Divine wisdom. Happiness, and its pursuit is a theme that occupies ibn Gabirol's attention. For him happiness is the result of wisdom.

He also wrote *Mukhtar Al-jawahir* [Choice of Pearls]. This book is an anthology of ethical maxims and wise sayings drawn from Arabic sources and arranged in sixty categories. This too was translated by Yehuda Ibn Tibbon and became very popular in Europe.

Ibn Gabirol's third book is by far the most important of his works that have survived history: It is a philosophical work called *Mekor Hayim* [The Source of Life]. This is an esoteric work, a sort of guide to mysticism and higher consciousness. The Arabic original is lost and for a long time was represented by the Latin translation commissioned in 1150 C.E.by the Archbishop of Toledo and translated by the converted Jew John deSeville. The Latin version has as the author of the book "Avicebron." This work was very popular in medieval religious Christian circles, especially among the Franciscans who had no idea of the true identity of the author. It was not until 1846 that Solomon Munk revealed the true authorship of the book based on some thirteenth century manuscripts of *Mekor Hayim* he found in the National Library of Paris. In this work ibn Gabirol presents the Jewish idea that the world was created *ex-nihilo*, from absolutely nothing. Andalusian Jewry parted ways with Aristotle on this issue. In fact, this philosophical concept is later developed more fully by HaRam-

---

[7] HaRambam will later develop the concept of forming good habits and training good ethical behavior.

bam.⁸ Shelomo ibn Gabirol expresses through his poetry and teaching how God is completely transcendent but also intimately immanent and personal. He reconciles this theological contradiction by stating that while the Divine Essence is immutable and wholly transcendent the Divine Will acts as an active extension that connects with the finite. And yet, in His ultimate essence God is both Will and Essence. To know this, writes ibn Gabirol, is to experience supreme happiness.

Ibn Gabirol's religious poems are exquisite. His poems are full of anxious emotional stirring and were probably written in a deep state of mystical ecstasy. He blends mysticism, science, and philosophy per his Andalusian education. As is reflected in ibn Gabirol's esoteric writings and later developed by Bahya ibn Pakuda and HaRambam, the Jews of Andalus recognized that authentic mystical pursuits must be in line with the science of God's created universe and consistent with philosophical principles.⁹ European Jewry created what is called Kabbalah which rejects philosophy and science. Alexander Altmann in a groundbreaking article called, "Maimonides' Attitude Toward Jewish Mysticism," distinguishes between Jewish mysticism and European kabbalah. Kabbalah is not mystical in the strict sense of the term, he writes, but he admits that it is a form of esotericism.¹⁰

Ibn Gabirol is most famous for two long poems. One is titled *Azharoth* [Warnings] and the other *Keter Malkhut* [the Kingly Crown]. *Azharoth* is a poetic version of the six hundred and thirteen mitzvoth. The poem appears in Sephardic *machzorim* [holy day prayer books] and is recited on Shavuoth to celebrate the giving of the Torah. *Keter Malkhut* is arranged in three parts. The first part celebrates God's goodness in lyrical language of sublime grandeur. He references Di-

---

⁸ See Guide 2:13 were he writes: "God brought everything existing outside Himself into existence after complete and absolute nonexistence." and 2:19 See Commentary on Mishna Sanhedrin 10:1 Principle number four Kafikh edition (Jerusalem 1963) page 212 see also MT Hilkhot Avodat Kochavim 1:3

⁹ In Europe, philosophy and science were viewed as having nothing to do with mystical aspirations and were seen as mutually exclusive. European Jewry created what is called kabbalah, which rejects philosophy and science.

¹⁰ Altmann, "Maimonides' Attitude Toward Jewish Mysticism," 200-219.

Ibn Gabirol's Keter Malkhut
Cairo Genizah Collection (University of Pennsylvania. Center for Advanced Judaic Studies. Library).

vine wisdom and the active intellect, an important idea in HaRambam's mystical writings that will later be developed in the *Moreh Nevuchim*. In this first part of the poem, ibn Gabirol describes how Creation is an act of God's will and how the ultimate goal of all human beings is to know God. In the second part of the poem, he describes the wonders of Creation per the philosophic and scientific ideas of the time. The third part of the poem focuses on awakening the human being to the depth of worship and love of God, the pursuit of repentance, and the need for supplication. The poem ends with a hymn of glory of God, both personal and universal. This poem can be found in many Sephardic Yom Kippur *machzorim* and is recited between services during the day of Yom Kippur. Ibn Gabirol considered this poem his greatest achievement. The frequent quotations from the book of Iyov suggest the poem may be a self-reflection of his own personal suffering.

His religious and liturgical poetry reveals a deep-felt attachment to the land of Israel and the Jewish holy days, a desire for the service of the Bet HaMikdash, and a profound stirring of religious fervor. All his poetry is addressed to God.[11]

His Legacy

Shelomo ibn Gabirol, is, in my opinion, one of the most illustrious scholars to emerge from Andalusia. His poetry not only made numerous cultural, literary, and philosophical breakthroughs but demonstrates how the Andalusian mystical tradition was alive and vibrant.[12]

While he is cited favorably by Moshe ibn Ezra, Avraham ibn Ezra, Yoseph ibn Zaddik, and others, surprisingly Avraham ibn Daud, the medieval chronicler and historian did not show much care for ibn Gabirol.

Rabbi Avraham ibn Ezra considered ibn Gabirol's interpretations of rabbinic allegories especially profound. He introduces ibn Gabirol in his commentary on the story of Gan Eden [Paradise]. For ibn Gabirol, the lost paradise, soul, matter, and the Cherubim protecting the gates of Gan Eden are all a metaphor for man's quest for knowledge. While HaRambam does not mention ibn Gabirol even once, it is evident that he was influenced by his works and developed many of his theological ideas. Ironically, there is considerable evidence that the kabbalists of Gerona were influenced by his writings as well.[13]

Ibn Gabirol's only experience of true love was the love he felt from

---

[11] Jefim Schirman, "Salomon ibn Gabirol, Su Vida y Su Obra Poetica" in *Seis Conferencias en Torno a Ibn Gabirol*, (Malaga, Spain 1973); also see *Hebrew Poetry in Spain and Provence*, Volume 1 (Hebrew) (Jerusalem: Bialik Institute, 1954).

[12] See note 150 below

[13] Gershom Scholem, *Kabbalah* (New York: Dorset Press, 1974), 93 and 392.

God and the profound love his soul had for God. Early scholars of ibn Gabirol's work and life, such as Solomon Munk, were convinced (as I am) that Shelomo ibn Gabirol was a mystic in the truest sense and his religious poetry is a product of his mystical ecstatic experiences.[14] He enriched Jewish prayer and discovered God's abundant love in his own suffering:

> When to the left and to the right I have sought for a helper
> I could look for dear life to no aid but Your power
> More than all earthly treasures I have made You my portion
> Through all the cares of Your love I have rapture eternal
> And prayer is but an occasion for praise.[15]

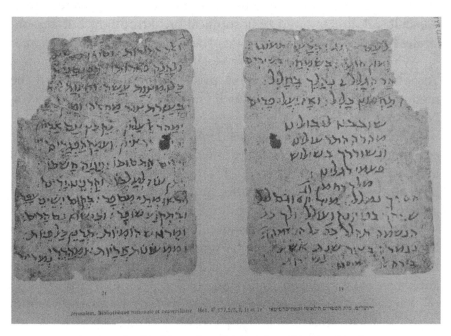

A poem by Shelomo ibn Gabirol found in the Geniza

[14] Jochanan Wijnhoven, "The Mysticism of Solomon ibn Gabirol," *The Journal of Religion*, Volume 45, No 2 (1965).

[15] Shirman, 239.

Three poems by Shelomo Ibn Gabirol, translated by Israel Zangwill

MY HEART CLAMOURS

My heart craves to praise Thee,
But I am unable.
Would my understanding
Were as spacious as Solomon's.
Without it my wisdom
As yet ill suffices
For expounding Thy wonders
And Thy deeds of beneficence
Wrought for me and all mankind.
Without Thee all's hopeless,
And where is the rock
Sustaining, suspending
The weight of the world?
I am as one orphaned;
Nay, on Thee I am cast.
What then can I do
But look to Thee, wait on Thee,
In whose hand is the spirit
Of all that is living,
In whose hand is the breath
Of all the creation?

MY SOUL SHALL DECLARE

My soul shall declare to Thee Thou art her former
    And shall Thee as her maker, O God, testify,
At Thy word "Be, O Soul" did she take on existence,
    And from naught didst Thou draw her as light from the eye.

Of Thee she shall own and affirm, hand uplifted,
    'Twas Thou that didst breathe her in me, and as due
For that work she shall pour out her thanks and bear witness
    That to me she was given Thy bidding to do.

She serves Thee as handmaid while yet in the body,
    And the day she returns to the land whence she came,
In Thee will she dwell, for in Thee is her being,
    Doth she rise, doth she sit, Thou art with her the same.

She was Thine when unborn ere the day of her breathing,
    With wisdom and knowledge by Thee she was fed,
And to Thee for her ordinance looks, and subsistence,
    Indebted to Thee for her water and bread.

Her gaze is to Thee, and in Thee is her hoping
    When like novice in child-birth she cries in affright.
O take her torn heart as a sacrifice offered,
    And her ribs lacerated for fiery rite.

To Thee let her pour out her tears as drink-off'ring,
    Let the breath of her sighing as incense-cloud be,
At her gate and her doorway she watches with prayer,
    She is burning like flame with her passion for Thee.

She must ever approach Thee as servant his master,
    Or as handmaiden looks to her mistress's eye,
She must spread out her palms in request and petition
    And turn herself humbly to Thee in her cry.

For call Thee she must, nor endure to be silent,
    Like a bird in the net her one hope is in flight,
In the depth of the night she must rise and keep vigil,
    For her work is Thy works to declare and recite.

For Thee she must pine and of Thee make entreaty,
    Her hand must be clean and as stainless her thought.
Her breach do Thou heal, be her hope and her helper,
    When she draws nigh redeem her, her sin count as naught.

Behold her affliction, and hark to her weeping,
    In the sphere of the soul she with Thee is alone,
Repay and restore her, attend to her anguish,
    When her sobs and her tears her backslidings bemoan.

Bemock, O Almighty, the foes that bemock her,
    Avenge with due vengeance her insults and shame,
In her stress be a rock of support 'gainst her foeman,
    Nor yield up the child Thou to manhood didst frame.

No enemy came, whose reproach could be borne with,
    No cruel one hunted her down in her track,
'Twas the friends of her household betrayed her—her passions—
    'Twas her comrade who bloodily stabbed in the back.

I ever am seeking my body's best welfare,
    Yet it in return would my spirit undo.
Ah, truly the fruit of the tree in its root is,
    The proverb "Like mother, like daughter" is true.

POUR OUT THY HEART

Pour out thy heart to the Rock,
    Pour out thy inmost soul
To the stronghold naught can shock,
    As the mornings and evenings roll.
To Him who around and before
    Is, whether thou rest or roam,
To Him let thy thoughts up soar,
    Be thou on the road or at home.
Thus, tested by praise and belief,
    Thou favor divine shalt gain,
He will turn His ear to thy grief,
    He will bend His eye on thy pain.
Behold, He will pay thy reward,
    Thou shalt share the abode of the blest,
For the day thou return to the Lord,
    He will draw thee close to His breast.

> In all your ways know Him
>
> MISHLE 3:6

Rabbi Bahya ben Yoseph ibn Pakuda
1050-1120 C.E.

VERY LITTLE IS KNOWN of the life of Rabbi Bahya ben Yoseph ibn Pakuda (hereon ibn Pakuda) other than the fact that he lived in Zaragoza, Spain where he served as a revered Dayan [judge on the rabbinical court], a position of great prestige. His legacy is the work he wrote late in life called *Al Hidayah ila Faraid al-Kulub* [the Direction to the Duties of the Heart]. This work was translated to Hebrew by the famous Yehuda ibn Tibbon and came to be known as *Hovot HaLevavot* [*Duties of the Heart*]. This book enjoyed immediate success both in Andalusia and in Ashkenaz, Europe. It has been translated into most languages, including Yiddish. It is indeed interesting that it can be found on the shelves of Lithuanian Yeshivoth even today and yet many of the core values the author promotes such as the pursuit of philosophical precision, the study of secular sciences and a non-theurgic approach to mitzvoth would not be wholly embraced by most Lithuanian or Hassidic *Roshei Yeshiva*.[1]

In the introduction to his book, ibn Pakuda states that his goal is

---

[1] Ibn Pakuda and his work *Hovot HaLevavot* is anti-superstition and anti-magic. While the Zohar was not yet written the ideas in *Hovot Halelvavot* are contrary to the Zohar and kabbalistic thinking.

to place Judaism's ethical, spiritual, and mystical teachings into a coherent system. Not enough emphasis has been placed on the observance of the duties of the heart, writes ibn Pakuda. One cannot observe rituals without being conscious of the spiritual elements associated with Jewish observance of the commandments. There is an intimate relationship between the physical body and the soul. Ibn Pakuda notes it is impossible to perform even one external duty appropriately, or one movement of the limbs, without the total consent of the mind and spirit. The ideal state of intent when performing mitzvoth is what he calls "whole-heartedness" – where the body, mind, and soul are in perfect harmony.

> The believer's faith is not perfect unless he acknowledges both the elements of knowledge, and he practices the duties of the heart.[2]

Alas, writes ibn Pakuda, the human condition is such that achieving the ideal state of "whole-heartedness" is difficult and rare indeed but must be pursued and practiced.

He ends his introduction with a parable of a palace and a king who wishes to test the intelligence of his most trusted servants:

> A king wishing to test the intelligence of his servants distributed among them bundles of silk. The diligent and sensible one among them sorted the portion allotted to him, again and again and divided it according to its quality into three parts: the superfine, medium, and inferior silk. He did the best that could be done with each of these – he had the material made up by skilled workmen into fine clothing of different styles and colors which he wore in the royal court, selecting the garments suitable to each occasion and place. The fool among the king's servants made out all of his silk that which the wise servant made out of the worst silk; he sold it for whatever it would fetch and hastened to squander the proceeds in eating and drinking. When

---

[2] Bahya ibn Pakuda, *The Book of Direction of the Duties of the Heart*, Introduction, translation by Menahem Mansoor, 93, (London: Routledge and Kegan Pal, 1973).

these things came to the attention of the king he was pleased with the conduct of the intelligent servant, promoted him to a position near himself, and raised him to the rank of one of his favorites. But he was displeased with the actions of the fool, drove him away, and had him transported to some desolate parts of his realm to keep company with those who has incurred his royal anger.[3]

Ibn Pakuda proceeds to explain the meaning of the parable. The bundle of silk is the Torah God gave the Jewish people. The finest threads of the silk are the duties of the heart, the inward spiritual world that the seeker taps into when serving God. The medium threads represent the external or practical duties, while the least of the silks threads represent the historical elements of the Torah. The wisest know how to distinguish between the different elements of Torah and religious practice. The wise know how to weave the different elements into their service of God and their pursuit of love of God. It is the fool who cannot distinguish between the different levels of spiritual practice, beliefs, and observances.

The strength of Andalusian Jewry was indeed their ability to distinguish between Halakha (Jewish Law) and minhag (custom). They understood within this formidable body of rabbinic law three different types of minhag developed. First is *Minhag* that emerges from *Halakha* and is rooted in Halakhic practice and emerged possibly because there were two valid yet conflicting views. Alternatively, there are *Minhagim* that have no *Halakhic* source but are established by the practice of the Jewish people and ratified by the Sanhedrin. Regarding these two types of *Minhag*, HaRambam writes:

> "Whoever goes against any one of the regulations of the rabbis is transgressing a negative commandment, inasmuch as it says in the Torah 'You must follow according to all that they teach you.' This includes amendments, decrees, and **customs** that they teach to the multitudes in order to strengthen their minds and improve the world." (*MT Mamrim 1:2*)

[3] Ibid, 106.

A third type of *Minhag* emerges locally within a community or even a family and is often based on local culture and customs of the host society. The first two types of *Minhagim* are very hard to differentiate from rabbinically-ordained *Mitzvoth*. The third, while still called *Minhag*, is significantly less binding. The Jews of Andalus also knew how to distinguish between *Peshuot shel Mikra* (the original meaning of the biblical text) and *Midrash* (hermeneutics). They invested a great deal of intellectual energy determining how to apply each of these concepts and when. Within Midrash there are distinctions between Midrash Halakha and Midrash Aggadah. Ibn Pakuda's point is that recognizing and understanding the various elements and their nature of the vast corpus of rabbinic literature is critical to achieving mastery of the material which is a fundamental principle in the service of God.

For Rabbi Bahya ibn Pakuda, an action without the inner spiritual intent is null and void. Religious practice lies primarily in the clear conception of what the ideal conduct should be. He emphasizes consciousness, knowledge, and understanding in addition to intent. *Kavanah* [intent] must be framed in the context of the intellect and reason. Without knowledge and reason, all of one's best intentions will fall flat.

For Bahya ibn Pakuda reason and philosophical precision is the most central element of Torah study and observance. This is consistent with the religious and spiritual approach embraced by Andalusian Jewry. Knowing and learning about the created world, the natural order of things, physics, psychology, and natural sciences is a means to knowing God, loving God and being in awe of God.[4] The Torah is the written word of God and the source of Divine wisdom and yet it is but a part of the greater pursuit of knowledge which leads to love of God and proximity to God. In ascending order, Ibn Pakuda

---

[4] HaRambam develops this idea throughout his writings. See MT Hilkhot Yesodei HaTorah 2:2

presents a hierarchy of material that one should endeavor to know: One must master the natural sciences and physics, then one must master Torah, TaNaKH and all that is included in Divine wisdom, and finally one must have full engagement with the heart. The duties of the heart are themselves organized in a hierarchy of ten gates, each of which takes the seeker to higher level – what he calls "roots" – leading to a wholehearted mystical union with God.

The spiritual trajectory of *Duties of the Heart* begins with the root of roots, the most basic premise of one's relationship with God: knowing the Unity of God. Knowing that God is a singularity unlike any other singularity. The spiritual trajectory of the remaining nine gates leads one to a deep-felt love of God that leads to a union with the Divine. Ibn Pakuda is not writing for philosophers; he is writing for the seeker whose spirit yearns for God. Therefore, at the most basic level one has to understand that which God is not. Any kind of corporeality or any form of ascribing to God human qualities, emotions, or the like is a movement in the wrong direction – a movement away from God.

He reiterates numerous times that his goal is not to refute those who dispute the most fundamental principles of faith. Rather his aim is to illuminate the way to God for those who seek the Divine and for whom the fundamental principles are evident like a lightning bolt illuminates a dark night.[5]

Ibn Pakuda argues that the religious practices associated with duties of the heart are obligatory both by revelation through the Torah and by reason. Actions of course can be commanded, but how does a legal system command thoughts or beliefs? Isn't that a form of human brainwashing and coercion? How can the Torah possibly command what one must believe, think, or feel? If someone already believes in God, then the command is superfluous; if someone chooses not to believe, how can it possibly be enforced?

The Jews of Andalusia assumed that belief can and is indeed commanded. The Torah is unequivocal when it states:

Know therefore, this day, and take to heart that the Lord is God

---

[5] HaRambam frequently uses the image of lightning illuminating a dark night.

in heaven above and on earth below, there is no other.[6]

HaRambam, based on this verse, begins his *Mishneh Torah* (his legal code of law) with:

> *Yesod Hayesodot*, the basic principle of all basic principles and the pillar of all sciences, is **to know** (believe) that there is a First Being who brought every existing thing into being. All existence, whether celestial, terrestrial, or belonging to an intermediate class, exist only through His true existence.[7]

Ibn Pakuda explains the philosophy behind such a ruling. According to ibn Pakuda, Judaism mandates certain beliefs and creeds that are essential to being identified as a "good Jew." He differentiates between outward observances – such as fasting, prayer, or resting on Shabbath, and inward observances such as love and fear of God. To observe the law correctly, ibn Pakuda argues, one must have substantial knowledge of the principles upon which they are based. Knowledge implies the study of God and therefore the entire enterprise of outward and inward observances are built upon belief. The quality of a person's belief has a direct bearing on the level of his or her observances.

In other words, one cannot correctly observe the biblical commandments to recite the *Shema Yisrael* if he or she does not completely believe in God and understand that God is *One* in the sense of unique and completely non-physical.

Ibn Pakuda makes a second argument, which is as compelling as the first argument, if not more so. He argues that it would be absurd of God to issue commandments that involve our arms—such as *tefillin*, our legs – such as *aliyah leregel* [pilgrimages to Jerusalem], our mouths – such as reciting prayers, our gastronomy – such as eating *matza*, and not our mind the noblest of our organs. If our entire bodies must serve God, then surely our mind must serve God as well. He cites the verse in Devarim quoted above and maintains that it is a bib-

---

[6] Devarim 4:39.

[7] HaRambam *MT Yesodei HaTorah* 1:1.

lical duty to believe in God, Creator of heaven and earth!

Ibn Pakuda's third answer, while less creative, might be the most convincing. Commanding internal obligations is not new in the Torah. One of the Ten Commandments forbids us from coveting one's neighbor's wife and another's belongings. We are forbidden to hate our brother in our heart,[8] similarly, we are obligated to love our neighbor as ourselves. Additionally, repentance [teshuva] requires a degree of sincerity to be fulfilled appropriately.

Ibn Pakuda argues God is not only concerned with what we want or how we feel, but God is also concerned with what we believe.

It is not enough, insists ibn Pakuda to repeat what others have said about belief or to accept belief in God on the authority of others, but rather one must seek to understand the nature and scope of belief in God. The duties of the heart are not only commanded, but reason dictates their observance.

The above discussion sets the framework for how Andalusian Jewry understood the relationship between Jewish law, the Jewish people and God. Law for the Jews of Andalus was understood in radical terms with no parallel in legal thought. From this perspective law is the ultimate authority, not the people, not the sovereign and not even God.

Jewish law is the result of a bilateral agreement between God and the Jewish mediated by Moshe Rabbenu at the foot of Mount Sinai some 3300 years ago. Based on rabbinic tradition the bilateral agreement contains six-hundred and thirteen mitzvot, commandments regulating all aspects of Jewish life. The agreement between God and the Jewish people is regarded as divine and immutable.[9] Being that it is divine it requires no promulgation or declaration. All Jews at all times no matter where they may physically be obligated to observe the commandments. This then is not a theological doctrine but rather a purely legal principle that does not require an authority or institution to sanction it. God, therefore, and the belief in God is a function of the law. Belief in God is the consequence of the law and not the cause of one's

---

[8] Vayikra 19:17

[9] HaRambam Thirteen Principles of Faith, Commentary on Mishna Sanhedrin 10:1

observance of the law.

This idea is codified by HaRambam in his Mishneh Torah where he states unequivocally that Belief in God is a mitzvah a result of the bilateral agreement between the Jewish people and God.[10] As ibn Pakuda states the ultimate grounds for belief in God is legal, not theological, and not metaphysical.[11]

Judeo Arabic Translation of the Bible

[10] MT Yesodei HaTorah 1:1 and Sefer HaMitzvaooth Mitzvat Aseh #1 ,

[11] See MT Hilkhot Yesodei HaTorah 8:2. See also Yoseph Faur *Studies in Mishneh Torah* (Hebrew) (Mosad harav Kook, Jerusalem 1978) page 18.

Knowing God

Ibn Pakuda introduces his readers to a practice that is well known in Andalusia and that would later be developed by HaRambam in his *Moreh HaNevuchim*, The Guide of the Perplexed. The premise is that language cannot describe God – God is indescribable. Anything we can possibly know about God is deduced from the principle of His absolute unity and from what we can observe of God's creations in the universe. The only things that can be said about God are things that God is not because articulating anything positive about God will always be false. God is wholly and completely transcendent not depending on or even related to any other existing species, genus, or group of creation. And while rabbinic literature has a great deal to say about God in its various writings at the end of the day all we can know about God is what God is not and what He has created.

And yet the gap can be spanned. The gap between man and God, writes ibn Pakuda, is bridged by the human being transcending his or her physicality and elevating one's consciousness to higher levels. Even revelation and prophecy are only possible if the human being rises to the spiritual challenge.

As noted, Ibn Pakuda teaches that one can achieve knowledge of God through knowledge of God's universe. The universe is a manifestation of God's actions and represents God's attributes of action. Reflecting on the created order is the only positive knowledge of God that one can aspire to achieve. For ibn Pakuda there are no astral intermediaries between man and God; rather, knowledge of God's world is the most direct venue to God.

Appreciating the vast wisdom and the intricate physics of God's creations leads to a state of profound love and radical awe of God. It is that experience that bridges the eternal gap between the transcendent God and the human soul. HaRambam will later develop this idea of a passionate love of God that reflects the Andalusian mystical aspirations.[12]

---

[12] See my *The Mysticism of Andalusia: Exploring HaRambam's Mystical Tradition*, (MHC Press, NY 2023)

Ibn Pakuda puts forth the Andalusian belief that philosophy is an essential discipline in strengthening one's religious convictions. This explains HaRambam's placement of *Sefer Mada* [Jewish philosophy] before *Sefer Ahava* [devotional laws]. Similarly, Ibn Pakuda's early chapters of his book *Hovot HaLevavot* introduce the idea that the absolute "oneness" of God precedes time and all the duality that matter introduces into our existence. He alludes to concepts that were taken for granted in Andalus and later fully developed by HaRambam, such as creation *ex nihilo,* and the concept of the Prime Mover.

Regarding providence as well, Ibn Pakuda begins the task of charting the Andalusian approach that HaRambam fully develops later. He writes that the closer one comes to perfection, the more one is graced with God's protection and providence. Similarly, writes ibn Pakuda, abstinence from excessive physical pleasures, materialism, and self-aggrandizement is what nurtures the soul and brings one closer to God.

Like his predecessors, Ibn Pakuda had a strong aversion to the use of anthropomorphism. He felt that such images prevented students from achieving spiritual heights. Genuine knowledge of God means transcending the limitations of language and thought. In one of his parables, Ibn Pakuda describes men who cannot correctly identify the road that leads them to their destination. Similarly, following tradition and authority is indeed a step in the right direction for Ibn Pakuda and the scholars of Andalus, but it can only take one so far. To know God and arrive at true knowledge of God one must know the correct road, which is the pursuit "rational investigation."[13]

The Ten Gates Toward Spiritual Perfection

1. *Yichud Ha'El:* The Unity of God

There can be no knowledge of God, love of God, or proximity to God without a clear understanding of the concept of the unity of God. Ibn Pakuda's proofs and deductions are beyond the scope of this work.

---

[13] This of course recalls HaRambam's analogy of the Palace.

However, he establishes that corporeal language of the Torah must be interpreted metaphorically, and the Divine attributes as described in chapter thirty-three of the book of Shemoth are attributes of the name of God and not of God's essence.[14]

He explains the abundant anthropomorphism found in the TaNaKH in terms of it needing to be accessible to all people even those who are less philosophically sophisticated. The Torah writes Ibn Pakuda was written in "the language of man"[15] so that it be understood by all.

He does however concede that while God cannot be known in the way people know things, the soul can know God even while still in a physical body. This is the goal and purpose of religious life.

2. *Be'ur HaBeru'im:* The Examination of Created Things

Divine wisdom manifests itself in the composite nature of man and in the general and detailed order of the world. Mankind is created differently and is superior to all other created beings in the world. Divine wisdom can be revealed through mankind's soul. Through reason, the existence of God is known. If man loses reason, he cannot hope for reward and redemption.

The soul of man (and woman) is made up of two opposing parts with dual functions - the soul is very much a part of the physical experience, but it also yearns to reach for the spiritual.

3. *Avoda:* Service of God

This "gate" deals with reward and punishment. Reward is the consequence of service. The highest reward one can attain is the world-to-come. Only the few who can appreciate the spiritual rewards of the world-to-come pursue it; most others only understand and appreciate physical rewards. Here Ibn Pakuda discusses the problem of free will. "Let man live as if he has free will," writes Ibn Pakuda, and

---

[14] See my discussion on this subject in The Mysticism of Andalusia pages pages 341-345

[15] Ibid page 106-108

at the same time believe that everything is determined. This paradox writes Ibn Pakuda provides the soul of the human being the opportunity to strive for spiritual heights while remaining humble.

Two paths lead to the world-to-come: the path of Torah and the path of reason. One must first establish unequivocal conviction of all the foundations of religious certainty through reason, and only then can Torah be observed at the highest level. As a result of this system, he makes a distinction like Rav Sa'adia Gaon did before him, between the mitzvoth that make reasonable sense and those that had to be revealed. All mankind is bound to observe the mitzvoth of reason while only the Jewish people who experienced revelation are bound by the mitzvoth of Torah.

The revealed commandments are pedagogical in nature. They serve to remedy the excesses and desires that mankind is driven to pursue. The human soul gradually connects with the spiritual at every opportunity presented. The soul's created objective is a wholehearted worship of God.

Being chosen, writes ibn Pakuda, has its benefits but also its dangers. The chosen ones will always suffer more.

4. *Bitachon:* On Trust of God

Here Ibn Pakuda begins a new part of the book, where ethics and the working of the inner world take center stage. Trust in God comes from absolute understanding of the Unity of God, and complete trust means the exclusion of worship, service, and recognition of any agent other than God. One must reject all forms of sorcery, magic, astrology, and that which the Middle-Ages called "untested science." Only absolute trust in God and in God's providence leads to reward and perfection of the soul. Trust only in God Who knows what is beneficial to mankind, both externally and internally.

Ibn Pakuda addresses the problem of theodicy in this chapter. Why do the wicked prosper while the righteous suffer? No single answer fits all, writes Ibn Pakuda. Each case must be analyzed separately. Perhaps the pious suffer in order to teach the masses a lesson? Or maybe because he was not zealous enough on behalf of God. Ibn

Pakuda asks why God made Iyov, the biblical Job suffer so much if he was a righteous man. He quotes Rav Saadia Gaon, who explains that this is the role of a *zadik*. The righteous must lead by example and show the world how to serve God even when times are difficult.

In this chapter he also discusses the importance of good health. One is not permitted to neglect the body, this, he writes, is a form of testing God and that is forbidden. God will not protect those who do not care for themselves, their physical bodies, and the society. One must be engaged in whatever occupation provides sustenance and maintenance.

The chapter ends with a discussion of why there is no mention of the world-to-come in the Torah. Ibn Pakuda answers that the wise who know how to read between the lines can clearly see the mention of the world-to-come in the Torah.

5. *LeYached Ma'asim Lishmo:* Wholehearted Devotion to God

One's deeds must be consecrated to God alone. One's actions must be pure with heavenly intention. This is the highest level of human existence. The value of each of one's deeds is determined by their purity of thought and wholeheartedness.

The primary obstacle to fulfilling pure deeds is ignorance of God and forgetfulness of Divine grace. This is a form of paganism because it leads to men worshiping themselves and the material world. The second obstacle is ignorance of the Torah and Jewish law. Observed correctly and with *kavanah*, intent Jewish law leads to the perfection of the body, society, and the soul. The third obstacle is the *Yezer HaRa* [the evil inclination]. Although the evil inclination is the least serious obstacle, Ibn Pakuda devotes the rest of the chapter to an explanation of its seduction.

The *Yezer Hara*, writes Ibn Pakuda, works in two ways. It will stir up doubts and nagging questions, or it will devise arguments designed to dissuade the believer. The *Yezer Hara* is constantly alert, always trying to render good deeds useless. The best protection against the *Yezer HaRa*, Ibn Pakuda suggests that one master the first four chapters of his book.

6. *Anava:* **Humility**

For Ibn Pakuda, humility is not false modesty or the lowliness of spirit that results from a lack of self-confidence. True humility is a reflective activity – it is the soul reflecting upon itself and recognizing how truly humble one is in the scheme of the greater universe. Once again, Ibn Pakuda emphasizes the importance of consciousness and self-awareness.

For Ibn Pakuda, self-pride is a form of self-worship and worse – idol worship. There is another kind of pride that he calls spiritual pride. This form of pride has both a negative and a positive side. Its negative effect is that spiritual pride stops the seeker from pursuing their upward trajectory and makes one self-satisfied. However, when it encourages the seeker to see in himself the possibilities of spiritual growth, see God's greatness, and be thankful for the spiritual opportunities available, then this variety of pride is positive. Spiritual pride can help increase one's humility before mankind and God.

Ibn Pakuda distinguishes between humility before man and humility before God. Humility before man always must be measured in context. It is not always appropriate, though it is very important. Humility before God, however, is universal and always relevant. It is a state of mind and consciousness that deepens one's awareness of God. True humility does not only exist in unfavorable circumstances. In fact, the opposite is true: One should learn to induce humility even when the natural feeling should be pride. The seeker must be humble even when life circumstances provide good reason to be arrogant. Knowledge of God is what inspires true spiritual humility. Recognizing the vast universe and how insignificant the human being is in the scheme of things leads to radical awe and spiritual humility.

True service and worship of God is dependent on profound humility before God. Just like there cannot be a servant without a master "there cannot be worship without humility." Ibn Pakuda sees humility as part of one's larger social and moral qualities. The truly humble person is easily recognized in a crowd. The humble person never takes revenge even when he has the power to do so. He does not rebel against God's judgements even in the face of death and rejects praise even when he has earned it. The truly humble never denies responsibility when it is pointed out to him or alters his behavior when his fortunes improve. He will always reflect on his own deeds even if he is not reproved by others.

Humility, writes Ibn Pakuda, can be induced by proper thoughts, meditations, and imagination. One should ask oneself, "Know from where you come and to where you are going and before Whom you will be judged."[16] One must live each day as a step closer to death and judgement and remember that life is full of changes that can occur in moment's notice.

Ibn Pakuda ends this gate by teaching that there is great reward for living a life of spiritual humility.

7. *Teshuva:* **Repentance**

All avenues of repentance are always open as long as one's heart is open to it, writes Ibn Pakuda. For him, repentance means the return of man to the service of God. In this chapter he is only interested in the return to God through consciousness and actions. Repentance is a gift that God has given the seeker to repair one's ways. He introduces a method that will later be developed more fully by HaRambam,[17] where one goes to the opposite extreme of ethical behavior in order to arrive at the ideal middle road. For example, if one is frugal with his money he must, for a period of time, go to the opposite extreme and give it away so that he will learn to be charitable in the correct Jewish way.

Repentance without knowledge and consciousness of wrongdoing is worthless. The process begins with *Viduy* [confession of wrongdoing], regret of sin, and finally affirming never to repeat the sin. Each of these stages of repentance are then broken down to five levels of inner consciousness.

The chapter ends with a discussion of the status of the one who sinned and repented. Is the sinner who repented equal or better than

---

[16] Pirke Avot 3:1

[17] MT Hilkhot Deot chapter 1-4. See Also *Shemoneh Perakim* chapter 4

the one who has never sinned? What did the sages mean when they said:

> The place where on the penitent stands the wholly righteous could not stand; as if saying: their degree is above the degree of those who never sinned because it is more difficult for them to subdue their passion.[18]

Ibn Pakuda explains that this principle only applies to the neglect of ritual sins. When one begins to perform rituals once again, he or she is equal in status to the righteous. Even if one repents after committing moral and ethical transgressions or the transgression of the negative commandments, Ibn Pakuda writes, he is never equal to those who haven't sinned. It is always better to never sin than to sin and repent.

8. *Cheshbon HaNefesh:* Self-Reckoning: The Soul

In this chapter Ibn Pakuda examines in great detail the nature of the soul. He revisits many themes already discussed in earlier chapters. As an analogy he uses the metaphor of a lowly servant in the presence of a great king.

Ibn Pakuda discusses the importance of organized religion in the life of those who seek out God. He notes how prayer, which is rooted in the heart of man and is a personal expression of devotion to God, is nevertheless most optimal when it is scheduled, fixed, and with a Minyan [a quorum of ten men]. The liturgy affords everyone the opportunity to be present before God with the correct words. This mechanism is a prescription against forgetfulness. Precisely because prayer is fixed and scheduled, it requires intent and wholeheartedness.

While one embraces the teachings of the rabbis one must always seek to deepen the meaning of their teachings and find new insights in their philosophy. All seekers require custom and rote practice, but the wise know how to infuse their practice with passion.

Pursuit of God is the highest form of religious expression. For Ibn

---

[18] TB Berakhot 34b; *Mishneh Torah Hilkhot Teshuva* 7:4.

Pakuda, the seeker desires God so passionately that he loses himself in the love and service of God. Such a level of spirituality is never arrived at suddenly. One must embrace the outward practices in order to fully develop the inward trajectory. Ibn Pakuda uses Euclidean geometry as an example as to how one must fully understand the concrete forms before engaging in the theory.

9. *Perishut:* Abstinence

Abstinence was part of the religious and mystical practices taught by Ibn Pakuda and the Jews of Andalus. The human being is made up of both body and soul; the physical body has to be harnessed and controlled in order to achieve an appropriate equilibrium.

The mystic, however, engages in what he calls "special abstinence" where emphasis is placed on the wellbeing of the soul over the needs of the physical body. Abstinence, in Ibn Pakuda's worldview, is a means to a greater purpose and not an end in itself. It must be an act of free will. For it to have its complete spiritual effect it must be practiced by one who has the power and does not use it. Jewish law is a means to abstinence and the ideal middle-path. It is an abstention that lies in one's consciousness and not in one's physical body.

The ideal seekers are modeled by our forefathers who combined spiritual life with work and self-maintenance.

10. *Ahavat HaElohim:* True Love of God

This is the culminating chapter of the ten gates towards spiritual perfection. Ibn Pakuda began the spiritual flight with unity of God and here he ends with union with God – the love of God. He states explicitly that love of God is the ultimate goal and the most noble form of worship. By placing this goal in the last chapter, he is suggesting that achieving love of God is a process that requires elf-examination, humility, and understanding the nature of the soul. HaRambam also places love of God at the end of the ten chapter on *teshuva* [repentance]. The soul is naturally inclined towards God but must be freely guided and educated by the body.

The Jewish Quarters in Lucena Spain, Andalusia

The verse in Devarim states that one must love God with "all of one's heart, soul, and means." The intensity of one's love is indicated by how much one is willing to sacrifice for that love.[19] Since the giving of the soul is the ultimate sacrifice, very few attain it.

The true lover of God is always in awe of God's wonders. He recognizes the importance of teaching and directing others toward God. One who is focused solely on his or her own spiritual development is like a merchant with only one item to sell. Even if this one item is valuable, the merchant can only profit once from the sale. A savvier merchant will sell many products even though they may be of lesser value. By bringing others to the love of God and Torah, one earns greater reward and reaches greater heights of spirituality. HaRambam develops this idea beautifully in his *Sefer HaMitzvoth*, where he writes that Avraham was the perfect example of one who loved God and brought others under the "wings of the Divine providence."

[19] TB Yoma 82b.

"And you shall love the Lord your God," this means that you shall make Him beloved to all like Avraham your father did as the verse states: "And all the souls that they had gotten in Haran" (Bereshit 12:5). That is to say that just as Avraham, being a lover of the Lord – as the Torah testifies "Avraham My friend" (Yeshayahu 41:8) – by the power of his conception of God and out of his great love for God, he summoned mankind to believe, you too must so love Him as to summon others unto Him.[20]

---

[20] HaRambam, *Sefer HaMitzvoth, Aseh* #3.

> The world is divided into men
> Who have wit and no religion and
> Men who have religion and no wit
>
> AVICENNA

Rabbi Yoseph ben Meir ibn Migash HaLevi
(1077-1141 C.E.)

HaRambam reserved his praise for only one Torah scholar of his generation – Rabbi Yoseph ben Meir ibn Migash HaLevi (hereon Ibn Migash). In his introduction to his commentary on the Mishna, HaRambam wrote about Rabbi Ibn Migash:

> The understanding that this man had of Talmud was unparalleled and awe inspiring . . . so that it could be said of him that never before had there been his like.

HaRambam was so attached to Ibn Migash that many scholars erroneously assumed he had been his pupil. Although Rabbi Ibn Migash was especially close to Dayan Mimon ben Yoseph, HaRambam's father, and HaRambam was indeed precocious, it is very unlikely that the three-year-old studied Talmud with the elderly and dying Rabbi Ibn Migash. HaRambam often quotes Rabbi Ibn Migash and adds that this is the interpretation he received from his father who learned it from his teacher, Rabbi Ibn Migash.

Rabbi Ibn Migash may have been the greatest Talmudic scholar to have lived following the close of the Talmud. Throughout his lifetime, Ibn Migash enjoyed an outstanding reputation; unlike most of his predecessors, he avoided all kinds of disputes and communal disagreements. The famous poet and philosopher Rabbi Yehuda HaLevi composed numerous poems about the rabbi. And it was Rabbi Yehuda HaLevi who first introduced Rabbi Ibn Migash to the scholars of Provence, France through direct correspondence. This letter is the earliest known document that suggests religious ties between the Southern French Torah centers and Andalusia.

We know very little about the life of Rabbi Ibn Migash. We know that at twelve years old he studied at the feet of the then-famous Rabbenu Yitzchak Alfasi in Lucena. At twenty-six, Rabbenu Alfasi appointed him successor as head of the Yeshiva even though Rabbenu Alfasi had a very eligible son. Rabbi Ibn Migash occupied the position for thirty-eight years, until his death.

Rabbi Ibn Migash recognized the difficulty of Talmud study and was wary of those who claimed to know Talmud well enough to teach it. He felt that a teacher who studies and masters Geonic literature or codified *halakha* is more reliable that one who is teaching Jewish law based on the Talmud. He was asked the following question:

> I am asking what our master would have to say regarding someone who has never studied under a rabbi and who is unfamiliar with the way of *halakha* – its interpretation and its reading. Rather he studied a large amount of Geonic responsa and books of law. He cannot, however, say from where in the Talmud it derives. Is it proper for this person to teach or is he unreliable in all contexts?

His response was fascinating and very relevant in understanding HaRambam's motivation in writing the *Mishneh Torah*. Rabbi Ibn Migash, as is evident from his response had more confidence in a teacher who knew the law based on Geonic literature but had no experience with Talmudic study than in one who claimed proficiency in Talmud but had no exposure to the codes and rulings of the Geonim. His response:

> Know that it is more proper that this person be allowed to teach than it is for the many self-styled teachers, most of whom lack one

of two things: understanding of the *halakha* and knowledge of Geonic rulings. Those who purport to teach based on their study of *halakha* and Talmud are the ones who should be prevented from doing so since in our generation there is no one worthy of this or anyone who after studying the wisdom of the Talmud has arrived at a level that he can then teach without relying on the commentaries of the Geonim. The one who teaches Geonic responsa and Geonic rulings – even though he might not be proficient in Talmud – he is finer and more decent that the person who thinks he knows Talmud and relies on himself.[1]

Tragically, very few written works of Rabbi Ibn Migash have survived the ravishes of history. We have his commentary on Baba Batra, and on Shevuoth. He is often quoted by medieval Talmudic scholars. A small number of his responsa have been published, translated from the original Judeo-Arabic. He is known to have composed a commentary on Rabbenu Alfasi's *Halakhot* but it has not survived. Nachmanides transmitted Rabbi Ibn Migash's Talmudic commentary to his students Rashba and Ritva, though Ibn Migash is seldom quoted by name.[2]

---

[1] Cited by Yoseph HaLevi Ben Migash, *Responsa*, edited by Simha Hasida (Jerusalem: *Mehon Lev Same'ach*, 1991, Hebrew), #114.

[2] Israel Moses TaShma, *Encyclopedia Judaica* (Keter Publishing House, NY Macmillan, 1973)

> And the Lord God of truth
> Shall direct his servant on the way of truth.
>
> IBN EZRA

Rabbi Avraham ben Meir ibn Ezra
(1089-1164 C.E.)

LIKE HaRambam, Rabbi Avraham ibn Ezra (hereon ibn Ezra) was one of the last great scholars to escape from Andalusia. And like HaRambam he also devoted his life and creative output to preserving and transmitting the intellectual, religious, and spiritual culture that he was heir to and that was on the verge of being lost.

Any record of medieval Jewish history must include Ibn Ezra. He was a biblical exegete, a poet, philosopher, grammarian, mathematician, astronomer, and Talmudic scholar. He is mentioned by Moshe ibn Ezra by his Arabic name, *Abu Iskhak Ibrahim ibn al-Majid Ezra*. According to Moshe ibn Ezra, Rabbi Avraham ibn Ezra and Yehuda HaLevi* were both from Toledo and later emigrated to Cordova. According to Tzvi Langerman, there is evidence that Ibn Ezra was born in Tudela, Spain, which was within the northern reaches of Andalusia.[1]

Ibn Ezra writes about himself that he was a troubled spirit. He refused to accept money or any form of compensation for his Torah scholarship, as was the tradition in Andalusia per Jewish law.[2] His

---

*Rabbi Yehuda Halevi was actually born in Tudela Spain.

[1] Tzvi Langerman, "Abraham ibn Ezra," ResearchGate October 2018, https://www.researchgate.net/publication/328432579_SEP_October_2018_Abraham_Ibn_Ezra

[2] See chapter on HaRambam below.

various attempts at business ventures failed. He decries his poor luck and lack of business savvy in a satiric poem where he writes that if he went into the candle business it would never get dark and if he sold shrouds no one would die.

> To my birthplace, they incline as they rise
> Were candles to be my merchandise
> The sun would not be taken in until my demise
> I try to succeed, but I am not able
> For they have wronged me in the skies
> Were I a merchant of burial shrouds
> As I live, no man dies[3]

In his commentary on Shemoth[4] Ibn Ezra speaks of his wife and four children who died at a young age. His one surviving son, Yitzchak, became a poet and befriended Rabbi Yehuda HaLevi. Yitzchak explored Islam and then returned to his Judaism. Despite Ibn Ezra's misfortunes, he was a gifted scholar whose works were so impressive they survived the ravages of time and proved to have permanent value. Could Robert Browning's (1812-1889) optimistic poem titled Rabbi Ben Ezra be about Rabbi Avraham ibn Ezra?

In or around 1140 C.E., as the Almohad invasion made life in Cordova impossible for the Jews, unlike HaRambam, Ibn Ezra followed the more popular migration north towards Christian Spain, Europe, and Italy, in search of a place to feel religiously, culturally, and intellectually at home.[5] The destruction of Andalusia and the annihilation of its rich Jewish legacy is lamented by Ibn Ezra in an elegy he wrote called *Eicha Yarad Sepharad* [How did Sepharad Fall]. The Hebrew word *Eicha* is an allusion Yirmiyahu's description of the destruction of Jerusalem.

---

[3] Kolatch, Y. *Masters of the Word* Volume II (Ktav Publishing NJ 2007) page 274

[4] Shemoth 2:2.

[5] See Gidon Freudenthal, "Abraham ibn Ezra and Judah Ibn Tibbon as Cultural Intermediaries" in *Exchange and Transmission Across Cultural Boundaries: Philosophy, Mysticism and Science in the Mediterranean World*, edited by H. Ben-Shammai, S. Shaked, and S. Stroumsa (Jerusalem: Israel Academy, 2013).

> Alas! The rain / upon Spain / from heaven was foul.
> Greatly distressed stood the west hands trembling to howl
> The Torah was withdrawn, the holy writ gone, and the Mishna hidden
> And the Talmud, barren stood, for all its glory was overridden
> Cordoba was stunned, and wholly abandoned, became like the sea's desolation
> The names of the Sages, and warriors for ages, died of famine and privation[6]

While in Europe, Ibn Ezra could not help but notice how even reputed Torah scholars did not know Hebrew grammar, basic philosophy, Jewish theology, or sciences. He undertook the task of translating the works of the Andalusian scholars for the benefit of the European Jewish communities in the hope of preserving the religious, spiritual, and cultural traditions of the Jews of Southern Spain and in the hope of educating his European coreligionists. He translated three grammatical treatises of Rabbi Yehuda ibn Hayyuj from Arabic into Hebrew and composed basic Hebrew grammar books for the European Torah scholars whose knowledge in grammar was deficient.

In his commentary on Kohelet[7] he bemoans the poor poetic style of Ashkenaz linguists. He notes how they are sloppy and imprecise in their Hebrew writing. He specifically notes the inferior style of Rabbi Eliezer HaKalir, the poet from Israel who was the primary influence of European Jewish poetry.

> We are obligated to know the grammar of our language, so that we will not make mistakes. For example, there are those who say while reciting the Grace After Meals and pronounce the word *"zunenu"* not knowing that *"zunenu"* is from the word *zona* [to

---

[6] Abraham ibn Ezra, Yalkut ed. Israel Levin (NY Keren Israel, 1985) #35 also see Translation by Peter Cole, The Dream of the Poem (Princeton University Press, 2007) pages 181-182. See S. J. Pearce *The Andalusi Literary Tradition: The Role of Arabic in Judah ibn Tibbon's Ethical Will*, (Indiana University Press, 2017) page 20

[7] Kohelet 5:1.

stray] just as *"anenu"* come from *"ana"* [to answer]. They do not realize that the correct root is *"zan"* [to provide food] . . .[8]

He then goes on to provide specific guidelines for poetic writing. While in Italy Ibn Ezra composed his short commentary on the Torah as well as his commentary on the *Neviim* [prophets], most of which is tragically lost. During that period, he also composed a book on the Jewish calendar called *Sefer HaIbur*. Although Rome had a vibrant Jewish community and a place of presumed intellectual activity, Ibn Ezra did not find a cultural home for himself there, based on the criticism described in his writings.

> There is no glory among the Edomites (Christians)
> For any scholar who there alights
> In the land of the Kedarites (Christians)
> And they hoot at us[9]

From Italy Ibn Ezra moved to Southern France around 1148 C.E., in the hope of finding like-minded scholars. There he found a more welcoming community of scholars and thinkers who appreciated the Andalusian tradition he represented. The famous translator Yehuda Ibn Tibbon,[10] who also migrated from Andalusia to Southern France, wrote about Ibn Ezra's arrival:

> But the exiles in France and throughout the borders of the Edomite (Christian) lands did not know Hebrew and they held these books as sealed tomes . . . until the sage Rabbi Avraham ibn Ezra arrived in their lands and helped them in this respect with his brief compositions, including many precious and valuable matters . . . Thereafter some of them followed this discipline, and they occupied themselves a bit in it. Then I encountered those who diligently are at its doors who travel by its light; men began

---

[8] Avraham Ibn Ezra, Introduction to *Commentary on Kohelet*.

[9] Ibid.

[10] Ibn Tibbon was responsible for translating the works of Rav Saadia Gaon, Bahya ibn Pakuda's *Hovot Halevavot*, Rabbi Yehuda HaLevi's *Kuzari*, and most famously HaRambam's *Moreh Nevuchim*.

to seek it and they tasted the sweetness, and when they saw that their eyes would light up, their ears opened up and they were drawn after it. Thus, they desire to understand literature.[11]

Ibn Tibbon here attests to the differences between the Andalusian and European cultures when it came to Jewish scholarship. Despite Ibn Tibbon's enthusiastic reception, Ibn Ezra was not at home intellectually in Southern France either. In 1152 C.E., just four years after arriving, he set out to Northern France, the home of the Ashkenaz Tosafists who were renowned for their Talmudic excellence. When he arrived in the city of Dreux he fell ill and was bedridden. In his introduction to his more elaborate commentary on the Torah, Ibn Ezra explains that in the city of Dreux he made a vow that if he recovers from his illness, he will write a second commentary on the Torah. After recovering from his debilitating illness, he wrote his second commentary called *Perush HaArokh*, the long commentary.

In Northern France Ibn Ezra met with the illustrious Rabbi Yaacov ben Meir, known as Rabbenu Tam (1100-1170 C.E.). Rabbenu Tam was very impressed with Ibn Ezra. Ironically but not surprisingly, Ibn Ezra was very impressed with Rabbenu Tam's Talmudic abilities but disappointed in his linguistic abilities. We know this from a beautiful and cordial poetic exchange between the two Torah giants. Ibn Ezra wrote about Rabbenu Tam:

> **What gall brings the Gaul in verse's abode?**
> *[What makes this Frenchman think he can write poetry]*
>
> **Like a stranger in the temple, no fear to tread.**
> *[Rabbenu Tam is trampling on the sacred grounds of poetry.]*
>
> **Were Yaacov to make sweet and Manna his ode.**
> *[If Rabbi Yaacov Tam would write poetry as sweet as Manna.]*
>
> **I am the sun that melts his heavenly bread.**[12]
> *[Then I(Ibn Ezra), will be like the midday sun that melts the Manna.]*

---

[11] Avraham Ibn Ezra, Introduction to *Commentary on Kohelet*.
[12] Brilliant references are made in this poem to Shemot 16:21.

Rabbenu Tam responded beautifully and poetically, conceding that indeed Ibn Ezra is the greater linguist. Ibn Ezra responded with another beautiful poem expressing his humility and Rabbenu Tam's superiority:

> Is it right for the bull [*abir*] of God's people, their Shepherd prized
> [*the term* abir *is used for as a term for our Patriarch Yaakov*] [13]
> To bow his head in a missive to the people's despised?
> Heaven forfends that God's own angel
> Should bow and prostrate before Bilam[14] chastised

While in Northern France Ibn Ezra wrote his commentary on Kohelet and Tehillim. He also produced important works on mathematics, astronomy, and astrology.[15] In his commentary on the book of Shemoth, when the Torah says that God filled Bezalel with the spirit of wisdom, he writes:

> Bezalel was knowledgeable in every aspect of mathematics, algebra, geometry, astronomy, science, and the secrets of the soul. He had an advantage over all the men of his generation; he knew every discipline while many of the "wise of heart" did not even know one discipline. This is why it says in "every discipline."[16]

It is an accepted fact among historians that the decimal number system, which had been known and used in India, first appeared in Europe in Ibn Ezra's writings. In one of his mathematic notebooks, he wrote:

> Now, if he does not have any *one*, but he does have the next level, for example tens, he should put a circular symbol first, to indicate

---

[13] Bereshit 23:18 and 24:34.

[14] Ibn Ezra compares himself to Bilam, the Moabite soothsayer.

[15] Unlike his Andalusian countrymen, ibn Ezra was fascinated by astrology. It is possible that was exposed to it in Europe and related it to his lack of fortune in life and the death of his wife and children. See Langerman Tzvi, "The Hebrew Mathematical Tradition," *Mathematics Across Cultures* online at *https://www.academia.edu/3434991/ The_Hebrew_mathematical_tradition*

[16] Shemoth 31:3.

that in the first level there are none, and then he should write the number of tens afterward.

In 1158 C.E., Ibn Ezra left Northern France and travelled to England; he died there in 1164 C.E. at the age of seventy-five. On his deathbed Ibn Ezra jokingly and wittily applied the following verse to himself and his impending death: "And Avraham was seventy-five years old when he left *charon*."[17] Instead of the city Charan, Ibn Ezra said *charon*, which means the furious wrath of this world.

Despite his constant travels and difficult life, Ibn Ezra produced over one thousand poems, mathematical and biblical riddles, and various mind-bending exercises in addition to his commentaries and translations.

His Biblical Commentaries

Ibn Ezra is most famous for his elaborate and extensive commentaries on the TaNaKH. The commentaries that have survived are on the Torah, the Five Megilloth, Yeshayahu, Trei Asar, Tehillim, Iyov, and Daniel. He wrote two commentaries on the Torah, the *Perush HaKatzar* [the short commentary] and *Perush HaArokh* [the long commentary].

Ibn Ezra understood that the world of Andalusia and the Judeo-Arabic culture was gone forever and so he wrote his commentaries in Hebrew, the universal language of the Jewish people. In the tradition of Andalus he wrote introductions to each of his compositions. In his introduction to his commentary on the Torah he expresses strong opposition to the way the Torah was being studied in some Northern Spanish schools and especially in Europe. He was against those who weave life lessons into their commentary. He wasn't against the study of pseudo-philosophy, but he felt the Torah needs to be learned as an independent text whose *peshat* meaning is most profound. He was against the Karaite interpreters of the Torah who opposed rabbinic teachings and interpretations. He opposed those

---

[17] Bereshit 12:4.

who neglected the *peshat* reading altogether and only read the Torah as allegory. And he of course opposed those who mimic the Christian readers of the Torah and interpret it as homily and solely through Midrashic lenses.

Ibn Ezra describes his own approach as one that is dedicated to the *peshat* reading of the text,[18] stylizing the "fundamentals of grammar" to arrive at the true meaning of the text. He writes:

> And it is right in my eye
> Before God's face on High
> His awe alone I savor
> In the Torah, I will never show favor
> I will explicate each word's grammar with all my strength
> And afterwards as I am able, I will explain it at length
> Because *derash* does not make the way of *peshat* mistaken
> For the Torah has seventy faces which may be awakened
> Only when it comes to laws and decrees
> If the verse has two reasons which may please
> And the one reason relies on the scribe's expertise
> For they are all righteous, we need no guarantees
> We will doubtless rely on their truth, with strong hands and ease
> God forbid that we may involve with Sadducees (Karaites)
> Who says that the scribes contradict the details written in these
> Rather, our predecessors embody truth
> And all of their words are truth
> And the Lord God of truth
> Shall direct his servant on the way of truth.

With regards to the narrative portions of the Torah, Ibn Ezra states that he is not committed to earlier commentaries that were based on Midrashic interpretations ("I will never show favor"). He interprets the text based on rules of grammar, linguistics, and reason. When it comes to the legal portions of the Torah, Ibn Ezra clearly states that he is bound by the rabbinic rules of interpretation.

---

[18] For an analysis of what *peshat* meant to the scholars of Andalus, see my book *The Mysticism of Andalusia*, (NY, NJ: MHC Press, 2023) Page 176 -190

Indeed, Ibn Ezra's commentary is characterized by a significant emphasis on grammar, language, and a sensitivity to the biblical style. His commentary is based on reason and includes his multi-disciplinary knowledge. He sets himself apart from his European counterparts by his sharp and precise commentary of the biblical text. While he writes in his introduction that he is bound by the rabbi's legal interpretations, at times he diverges from their exegesis. In other words, Ibn Ezra understood that there is a difference between *peshuto shel miqra* and rabbinic legal interpretations. There are times when the rabbis will use a biblical verse as a means of presenting a law or legal principle by using a creative mode of interpretation. For example, the biblical verse states "Be fruitful and multiply" (Bereshit 1:28). The rabbis understood this as a biblical mitzvah, a command to populate the world. Ibn Ezra writes that the *peshuto shel miqra* is that this is a blessing that God bestowed on man and the rabbis used the verse as a means of transmitting the law. In his commentary on the difficult verse *aharei rabbim le-hattot*,[19] which literally means "after the multitude to pervert justice," Ibn Ezra explains that the rabbis interpreted the verse to mean that all legal disputes must be solved in accordance to majority opinion.[20] Ibn Ezra here argues that while this is not *peshuto shel miqra* it is a means by which the rabbis anchored the legal principle of majority rule on the biblical text.

When Ibn Ezra presented a *peshat* that differed from rabbinic interpretation or from the standard *halakhic* practice, he always adds a note that one is obligated to follow the *halakha* as ruled by the sages because the "minds of the sages were greater than our minds."[21]

Ibn Ezra was a stickler for precision and consistency in his com-

---

[19] Shemoth 23:2

[20] TB Sanhedrin 2a

[21] Ibn Ezra wrote his *Iggeret HaShabbath*, his Epistle on Shabbath in reaction to a commentator who suggested the biblical Peshat is that a day really begins in the morning and not as the rabbis state in the evening. Ibn Ezra curses the author of this interpretation which may have been a European exegete with the words "may the hand of him who wrote these words wither and may his eyes darken." See "Sefer HaShabbath" in *Yalkut Ibn Ezra*, ed. Israel Levin (New York, Tel Aviv: Israel Matz Hebrew Classics Library Foundation, 1985)

mentary. He did not see the need to give meaning to trivial changes when stories are repeated in the Torah or to words that have variant spellings. For example, the Ten Commandments appear twice in the Torah, once in the book of Shemoth and the second time in the book of Devarim. Ibn Ezra writes:

> Behold, we have seen that from the beginning "*Anochi*" until the end of the section there is not difference between the two passages. From the beginning of "*Zachor*," until the end there are some differences . . . Avraham the author says: This is the way of those who speak the holy tongue. Sometimes they will explain their words in great detail, and sometimes they will state matters succinctly and tersely, so that the listener may understand their meaning. Know that the words are like bodies, while the meaning are the souls. The body is the soul's utensil; therefore, the rule of all the wise in every language is that they maintain the meanings, but they do not worry about changing the terminology as long as the meaning remains the same . . . there are many examples of this . . . nevertheless, the members of this generation look for a reason in all variations, even in spelling.

Another of Ibn Ezra's many rules is what he called in Hebrew *"moshekh atzmo ve'acher immo"* which means "it draws itself and another along with it." What this means is that often times the text will utilize a word or a letter to include a list of other items even though the word does not appear to be qualifying the list. For example, the verse states:

> For I am more of an ignoramus than any man; I do not have human understanding, and I did not study wisdom, and knowledge of the holy I know.[22]

If he is ignorant and did not study wisdom, how can he possibly know the holy? Ibn Ezra applies his principle here and interprets the verse to mean that the subject is ignorant, and he did not study wisdom or knowledge of the holy.

---

[22] Mishle 30:2-3.

Ibn Ezra's commentary is also characterized by reason and rationality. The Torah must make rational sense, as was the accepted outlook in Andalus. Ibn Ezra famously disregards the Midrash that states that Yitzchak was thirty-seven years old when Abraham was asked to sacrifice him to God.

> Our sages have said that Yitzchak was, at the time of the binding, thirty-seven years old. Now if these are words of tradition, we will accept them; but logically this is not proper, for Yitzchak's righteousness should be revealed and his reward would be double the reward of the father – for he gave himself over willingly to be slaughtered. However, the Torah tells us nothing about Yitzchak. Others claim that he was five years old, but this too cannot be because he carried the wood for the offering. What is most reasonable is that he was about twelve or thirteen years old, and his father compelled him and bound him against his will. The evidence of this is that the father hid the secret from his son.

Midrash aggadah for the Jews of Andalusia was meant to be taken seriously but not necessarily literally. And when reason defies the possibility of the Midrash, the unreasonable possibility can and should be disregarded. Another example appears in the book of Shemoth. According to Ibn Ezra, the Jews also suffered during most of the plagues that came upon Egypt. The verse in the book of Shemoth states, "All of Egypt dug around the Nile for water to drink, for they could not drink the waters of the Nile."[23] Ibn Ezra writes:

> Many say that when the water was in the hands of the Egyptians it was red as blood, but it turned clear again when it was in the hands of the Israelites. If so, why was this miracle not mentioned in the Torah? In my view the plagues of blood and frogs and lice included the Egyptians and the Hebrews, for we must follow what is written.

For Ibn Ezra, the Israelites in Egypt had to dig for water just like the Egyptians. If the Midrash was indeed true, the Torah would have

---

[23] Shemoth 7:24.

mentioned it because it is as great a miracle if not greater than the Nile turning into blood. There were some plagues where the Torah explicitly states that the Israelites did not suffer, such as the plagues of pestilence, hail, and wild animals.[24] Being that the verse explicitly states, "all of Egypt," there is no reason to assume it does not include the Hebrews.

Ibn Ezra is also well known for the concept that *en mukdam ume'uchar baTorah* [the Torah is not necessarily written in chronological order]. When the Torah alters the chronology, Ibn Ezra insists on understanding why. If the Torah intentionally places certain passages together that defy the historical chronology of events, then the juxtaposition must have some meaning.[25] Ibn Ezra is of the opinion that Yitro's encounter with his son-in-law Moshe Rabbenu occurred *after* the giving of the Torah even though it is recorded as having occurred prior to the giving of the Torah. Ibn Ezra writes:

> Now I will explain why the passage of Yitro was inserted here. Because we have mentioned above the evil done by Amalek to Israel, here we mention the contrasting good that Yitro did for Israel. It is written: "And Yitro was elated about all the good" (Shemoth 18:9), and he gave good and correct advice to Moshe and to Israel, and Moshe said to him, "And you will be our eyes" (Bemidbar 10:31), and this means that he enlightened their eyes. Now the king Shaul said while addressing the Kenites, Yitro's descendants, "and you did kindness with all the Israelites" (I Shemuel 15:6). Because it is written above: "God is at war with Amalek" (Shemoth 17:16), Israel must fight Amalek when God will grant them rest. So it mentioned the matter of Yitro here because his decedents reside near the nation of Amalek. This will remind Israel of the kindness of the ancestor, and they will not touch his seed.[26]

---

[24] Shemoth 8:17; 9:6 and 25.

[25] I. Gottlieb found 150 such cases in the Torah and presents how they are addressed by the medieval commentators. See *Yesh Seder LaMiqra: Chazal U'Parshanei Yemei Habeinayim al Mukdam Ume'uchar Batorah*, (Jerusalem Ramat Gan: 2009).

[26] Peruch Ha'arokh Shemoth 18:1.

Ibn Ezra is suggesting that the Torah purposefully altered the chronology of events in order to juxtapose Amalek's evil with Yitro's kindness. The reason for this juxtaposition is so that one should not get the impression that all gentiles are bad or against the Jews. Additionally, Ibn Ezra notes that the Kenites who are Yitro's descendants should always be remembered for their kindness, despite the fact that they dwell alongside the Amalekites.

The juxtaposition of commandments is also meaningful. In the chapter that deals with civil laws[27] Ibn Ezra writes:

> [The verse states] "When you buy" – before I am able to explain this, I must present the rule that each and every law or commandment stands on its own. If we happen to find a reason why this law is placed next to another or this commandment to that one, we will cling to it with all our ability. If, however, we are unable to do so, we will believe that the deficiency comes from our lack of intelligence.[28]

For example, verses fifteen to seventeen of chapter twenty-one in the Book of Shemoth list a series of laws with no apparent link.

15. Whoever strikes his father, or his mother shall be put to death.

16. Whoever steals a man and sells him, if he is found in his hands, he shall be put to death.

17. Whoever curses his father, or his mother shall be put to death.

Ibn Ezra here quotes Rav Saadia Gaon to explain the juxtaposition of these three verses:

> The Gaon says: Why does this verse come in between striking a parent and cursing a parent? He responds that the verse addresses reality, because minors who are kidnapped and grow up in a foreign place do not know their fathers, so it may come to pass that they may strike them or curse them – in such a case the punishment is for the kidnapper.

[27] Perashat Mishpatim, Shemoth chapters 22-28.
[28] Shemoth 21:2.

The juxtaposition addresses the tragic reality of human trafficking which often occurs with the kidnapping of children. If such a victim returns home as an adult and strikes or curses his parents without knowing who they are, the punishment is on the kidnapper. For Ibn Ezra and for Rav Saadia Gaon the verse then has a double meaning: its plain sense and the interpretation afforded based on the juxtaposition.

He often draws on his own life experience to elucidate biblical texts. For example, while he was in England, he visited a prison and saw prisoners eating flat, unleavened bread. In his comment on chapter twelve of Shemoth he writes how the matza [the unleavened bread the Torah commands the Jewish people to eat on Pesach] is symbolic of both the redemption from bondage but also a reminder of the bondage itself. In London he also experienced a thick fog rise from the Thames River, which led him to explain the plague of darkness as a thick fog rising from the Nile as opposed to a prolonged eclipse of the sun.

Ibn Ezra is both daring and honest in his commentary on the Torah. And yet he often will write cryptically so that he does not offend the more conservative reader. He recognized that his survival depended on his reputation. Because he was living in Europe among the more religiously conservative, he had to be tactful when presenting his more critical and philosophically precise ideas.

Ibn Ezra's daring nature goes to the core of fundamental Jewish beliefs about the biblical text. The Torah says right at the beginning of the Book of Devarim that Moshe Rabbenu spoke to the people of Israel "on the other side of the Jordan." On this ibn Ezra writes:

> And if you understand the secret of the twelve, then also "and Moshe wrote" (Devarim 31:22), "The Canaanites were then in the land" (Bereshit 12:6), "And God's Mountain shall be seen" (Bereshit 22:14), "Behold his bed is a bed of iron" (Devarim 3:11) – then you shall know the truth.[29]

Ibn Ezra here refers to "a secret" that reveals the "truth" about

---

[29] Devarim 1:1.

these passages. The foremost super-commentator of Ibn Ezra in the fourteenth century, Rabbi Yoseph ben Eliezer (14th Century Spain),[30] explains that Ibn Ezra is suggesting here that there are passages in the Torah that were written after Moshe Rabbenu's death.[31] Rabbi Yoseph ben Eliezer contends that Ibn Ezra and the schools of Andalus believed that the prophets of Israel were authorized to add verses or passages in the Torah.

> Since we are beholden to believe in the received tradition and the word of prophecy, what difference does it make whether Moshe Rabbenu wrote the passage or whether it was written by another prophet, inasmuch as all their words are true and prophetic?

Although this idea was common knowledge for the Jews of Andalusia, it was not publicized in writing because of enemies of the Jewish people, like ibn Hazm, who liked to claim that the Jewish people had tampered with the written text of the Torah.[32] The secret of the "twelve" has to do with Ibn Ezra's position, based on the Talmud, that Moshe Rabbenu did not write and could not possibly have written the last twelve verses of the Torah because they describe his death and what occurred following his death. He uses this conclusion as a model of verses added to the biblical text following Moshe Rabbenu's death. Afraid of sounding heretical – or worse, being labeled as such – when Ibn Ezra uses the expression *ve'zeh sod*, he is actually asking his intelligent readers to keep a secret.[33]

Ibn Ezra's secrets are fascinating in their own right. On the verse in Bereshit 35:22 where the Torah enigmatically describes an incident that involved Reuven and Bilha, his father's concubine, the sages of the Talmud warn the reader with the dictum, "Whoever says Reuven sinned is completely in error."[34] Ibn Ezra on this verse states, "Our

---

[30] Rabbi Yoseph ben Eliezer is from Toledo, Spain and author of *Tzafnat Pane'ach*.

[31] *Tzafnat Pane'ach* Bereshit 12:5.

[32] For an insightful discussion on this topic see Joshua Berman, *Ani Maamin: Biblical Criticism, Historical Truth and the Thirteen principles* (Jerusalem: Maggid Press, 2020), 257-259.

[33] And not offering some esoteric interpretation of the text.

[34] TB Shabbath 56a.

Image of Rabbenu Avraham Ibn Ezra's Grave Stone

rabbis have explained this well." He then quotes the following verse from Mishle: "The clever conceal the shameful."[35] In order to appreciate Ibn Ezra's comment one must consult his commentary on the verse he quotes in Mishle. There Ibn Ezra says that the clever person knows how to conceal that which is shameful. Ibn Ezra is saying the sages really believed that Reuven did something shameful, but it is best to conceal it. In exquisite Andalusian form, Ibn Ezra reveals the concealed and conceals the revealed.

He is not averse to speculating psychological interpretations on the biblical narrative. He writes that God designed by Divine providence that Moshe Rabbenu be raised in Pharoah's palace because he would never have been respected had he grown up among the Jews. They would have been too familiar with him and not believed in him. Additionally, the future leader of the Jewish people had to have a regal upbringing and an aristocratic background so that he can model nobility.

Ibn Ezra uses the expression *ve'zeh sod* [and this is a secret] over one hundred times in his commentary on Torah. Unlike Nachmanides who also uses a similar expression to titillate his readers and lull them into a mystical, fantastical reading of the text, Ibn Ezra uses the ex-

---

[35] Mishle 12:16.

Commentary on the Book of Exodus by Avraham ibn Ezra Naples 1488

pression to protect his readers from misleading them. Regarding the scapegoat of Yom Kippur described in Vayikra 16:8, Ibn Ezra writes:

> If you are capable of understanding the secret which stands behind the word *Azazel*, you will know its secret and the secret of its name, for there are others like it in scripture.[36]

Nachmanides on the same verse writes unapologetically:

> And behold Rabbi Avraham of faithful spirit conceals the matter, but I am a gossip, so I will tell his secret.

It is very unlikely that Nachmanides' interpretation of the Azazel is in any way related or relatable to Ibn Ezra's understanding of the subject. Based on what we know about Ibn Ezra, Nachmanides' interpretation would be considered blasphemous.[37]

While living in London in his old age Ibn Ezra entrusted a student, Rabbi Yoseph ben Yaacov of Moundville, to write some of his ideas on Torah. Only a few fragments of this composition exist, and it has been called *Peirush HaShelishi*, Ibn Ezra's third commentary on the Torah.[38] In this composition, Ibn Ezra tells us about Reuven's sin:

> "And Israel heard" – what Reuven did, therefore "And Yaacov's sons are twelve" and no more. For Bilha had been desecrated, Rachel was dead, and he despised Leah and her handmaid because of Reuven. Therefore, he never again came to a woman and did not bear children – thus, his sons were only twelve . . .

This is indeed a daring and powerful reading of the text. Here Ibn Ezra reveals what he had initially concealed. There is no doubt that his comment here reveals what he actually believed.

When it came to intellectual integrity, Ibn Ezra was extremely independent. Although he revered his predecessors, he had no issue

---

[36] Ibn Ezra Commentary on Vayikra 16:8.

[37] See my The Mysticism of Andalusia pages 216-221

[38] See Aaron Mondschein, "*Shitta Shelishit LePerusho Shel* Rabbi Avraham Ibn Ezra" in *Or LeYaacov: Mechkarim BaMikra U'beMigilloth,* (Tel Aviv: Tel Aviv University Press 5757), 179-182.

challenging their commentaries and conclusions. He unapologetically and without reservation criticizes Rav Saadia Gaon, Ibn Janah, Dunash ben Labrat, and others when he disagrees with them, and praises them when he feels their commentary is correct. Ibn Ezra was a lot more careful about the commentaries of European Jewry. In both his *Arokh* and the *Katzar* commentaries on Torah, Ibn Ezra never criticizes Rabbi Shelomo ben Yitzchak, also known as Rashi (1040-1105 C.E.). When Rashi is mentioned, ibn Ezra's commentary is always neutral. This was not the case in Ibn Ezra's less popular works that were not intended for mass consumption. For example, in his *Safa Berura* Ibn Ezra writes about Rashi:

> There is no doubt that they [European Rabbis] knew that the *peshat* reading of the text is as it is; that is why they formulated the rule, "no verse should deviate from its simple meaning." Therefore, the *derash* is merely supplemental. The following generation made every *derash* essential and crucial, as Rav Shelomo z"l [Rashi] does, so that the TaNaKH is explained by way of *derash*. Though he was under the impression that this is the way of *peshat*, in his writings one will find only one *peshat* out of a thousand. – yet the sages of our generation boast of these books.[39]

Ibn Ezra is unapologetic about the little regard he had of Rashi's commentary on the Torah.[40] In fact, he denigrates the rabbis of Europe for boasting of such works. Ibn Ezra understood however, that Rashi was a beloved sage in France and Europe and publicly taking Rashi to task would have led to his absolute excommunication.

Other Works

Ibn Ezra wrote two other short treatises each with a particular focus. He wrote a book called *Sefer HaShem* [The Book of God's Name]. This book is a study of the various names of God. The basic idea is that the

---

[39] Avraham ibn Ezra, *Safa Berura*, Wilensky edition (Jerusalem, 5738), 64.

[40] In his introduction, ibn Ezra sarcastically notes that indeed Rashi wrote a *peshat* commentary on the Torah "one out of a thousand times."

numerology, phonetic qualities, grammatical functions, convey some theological information about God.

He also wrote a short book called *Sefer HaEhad* [The Book of One] where he lists all natural things that come in twos and threes. Ibn Ezra was a mathematician and he was fascinated by the theological implications of arithmetic properties.

His two most philosophical works are poetic compositions. One is called *Hayy ben Mekitz* (Hayy son of Mekitz) and the other *Arugot HaBosem* [the beds of perfume]. *Hayy ben Mekitz* has been described as a "visionary recital"[41] or philosophical allegory.[42] In Ibn Ezra's tale, Hayy is a guide, an old man who has not aged. The narrator, who has had to flee his home, meets Hayy and is enchanted by his words of wisdom. Hayy invites him to immerse himself in the fountain of life and enjoy its pleasures. Hayy guides the narrator through eight "kingdoms" that include astronomical spheres described in vivid terms. The narrator asks if there is anything beyond the astral spheres and the guide responds that there is – "the One, who has no second," sublime and invisible. Hayy promises that if the narrator follows him and his instructions, he will be able to know and meet Him. My understanding of this short story is Ibn Ezra's attempt at presenting the Andalusian esoteric tradition in allegorical terms.

An important feature of Ibn Ezra's worldview and philosophy expressed in *Hayy ben Mekitz* is his focus on the salvation of the individual. While rabbinic Judaism focused primarily on the collective redemption of the people of Israel, Andalusian tradition introduced the idea of personal and individual theological salvation.[43] This idea finds expression in another of his works, *Yesod Morah* [The Foundation

---

[41] I. Levin, "Cling to the Ladder of Wisdom: The Influence of Neoplatonic Psychology on the Poetry of Abraham Ibn Ezra," in *Te'udah* volume 8 1992; *Studies in the Works of Abraham ibn Ezra* (Hebrew), edited by I. Levin (Tel Aviv: Tel Aviv University Press, 1992)

[42] The great tenth century Muslim philosopher ibn Sina wrote a philosophical allegory called *Hayy bin Yaqzan*, and the Andalusian ibn Tufayl as well as other Moslem and Persian writers each wrote a philosophical tale that suited the message the author wanted to convey. Ibn Ezra wrote a Hebrew version of this genre.

[43] Similarly HaRambam understands Shir HaShirim, the biblical book Song of Songs as a mystical expression of the individual's quest for God.

of Reverence], where Ibn Ezra charts the mitzvoth and explains their purpose. There he notes that the law does not only benefit the society but is also a system of improving the individual:

> The person [*ha'adam*] must set himself straight. He must know the commandments of God Who created everything. He must try with all his strength to understand God's works, then he will know his creator . . . and when he knows God he will find favor in His eyes . . . It is for this reason that man was created. Once one has perfected oneself, he may set others straight – if this be possible.[44]

Yesod Morah VeSod Torah was the first book of Andalusian Jewish philosophy written in Hebrew. Recognizing that the Jews of Southern France and Europe could not read Arabic, Ibn Ezra presented this work in beautiful Hebrew. Rabbi Yehuda ibn Tibbon (1120-1190 C.E.), the famous translator of Rav Sa'adia Gaon's *Emunot VeDe'ot*, wrote the following about Ibn Ezra's *Yesod Morah*:

> The Jews living in exile in France and all the borders of Edom (Christian Europe) do not know Arabic. Books written in Arabic are like sealed books to them. They cannot approach them until they are translated in the Hebrew language . . . this was so until the wise man Rabbi Avraham ibn Ezra came to their country and helped them by composing works in Hebrew . . .

In recent years *Yesod Morah* has been made available to the English-speaking seekers thanks to the translation of Rabbi Dr. Norman Strickman.[45]

In true Andalusian form, Ibn Ezra develops the idea that Torah is what gives life meaning. Knowing God means knowing God's creations, which ultimately leads to love and awe of God, which is man's true purpose. Ibn Ezra writes that he wrote *Yesod Morah* in response to a query about the commandments:

---

[14] J. Cohen, and U. Simon, eds., *Rabbi Abraham Ibn Ezra, Yesod Morah VeSod Torah* (Ramat-Gan: Bar Ilan University Press, 2002), 83-84.

[45] Published by Kodesh Press 2021. An excellent critical edition with annotations was recently published by Joseph Cohen and Uriel Simon (Bar Ilan University Press 2007)

> The awe-inspiring God knows my heart's sincerity. For I did not compose this book to show that I mastered the sciences or to glorify myself by showing that secrets have been revealed to me. Neither did I write this book to argue with our ancient sages, for I surely know that they were wiser and more God-fearing than I. I composed this book for a revered and noble individual whom I taught the books that wrote for him dealing with the commandments only because of my great love for him, for I found him to be a person of integrity whose fear of the Lord exceeded my men.[46]

In *Yesod Morah*, Ibn Ezra addresses mystical issues such as the nature of the soul and how it is destined to return to God after the body dies.

> Man's soul is unique. When it is first placed in the body . . . it is like a tablet set before the scribe. When God's writing is inscribed upon this tablet then the soul clings to God both while yet in man's body and later after it leaves the human body.[47]

He extols the role of Torah study as well as the importance of knowing philosophy and science. He argues that one cannot properly understand the Talmud without a strong background in science and mathematics.[48] He stresses the importance of knowing the Hebrew language, especially grammar.

Isaac Husik[49] and Julius Guttman[50] both note how Ibn Ezra saw himself as a transmitter and preserver of the Andalusian tradition, wisdom, and culture. He devoted so much of his creative and intellectual energies in grammar, mathematics, astronomy, philosophy, theology, and the "scientific rationalistic spirit" to preserve the Jewish culture he knew represented the rabbinic Judaism of the Talmud and the Geonim.

An anomaly in Ibn Ezra's thought and philosophy is his fascination with astrology. I call this an anomaly because the Jewish

---

[46] Yesod Morah 2:4 Uriel Simon edition (Bar Ilan University Press, Tel Aviv, 2018)
[47] Ibid 10:2
[48] Ibid 1:4-6
[49] Isaac Husik, *History of Medieval Jewish Philosophy* (New York: JPS 1969), 187.
[50] Julius Guttman, *Philosophies of Judaism* (New York: Schocken, 1973).

scholars of Andalusia completely rejected astrology. While his comments about astrology are brief and cryptic, they do suggest a belief in astral influences. He considered the material universe to be divided into celestial and terrestrial realms. The terrestrial realm is under the sway of the celestial realm. Humans who perfect themselves can, however, link themselves to a third, Divine realm, a kind of super-celestial realm, and outmaneuver the stars and take destiny in one's own hands.

Ibn Ezra translated into Hebrew certain Arabic texts on astronomy and astrology. Because he was the first to translate these works, he had to invent a new vocabulary. For example, he introduced terms for the center of a circle and the diagonal of a rectangle. He describes his own research in astrology as *hakmei ha-mazalot* (the science of the zodiac signs). His best-known work called *Reshit Hokhma*, Beginning of Wisdom is actually an introduction to both astrology and astronomy. There he discusses zodiac constellation, planet movements and their technical aspects. Ibn Ezra created a start list which appears as a section of his work the Astrolabe. The list is given in the form of a paragraph where the coordinates are listed in Hebrew letters and numeral while the Arabic names are transliterated into Hebrew. He used Astrology as a way of explaining some of the biblical commandments including reasons for details of sacrifices. Astrology may have also offered some sort of explanation and possibly comfort for Ibn Ezra's own suffering and tragic life experiences.

He wrote a short book while living in England called *Iggeret Ha-Shabbath* [Letter on Shabbath]. In that short composition he writes that the Shabbath came to him in a dream and urged him to compile a work refuting those who claim Shabbath begins in the morning and not in the evening as it is traditionally observed.

I Am The Lord Your God

Ibn Ezra's secular and religious poems are among the most celebrated Hebrew poems. For Ibn Ezra the soul of the human being is the only eternal entity other than God. As was the tradition that was taught in

Andalus, the *nefesh* of the human being separates from the physical body after death and continues its existence.

> Just as the passerby, who has been taken prisoner, longs to return to his homeland and to be with his family, so does the intellectualization spirit yearn to grab hold of the higher rungs, until she ascends to the formations of the living God, which do not dwell in material houses . . .[51]

For Ibn Ezra,[52] the soul is the spiritual part of the human being that grows spiritually until death; then it returns to *olam haba* [the world-to-come].

In a lengthy comment on the first of the Ten Commandments,[53] Ibn Ezra relates a conversation he had with a close friend and kindred spirit, the poet and philosopher Rabbi Yehuda HaLevi. Why? HaLevi wanted to know, did God choose to reveal Himself on Mount Sinai as the God Who took the Jews out of Egypt as opposed to the God Who created the heavens and the earth? Why does God identify Himself with an event that is particular to the Jewish people and not an event that has universal significance? The question is both revealing and an important launch for Ibn Ezra's thought. If God is known through his creations, as HaRambam writes in several places, why does God not reveal Himself at Sinai as the Creator of the world?

Ibn Ezra answers the question in a long comment (possibly one of the longest in his entire commentary) that may have been part of a debate with Rabbi Yehuda HaLevi.[54] He suggests that God of Creation is actually revealed in the first two words of the commandment "I [am] God." Indeed, writes Ibn Ezra, those two words are a hint at the pursuit of knowledge of God. God's self-introduction as "the One Who brought you out of Egypt" implies the truth of God's existence and adds the important detail that the Creator is also the Redeemer.

---

[51] Ibn Ezra *Introduction* to Kohelet.
[52] Like HaRambam's more detailed description of the *nefesh*.
[53] Shemoth 20:1.
[54] Yehuda HaLevi addresses the issue of Jewish particularism in his *Kuzari* 1:1

Final Thoughts on Rabbi Avraham ibn Ezra

The above is an incomplete and unsatisfactory summary of one of the greatest Jewish scholars to emerge from Andalusia. Unlike HaRambam, he made the choice to flee Andalusia and go north to Christian Europe. Tragically, in that culture he never found a home and yet his impact was both immediate and powerful. Throughout those European communities, the Andalusian Torah he was able to present was widely embraced, to a certain extent. His attempts at being a cultural broker were significant. His writings in grammar, linguistics, philosophy, and arithmetic that were standard curricula for Andalusians were, to an extent, a novelty to the European Jewish communities he passed through. His commentary on TaNaKH is unparalleled. The French philosopher and biblical commentary Rabbi Levi ben Gershon (1288-1344) was very much influenced and regularly quotes both HaRambam and Ibn Ezra, the two beacons of Andalusian thought and culture.

Like HaRambam, the number of Ibn Ezra's writings that have survived the Middle Ages is a tribute to his influence and importance. His writing generated interest in a wide range of cultural and historical setting. They were sought and studied.

Wikipedia provides a extensive and what appears to be a complete list of ibn Ezra's written works:

Biblical Commentaries:
Perush HaKatzar – The Short Commentary
Perush Ha'Arokh – The Long Commentary

Hebrew Grammar
Sefer Moznayim – Book of Scales (1140 C.E.)
Sefer Hayesod or *Yesod HaDikduk* – Basics of Grammar (1148 C.E.)
Sefer Haganah Al Rabbi Saadia Gaon – Defense of Rav Saadia Gaon (1143 C.E.)
Tzakhot – on Linguistic Correctness (1145 C.E.)
Sefer Safa Berura – Book of Purified Language (1146 C.E.)

Sefat Yeter – In Defense of Rav Saadia against Dunash ibn Labrat
Sefer HaShem – The Book of God's Name
Yesod Mispar – Monograph on Numerals
Iggeret Shabbath – The Letter of Shabbath (1158 C.E.)

Religious Philosophy

Yesod Mora Vesod HaTorah – Fundamental of Reverence and the Secrets of the Torah (1158 C.E.)

Mathematics

Sefer HaEchad – The Book of One
Sefer HaMispar – Arithmetic
Luchot – Astronomical charts
Sefer HaIbur – Book on the Calendar
Keli Hanechoshet – On the Astrolabe
Shalosh She'elot – Answering three chronological questions of Rabbi David Narboni

Astrology (1147-1148 C.E.)

Mishpetei HaMazalot – Zodiacal sings
Reshit Hokhma – The Beginning of Wisdom
Sefer HaTe'amim – The Book of Reasons on Arabic Astrology
Sefer HaMe'orot – The Book of Luminaries on Medical Astrology
Sefer HaShe'elot – The Book of Questions
Sefer HaMivharim – The Book of Elections on Optimum Days for Activities
Sefer Ha'Olam – The Book of the World

He wrote over one thousand poems scattered throughout his works and fragments.

> In their day the wise of the world climbed
> To heights lofty and exalted
> They reached the peak of intellect, but
> Moses, only, unto God ascended.
>
> JUDAH AL HARIZI (THIRTEENTH CENTURY)

Rabbi Moshe Ben Mimon, HaRambam
Maimonides, Rambam
1138-1204 C.E.

HaRambam

HaRambam was one of those historical personalities whose impact on the world can be celebrated, denounced, or debated but never dismissed. At the young age of sixteen he published a credible lexicon of the logical terms and philosophical concepts basic to Aristotelian philosophy called *Millot ha-Higayon* [Treatise on Logic]. By the age of thirty he had systematically organized the entire corpus of rabbinic Jewish law into a complete and original code. His communal leadership is characterized by the countless responsa, introductions, monographs, and astronomical and medical works that he wrote and published. He sealed his legacy on the Jewish world and beyond by writing the classic text of what has been described by scholars as medieval Jewish philosophy, theology, and spirituality, but is actually the most exquisite post-biblical Jewish mystical text that has ever been written, titlted *Dalalat Al-Hairin in Arabic, Moreh HaNevuchim* in Hebrew,[1] and in English it is known as the

---

[1] Shemuel ibn Tibbon translated the title from the Arabic to *Moreh HaNevuchim* but throughout my writing I simply refer to it as Moreh Nevuchim

Guide of the Perplexed.² In a nutshell, he branded his presence on all subsequent Jewish scholarship, culture, and learning.

HaRambam, known in the world of academic scholarship as Maimonides, was named Moshe by his parents. The name RaMBaM is an acronym for **R**abbi **M**oshe **B**en **M**imon [Moses, son of Mimon]. Sephardic scholars have always referred to him as *Ha*Rambam [*The* Rambam, with the *hay hayediah*]. In medieval Egypt and in Arabic sources he was referred to as Al-Ra'is Abu Imran Mousa ibn Maymun ibn Abdallah al-Qurtubi al-Andalusi al-Israeli. This honorific appellation was reserved for the very few elites among the elite of Islamic society. *Al-Ra'is* means the head while *Abu Imran* means whose father was the biblical Amram. In Islam an honorable person was always given an honorific byname. Since HaRambam's name was Moshe, like Moses in the Bible whose father was Amram, his honorific is son of Amram in Arabic Abu Imran. This is then followed by his name Mousa, which is the Arabic form of Moshe. He is then referred to as the son of Maymun, followed by his father's father Abdallah which is the Arabic for Ovadia. After the names come his place of origin, *Al-Qurtubi* means from Cordova, then Andalusia, and finally his ethnic origin *al-Israeli* [the Israelite]. In most places HaRambam simply signed his documents as Moshe ben Mimon *HaSepharadi*, but at the end of his commentary on the Mishna HaRambam signs off as *Moshe ben Mimon HaDayan ben Yoseph HaHaham, ben Yitzchak HaDayan ben Yoseph Hadayan ben Ovadia HaDayan ben Shelomo HaHaham ben Ovadia HaDayan.*³

אני משה בר׳ ⁷⁵ מימון הדיין בר׳ יוסף החכם בר׳ יצחק הדיין בר׳ יוסף הדיין בר׳ עובדיהו
הדיין בר׳ שלמה הרב בר׳ עובדיהו הדיין זכר קדושים לברכה. התחלתי לחבר פירוש זה ואני
בן שלש ועשרים שנה⁷⁶ והשלמתי אותו במצרים ואני בן שלשים שנה שהיא שנת אלף וארבע
מאות ⁷⁷ ותשע ושבעים לשטרות ⁷⁸.
ברוך הנותן ליעף כח ולאין אונים עצמה ירבה ⁷⁹.

---

² I make the case that the Guide of the Perplexed is indeed a Guide to the esoteric and mystical tradition of Judaism in my book *The Mystical Tradition of Andalusia: Exploring HaRambam's Mystical Tradition*, (MHC Press 2023). HaRambam is unambiguous when describing the purpose and goals of the Guide see Guide 2:2, 2:29 and hid Introduction to part 3

³ *Commentary on the Mishna* Volume 6, page 738, of the Kafikh translation and edition (Jerusalem, 1963).

He was also referred to as *ha-Moreh* or *ha-Rav ha-Moreh* [the teacher or the rabbi of the *Moreh*], alluding to his great work ha-*Moreh Nevuchim*.[4] In some instances, he was called *Moreh Sedek* [the righteous teacher]. Some who wrote to HaRambam or wrote about him also referred to him as *Ish HaElokim* [the man of God], an appellation used only and exclusively for the biblical Moshe Rabbenu, as in the verse in Devarim.

> This is the blessing, that Moshe, *Ish HaElohim,* man of God, bestowed on the Jewish people just before his death . . .[5]

HaRambam was nicknamed *HaNesher HaGadol*, the Great Eagle, by Rabbi Yom Tov ben of Avraham of Seville (1250-1330), a name that stayed throughout the ages. The nickname is based on the verse in Yechezkel 17:3:

> Thus said the Lord God: The great eagle with the great wings and the long pinions, with the full plumage and the brilliant colors.

Or possibly the verse in Shemoth 19:4: "And I carried you on eagle's wings." Or the verse in Devarim 32:11:

> Like an eagle arousing its nest, hovering over its young, He spread His wings and took them, carrying then on his pinions.

The eagle, which is often considered the king of the birds and regarded with much awe, is indeed an apt image for the way in which HaRambam was viewed in his lifetime and remembered after his death. Like the great eagle in the verse in the book of Yechezkel whose enormous wings and bright colors soar into the heavens, HaRambam's fame and majestic legacy soared throughout the Jewish world. Eagles are an apt symbol of might, regality, and protection – all terms that describe how HaRambam was regarded among Jews and Muslims alike.

---

[4] The Hebrew title was given by Shemuel ibn Tibbon and ratified by HaRambam himself. For an in-depth study of the Arabic title *Dalalat Al-Hairin* see José Faur, *Golden Doves*, pages 74-76 especially footnote #66.

[5] Devarim 33:1; also Yehoshua 14:6.

More is known about the life of HaRambam than any other Jewish medieval scholar. We know that he was born in the Andalusian capital of Cordova on the fourteenth of Nissan in the year 4893 which corresponds to April 4th, 1138 C.E., and he died on the twentieth of Tevet 4964 corresponding to December 25th, 1204, in the Ayub capital city of Egypt, Fostat. Except for a brief visit to the land of Israel in 1165 C.E. while in transit from Morocco to Egypt, he lived his entire life within the then-Islamic world. He died in Egypt and asked to be buried in the city of Tiberias, Israel[6] alongside the *Tana'im* [authors of the Mishna], where the last Sanhedrin convened and where the next Sanhedrin will assemble before they go to Jerusalem.[7]

HaRambam's intellectual gifts were already legendary in his lifetime. As a young man he was being called the second Moses. Sephardic communities throughout the diaspora accepted his *Mishneh Torah* as the absolute standard for *halakha*[8] and many communities mentioned his name with great reverence in their Kaddish.[9]

However, in a letter by a well-known anti-Maimonidean, Rabbi Judah Alfakhar from Toledo, written to a Maimonidean scholar in Southern France around 1260 C.E., the author wonders facetiously if the followers of HaRambam have raised the *Moreh Nevuchim* to the status of another Torah and elevated HaRambam to the rank of a biblical prophet or into the inner circles of the celestial beings.[10] The famous Nachmanides[11] wrote a letter to the rabbis of Northern France

---

[6] Yamin Levy, https://mhcny.org/pdf/Burial%20Site%20of%20Rambam.pdf.

[7] *MT Hilkhot Sanhedrin* 4:11

[8] See Twersky, "The Beginning of Mishneh Torah Criticism," 171-177; also Septimus, *Hispano Jewish Society in Transition*, 39-43. For a more contemporary study of the influence HaRambam's *Mishneh Torah* had on Medieval Torah study see Ephraim Kanarfogel "Assessing the (Non-)Reception of Mishneh Torah in Medieval Ashkenaz," 123-147.

[9] It was the custom to mention names of revered rabbis and scholars in *Kaddish DeRabanan*.

[10] Letter of Judah Alfakhar KTR, III 2b.

[11] Rabbi Moshe ben Nachman of Northern Spain, who did not wholly approve of HaRambam's teachings.

asking them to rescind their ban on HaRambam because so many had aligned themselves with his teachings that to ban the teacher was to alienate the followers.[12] This was the nature of HaRambam's impact.

HaRambam grew up in a home and in a culture where Torah was the primary focus of study and was completely mastered. His home was a place where rabbinic texts were carefully explored and analyzed. He was an expert linguist, scientist, and mathematician. His world welcomed the great philosophers and thinkers of the age who were studied, discussed, and disputed. A letter written in Arabic by HaRambam to his translator Shemuel ibn Tibbon[13] affords us invaluable information regarding HaRambam's familiarity with the world of philosophy. He writes:

> The writings of Aristotle's teacher Plato are in parables and hard to understand. One can dispense with them, for the writings of Aristotle suffice, and we need not occupy our attention with the writings of earlier philosophers. Aristotle's intellect represents the extreme of human intellect, with the exception of those who have achieved divine inspiration.[14]

HaRambam continues in the same letter:

> The works of Aristotle are the roots and foundations of all works on the sciences. But they cannot be understood except with the help of commentaries such as those of Alexander of Aphrodisias, those of Themistius, and those of Averroes. I tell you as for the works of logic, one should only study the writings of Abu Nasr Al-Farabi. All his writings are faultlessly excellent. One ought to study and understand them. For he is a great man. Though the works of Avicenna may give rise to objections and are not as good as those of Al-Farabi, Abu Bakr ibn Bajja was also a great philosopher, and all his writings are of high standard.

---

[12] Letter of Nachmanides KTR III 9a.

[13] Edited by A. Marx in the *Jewish Quarterly Review* XXV, 378-380. Shlomo Pines discusses this letter in his Introduction to his Translation of the Guide on page iix.

[14] Ibid.

Remarkably, HaRambam intuited that certain book ascribed to Aristotle[15] were not written by him – a fact that has been proven only recently in academic circles. In that same letter,[16] HaRambam disregards the *Book of Definitions* and *Book of Elements,* works of an early medieval Jewish philosopher, Isaac ben Shelomo Israeli (855-955 C.E.). HaRambam is famous for having taught that one must accept "truth from wherever it emerges."[17] That HaRambam favored Greek and Muslim philosophers over Jewish philosophers is a function of the quality of the work.

Medievalists were known for lofty praising of HaRambam during his lifetime and after he passed away. Rabbi Dr. Isadore Twersky, of blessed memory, who collected the countless words of praise that had been showered on HaRambam said, "One reads these praises with awe – they exceed the most lavish of tributes."[18] For example, take the following anonymous poem:

> Moses was a faithful messenger of God
> He regulated scrupulously all matters of faith
> His pen took place of Moses's staff
> With which he did miraculous things.[19]

The poem suggests that HaRambam's pen performed miracles as did Moshe Rabbenu's staff. This unapologetic linkage to Moshe Rabbenu is extraordinary and unparalleled.

In 1148 C.E. the peaceful calm of Cordova, where HaRambam was born and lived, was disrupted by the Berber Almohad invasion. The Almohads were cruel and fanatical. Rabbi Avraham ibn Ezra (1089-1164 C.E.) laments the destruction of over a dozen Jewish communities in Southern Spain and North Africa, including Cordova and Fez. He

---

[15] Such as *Book of the Apple* and *Book of the Golden Palace.*

[16] The letter mentions numerous other philosophers and philosophical works, which suggests a remarkable familiarity with the material.

[17] Introduction to *Shemoneh Perakim.*

[18] Twersky, "Some Reflections on the Historical Image of Maimonides," 1-49.

[19] *Kobetz Al Yad,* I.

describes death, devastation, and captivity inflicted on the Jewish communities.[20] The Jews had few good choices. Rabbi Mimon and his family left Cordova and over the following ten years spent time in Morocco, and Israel. In 1167 C.E. the family finally settled in Egypt. Going north, like many Southern Spanish Jews such as Avraham ibn Ezra and others, was not an option for Rabbi Mimon and his family. The centralized religious control, the lack of progressive intellectual pursuits, and general religious superstitious culture of Christian Europe was not an option for the family of Rabbi Mimon. His goal was to raise his children in a culture that was open to intellectual pursuits, and a natural stage for the advancement of Torah study and Jewish practice. Although Egypt was not Andalus, HaRambam found a place where he could pursue his rabbinic learning, teaching, and writing in an environment that was not averse to philosophic speculation and scientific intellectual pursuits. Upon his arrival in Egypt, he was immediately accepted as a rising star in the Jewish community. However, his initial reaction toward the Jewish community in Egypt was ambivalent to a certain degree; as he bemoans, in his commentary on the Mishna:

" . . . unknown people are addressed as Rosh Yeshiva or by some other title. All these things are but vanities of title . . . "[21]

He nevertheless embraced the place that destiny had made his home until he died.

In 1168 C.E., HaRambam's father died in the city of Alexandria and around that time HaRambam moved to the city of Fostat [Cairo]. In a letter written to Yefeth Ben Eliyahu, HaRambam reports how he is blessed to be able to serve the community, to teach, and to write because his younger brother David would "conduct business in the marketplace and support the family."[22] Then tragedy struck. In the

---

[20] David Kahana, *Qobetz Hokhmat Rabbenu Avraham Ibn Ezra* (Warsaw: Ahiasaf Press, 1922); also H. Z. Hirschberg, *History of the Jews of North Africa: From the Ottoman Conquest to the Present Time* Volume 1, 123-124, (Leiden: EJ Brill, 1981).

[21] Commentary on Mishnah Berakhot 4:4.

[22] Shailat, Letter to Yafeth, *Letters and Essays of Moses Maimonides* (Ma'aleh Adumim, Jerusalem, 1995), 230.

year 1177 C.E. his beloved brother David drowned at sea on a business voyage and the entire family estate was lost. In a subsequent letter to Yafeth, HaRambam writes, "David had with him a large sum of money belonging to me, him and others, and he left me with his widow and a young daughter."[23] From then on HaRambam had the responsibility of supporting his entire family.

HaRambam served as a judge in Egypt, but he never took any money for his service as a judge, rabbi, or teacher of Torah. He lived his life based on a ruling of the Talmud that teaches that it is forbidden for a judge to take any money for his services other than compensation for the exact wages he would temporarily lose as a result of leaving his regular occupation to serve as judge.[24] HaRambam, based on rabbinic law, forbade a Torah scholar from commercializing their Torah knowledge. A Torah scholar is forbidden to take money from the community while studying Torah and for teaching Torah:

> Anyone who comes to the conclusion that he should involve himself in Torah study without doing work and derive his livelihood from charity, desecrates God's name, dishonors the Torah, extinguishes the light of faith, brings evil upon himself, and forfeits the life of the world to come, for it is forbidden to derive benefit from the words of the Torah in this world.
>
> Our sages taught: "whoever benefits from the words of Torah forfeits his life in the world." Also, they commanded and declared: "Do not make the words of Torah a crown to glorify yourself, nor an axe to chop with it." Also, they commanded and taught: "Love work and despise rabbinic positions." Torah that is not accompanied by work will eventually be negated and lead to sin. Ultimately, such a person will take from others.[25]

---

[23] Shailat, Letter to Yafeth, 229-230.

[24] HaRambam, Commentary on the Mishna Berakhot 4:6; *MT Sanhedrin* 23:5, TB Ketboth 105a.

[25] *MT Talmud Torah* 3:10; also, Commentary on Mishna Avot 4:7; also Commentary on Mishna Nedarim 4:3. Based on Geniza documents that reflect communal expenses in Egypt during HaRambam's time, Aryeh Leibowitz concludes that while HaRambam certainly objected to rabbis and teachers of Torah taking money for their services,

HaRambam supported himself and his family as a medical doctor. His reputation as a first-rate physician did not escape the notice of Saladin and Saladin's governor, Al Qadi al-Fadil. HaRambam's medical writings were sought after and many of them certainly reached a Jewish and non-Jewish readership. Those works were translated into Hebrew and Latin as early as the thirteenth century.

HaRambam's burdensome daily schedule included the medical care of the Sultan and his entourage, his over-subscribed medical practice in his hometown of Fostat, and his communal responsibilities as head of the Jewish community. Yet he still found time to write.[26] Here is a brief outline, in HaRambam's own words, about his daily schedule as he discourages his student and translator Shemuel ibn Tibbon from coming to visit him:

> God knows that in order to write this to you I have had to escape to a secluded spot where people would not think to find me, sometimes leaning for support against the wall, sometimes lying down on account of my excessive weakness, for I have grown old and feeble.
>
> With regard to your wish to come here to me, I cannot but say how greatly your visit would delight me, for I truly long to commune with you and would anticipate our meeting with even greater joy than you. Yet I must advise you not to expose yourself to the perils of the voyage for beyond seeing me and my doing all I could to honor you, you would not derive any advantage from your visit. Do not expect to be able to confer with me on any

---

the reality on the ground may have been different. See Aryeh Leibowitz, "The Pursuit of Scholarship and Economic Self-Sufficiency: Revisiting Maimonides' Commentary to Pirkei Avot" in *Tradition Magazine*, Volume 40:3 Fall 2007, 31-42.

[26] HaRambam attests to numerous other works that he wrote that were not published or preserved. For example in his introduction to his commentary on the Mishna (Kafikh edition page 25) he mentions a commentary composed on three sections of the Talmud. Additionally, in his commentary on Mishna Tamid 5:1 he references a commentary he wrote on the "Laws of the Yerushalmi." Rav Shilat, in Igerot HaRambam page 19 lists works attributed to HaRambam.

scientific subject, for even one hour even by day or by night for the following is my daily occupation: I dwell at Misr (Fostat) and the Sultan resides at Kahira (Cairo) these two places are two Shabbat days' journey (about 1.5 miles) distant from each other. My duties to the Sultan are very heavy. I am obliged to visit him every day early in the morning and when he or any of his children or anyone in his harem are indisposed, I dare not leave Kahira but must stay during the greater part of the day in the Palace. It also frequently happens that one or two of the royal officers fall sick and I must attend to their wellbeing. Hence, as a rule, I repair to Kahir very early in the day and if nothing unusual happens I do not return to Misr until the afternoon. Then I am almost dying of hunger. I find my antechamber filled with people, both Jews and Gentiles, nobles and common people, judges and bailiffs, friends and foes – a mixed multitude, who await the time of my return.

I dismount from my animal, I wash my hands, go forth to my patients and entreat them to bear with me while I partake of some slight refreshment, the only meal I take in the twenty-four hours. Then I attend to my patients, write prescriptions for their various ailments. Patients go in and out until nightfall, and sometimes even, I solemnly assure you, until two hours or more into the night. I converse and prescribe for them while lying down from sheer fatigue, and when night falls, I am so exhausted that I can scarcely speak.

In consequence of this, no Israelite can have any private interview with me except on the Shabbath. On this day the whole congregation, or at least the majority of the members, come to me after the morning service where I instruct them as to their proceedings during the whole week. We study together a little until noon when they depart. Some of them return and read with me the afternoon service until evening prayers. In this manner I spend that day. I have here related to you only a part of what you would see if you were to visit me.

Now when you have completed for our brethren the translation you have commenced, I beg that you will come to me but not with the hope of deriving any advantage from your visit as regards your studies, for my time is, as I have shown you, excessively occupied.[27]

Despite his ridiculously onerous schedule he made time to carefully and meticulously leave a written legacy of the Andalusian tradition for the Jewish people.

Commentary on the Mishna

HaRambam's first major work on rabbinic literature and Jewish Law was the commentary on the Mishna. In Arabic it was titled *Kitab Al-Siraj* [the Book of Light] while in Hebrew it is more commonly referred to as HaRambam's *Perush Al HaMishna* [Commentary on the Mishna]. He began writing this work in 1161 C.E. in Fez, Morocco, and completed it in Egypt in 1168 C.E., when he was thirty years old. This work is an extensive commentary on the entire six sections of the Mishna. He writes at the conclusion of the commentary:

I began the composition of this commentary when I was twenty-three years old, and I completed it in Fostat when I was thirty years old in the year . . .

The significance and magnitude of this commentary is often underappreciated. For starters, he personally copied the entire text of the Mishna. This is one of the earliest authoritative texts of the Mishna that we have today. He then appended the personal commentary he wrote in perfect Judeo-Arabic. In this work he explains the basic precepts of the Mishna and alludes to their ramifications discussed in later Talmudic texts. This work was later translated into Hebrew by several translators, including Shemuel ibn Tibbon.

The Mishna, which was compiled and edited by Rabbi Yehuda HaNasi around 200 C.E., is the first systematic compendium of the Oral Law. It consists of six sections which are then divided into sixty-three tractates. Each tractate is then divided into chapters which are divided into individual *mishnayot* [Mishna in the singular]. In English

---

[27] Letter to Samuel ibn Tibbon, in Twersky, *Introduction to the Code*, 4, note 5.

HaRambam's Commentary on the Mishna helped
authenticate the Misha text that is used today

the term Mishna means "that which needs to be studied." The Mishna is complete: it provides legal guidelines in civil, personal, criminal, constitutional, and religious law. It also contains material on ethical and moral modes of behavior.

HaRambam opens his commentary to the Mishna with a six-verse poem alluding to the six sections of Mishna. The name Moshe occurs three times in the poem. The first is a reference to Moshe Rabbenu, the second is a self-deprecating reference to himself:

> A book that was authored in accordance with Moshe's Law
> > Recording its laws and just ways
> Like the ways recorded by our elders,
> > The builders who strengthened the pathway
> A composition of a weak youth, Moshe son of Mimon who cries
> > To God to straighten his way and make the Torah alone his desires.
> Drop ropes for him to climb the mountain of knowledge
> > His only desire is to enjoy the fruit of wisdom
> Then I will rejoice when I will behold God's goodness
> > A beautiful gift presented by Moshe[28]

[28] For the original Hebrew per original manuscripts see Kafikh (Mosad HaRav Kook, Jerusalem 1976)

The third reference to Moshe remains ambiguous. The poem uses images of freshly picked fruit presented as a gift to those who will study the work.

HaRambam completed the *Commentary on Mishna* shortly after arriving in Egypt. At the end of the work as a postscript to the commentary HaRambam writes:

> I have completed this commentary as I promised. I ask and beseech the Exalted One to save me from errors. Whoever finds herein a dubious passage, or has an interpretation of any law that is better than mine, let him draw my attention to it and give me the benefit of the doubt. For what I have undertaken is no slight thing, and to carry it out is not easy for someone honest with good judgement especially as my heart has often been occupied with the vicissitudes of time and what God has determined for me by way of exile and wandering in the world from one end of heaven to the other. Perhaps I have been rewarded for this, for exile atones for sin.
>
> The Exalted One knows that there are legal precepts whose interpretations I wrote while I was travelling along the ways, and there are matters I wrote down when I was on ships in the Mediterranean. This would be enough to distract me, in addition to my studying other sciences. I only describe the situation to explain my apology for what may be vulnerable to an exacting critic, who is not to be blamed for his criticism. Rather he has a reward from God for this, and he is loved by me, for it is the work of the Lord. What I have explained of my situation during the time of composing this commentary is what caused me to take so long.

He gives strength to the weary
Fresh vigor to the spent
Youth may grow faint and weary.
And young men stumble and fall
But they who trust in the Lord shall renew their strength
As eagles grow new feathers (Yeshayahu 40:29-31).[29]

---

[29] Postscript to the *Commentary on the Mishna*.

In the above appendix to his Commentary on the Mishnah HaRambam informs his readers and students that he wrote this work under difficult conditions. He asks those who study it to consider those conditions if they find typos or errors. It is remarkable how HaRambam was able to study and compose a commentary of such magnitude at a young age under such trying and difficult conditions.

HaRambam's goals in writing the commentary on the Mishna included synthesizing and simplifying complicated ideas and laws that are linked to the Talmudic discussions. The primary novelty of this commentary is that it renders the six sections of the Mishna as an independent rabbinic work. He addresses the question of why he felt compelled to write such a work:

I saw that if this work encompasses the entire Mishna, as was the original intention, as we will explain, there would be four primary benefits [to such a composition].

1. We would present the correct explanation of the Mishna. If you ask one of the great geonim about the explanation of a halakha from the Mishna, he will be unable to tell you anything about it unless he remembers a relevant discussion in the Gemara by heart and it is impossible for any person to remember the entire Talmud by heart. This is especially true because one halakha in the Mishna may be explained over four or five pages as it moves from one topic to the next, together with proofs questions and answers. This makes it impossible for someone who is not an expert at analysis to extract the correct interpretation of the Mishna. This is all the more so when the explanation on one halakha is spread out among many tractates.
2. We would make known the halakhic rulings, together with the explanation of each halakha.
3. This commentary will serve as an introduction for those beginning to study Talmud in depth. He will learn the manner of deriving conclusions and he will be as one who has already studied the Talmud.

4. It will serve as a reminder to one who has already learned the Talmud, so that everything he has learned is available before him and he will remember it by heart.[30]

One cannot help but think of the influence Rabbi Afasi's Halakhot Gedolot had on HaRambam's goals in the study of Talmud. For the Jews of Andalusia, the halakhic, legal conclusions are the primary intent of one who studies Torah.

There is an interesting difference of opinion among the scholars as to whether or not HaRambam wrote the Commentary on Mishna as phase one of a much greater project or as an independent work not associated with his later writings. The late Professor Isadore Twersky was of the opinion that HaRambam, at an early age envisioned the three great works, commentary on the Mishnah, Sefer HaMitzvoth and Mishneh Torah.[31] Rabbi Nachum Rabbinivitch z"l disputes this claim and argues that the Commentary on Mishna must be seen as an independent work.[32]

The brilliance of HaRambam's *Commentary on the Mishna* is that it is a valuable tool of study for both the beginner and for the most advanced student of Talmud. One gets a panoramic view of the entire Talmud from this commentary. Without sacrificing precision and lucidity HaRambam was able to be clear and brief. He prepares the student with the necessary concepts, ideas and principles so that one can then embark on the Talmudic discussions associated with the particular Mishna. Additionally, he clarifies and records the legal decision of the Mishna based on the Talmudic debates.

As part of his Mishna commentary, HaRambam penned three major works often referred to as introductions, where he discusses history, theology, ethics, philosophy, and law. The first is an introduction to his commentary on Mishna. This essay can stand alone as a

---

[30] HaRambam, *Introduction to Commentary on the Mishna*, Kafikh edition

[31] Isadore Twersky, *Introduction to the Code of Maimonides*, (Yale University Press, New Haven, 1980) ages 7-12

[32] Rabbi Nachum Rabinovith, *Yad Peshuta*, Introduction (Jerusalem, 1987)

tour-de-force on the history and philosophy of Jewish law. Then there is the introduction to the tenth chapter of Tractate Sanhedrin, where he lays out the thirteen principles of Jewish faith. The third is an introduction to his commentary on Pirke Avot [Ethics of the Fathers], where he discusses his philosophy of ethics and psychology]. This work is referred to as *Shemoneh Perakim* [the Eight Chapters].

Introduction to the *Commentary on the Mishna*

In his general introduction to his commentary on Mishna, HaRambam discusses the historical development and the nature of the oral law as well as the role of the prophet of Israel. The oral law, according to the Jews of Andalusia, was revealed to Moshe Rabbenu along with the written law at Mount Sinai and expounded and developed through each generation's supreme court of Israel. The Mishna and subsequently the Talmud represent the authoritative and binding rulings of the last supreme court of Israel. Therefore, all Jews are bound by the rulings of the Talmud. A prophet, notwithstanding his or her spiritual and intellectual gifts, cannot be a part of the legislative process.[33] Law is determined by established principles that do not include prophetic visions or heavenly voices. Only Moshe Rabbenu enjoyed the dual status of prophet and legislator. The legislative process, to a certain degree, followed basic democratic rules.

A theme that runs through HaRambam's introduction to the Mishna is that Rabbi Yehuda Hanasi's compilation of Mishna is not so much a code of law as much as it is a launchpad for the study of Jewish law. It is a framework about how one thinks about law, as opposed to what the law is.

For HaRambam, the two great Jewish lawgivers were Moshe Rabbenu and Rabbi Yehuda Hanasi. Before Moshe's death, writes HaRambam, he wrote thirteen scrolls of the Torah and gave each of the tribes one scroll, placed one scroll in the Mishkan, and then ascended Mount Nevo on the seventh day of Adar.

---

[33] See my article Maimonides on Authority, Obedience and Reason also pages in My

Introduction to *Perek Helek*

HaRambam's introduction to *Perek Helek* is inspired by the Mishna that states:

> All members of Israel have a share [a *helek*] of the world-to-come as the verse states: "And Your people, all of them righteous, shall possess the land forever, they are the shoot that I planted, My handiwork in which I glory" (Yeshayahu 60:21).
>
> The following do not have a share of the world-to-come: He who says that there is no resurrection of the dead prescribed in the Torah; he who says the Torah is not from heaven and an Apikores. Rabbi Akiva says: Also, one who reads foreign books or who utters charms over a wound and recites the verse: "I will not bring upon you any of the diseases that I brought upon the Egyptians, for I the Lord am your healer" (Shemoth 15:26). Abba Shal adds: "One who pronounces God's name."[34]

As a commentary to this Mishna, HaRambam undertakes to put forth the core beliefs of a Jew. Rabbinic Judaism stresses practice but it is absurd to think that Judaism does not have certain fundamental principles of faith. The Mishna does not state which of an *apikorus's* beliefs disqualify him or her from sharing in the destiny of the Jewish people, but HaRambam explains that an *apikorus* is one who "disparages the Torah or its sages and does not believe in the principles of the Torah. Such a person despises the sages or the disciples of the wise, including his own teacher."[35] HaRambam's comment is consistent with the rabbinic saying in Mishna Avot in the name of Rabbi Elazar ben Arakh, "Be alert to learn Torah, and know how to answer the *apikorus*."[36]

Regarding Rabbi Akiva's statement that those who read foreign books do not share in the destiny of the Jewish people, HaRambam explains:

[34] TB Sanhedrin Mishna 10:1.

[35] HaRambam, Introduction to Sanhedrin, chapter 10.

[36] Pirke Avot 2:14.

They are heretical books, and also the books of Ben Sira,[37] who wrote books about the nonsense physiognomy,[38] lacking science and utility, rather a hollow waste of time such as the books found among the Arabs on chronicles, the lives of kings, Arab genealogies, books of songs and the like, in which there is neither science nor physical benefit but merely a waste of time.[39]

For HaRambam, the Arab books of chronicles and kings' genealogies were hagiographic books that recounted fantasies of Arab kings and heroes. He understood that people had a tendency to believe that the written word is truth, and so the sages banned books that were fantasy. In their view, books are meant to share practical, scientific, or philosophical knowledge.

The above quoted Mishna assumes that one's beliefs are critical in achieving a portion of the world-to-come. HaRambam seizes this opportunity to define precisely and clearly what it is a Jew must believe in order to avoid ambiguity and confusion and eliminate the possibility of this Mishna being a launchpad for nonsensical beliefs. One of HaRambam's primary goals as a teacher was to wean his community away from superstitious beliefs and corporeality of God. Therefore, he specified *Thirteen Principles of Faith*. Only those who believe in the following articles of faith belong to the community of Israel. Unlike their Muslim counterparts, the Jews of Andalusia insisted that even the common folk, children, and the uneducated must have correct beliefs about God and Jewish faith.[40] Here is a summary of the Thirteen Principles of Faith:

1. Belief in the existence of God, Creator of heaven and Earth, and His unity.
2. God is One, but not like the oneness of species or anything com-

---

[37] Rabbi Yitzchak Alfasi on TB Sanhedrin 19b also rejected the Book of Ben Sira.

[38] The belief that a person's facial features or expression is indicative of his character or ethnic origin.

[39] Introduction to Sanhedrim, Chapter 10.

[40] Yamin Levy, *The Mysticism of Andalusia*.

pound and divisible or simple; rather God is an absolute Unity.
3. God is neither body nor a force in a body and is not subject to the actions of bodies such as movement, rest, or emotions. When the Torah describes God in physical terms it is meant to be understood metaphorically.
4. God is eternal while every other existence is nonprimordial with reference to Him. God created and formed the world from absolute nothingness.
5. God is the only God and exclusively worthy of worship, extolled and obeyed. Nothing else in existence, including angels, heavenly bodies, the spheres, the elements nor what is composed of them, may be worshiped. Worshipping anything other than God is a transgression of idolatry.
6. Human beings can communicate with God through prophecy. Prophets are those who possess superior innate characteristics and human perfection.
7. Moshe Rabbenu is the father of all prophets who preceded him and who will come after him. All of them are inferior to him. He is God's chosen one who apprehended of God more than any other human being. God spoke directly to Moshe Rabbenu.
8. The entire Torah that is in our hands today was revealed to Moshe Rabbenu by God.
9. The Torah and the law of Moshe Rabbenu is immutable and will never be abrogated. God will never reveal another law to any prophet.
10. God knows people actions.
11. God will reward all those who observe the Torah and will punish all those who transgress its prohibitions.
12. Belief that the Mashiach [Messiah] will come and even if he tarries we must wait for him. One should not guess or set a time of his arrival nor interpret Scripture as a basis or when he will arrive. Whoever denies or doubts that the Mashiach will arrive denies the entire Torah.
13. Belief in the resurrection of the dead.

Shemoneh Perakim [The Eight Chapters]

Pirke Avot, literally translated as "Chapters of the Fathers" but generally known as "Ethics of Our Fathers," is a Mishnaic text that consists of five chapters. It presents the teachings and aphorisms of sages who lived between the second and third centuries. Like the rest of Mishna, Pirke Avot consists of short statements attributed to the rabbis of that era. While the rest of Mishna concerns itself with case law, Pirke Avot is primarily a series of ethical teachings and a presentation of the early rabbi's overall worldview.

Pirke Avot is therefore a perfect stage for HaRambam to expand and expound his understanding of the rabbis' ethics, culture, and views on Torah study, friendship, and numerous other teachings on Jewish life and living. HaRambam seizes this opportunity to write his third introduction, which is referred to as *Shemoneh Perakim* [Eight Chapters] because it consists of eight chapters.

The Eight Chapters of the *Shemoneh Perakim* are titled:[41]

Chapter 1: On the Soul of Man and Its Powers
Chapter 2: O the Disobedience of the Soul's Powers and on Knowledge of the Parts in Which the Virtues and Vices are Primarily Found
Chapter 3: On the Disease of the Soul
Chapter 4: On Medical Treatment for the Disease of the Soul
Chapter 5: On Directing All the Powers of the Soul Toward a Single Goal
Chapter 6: On the Difference Between the Righteous Man and the Disciplined Man
Chapter 7: On the Veils and Their Meaning
Chapter 8: On Man's Inborn Disposition

For HaRambam, "the improvement of moral habits is the same as healing the soul and harnessing its powers."[42] One who treats the

---

[41] Kafikh preserves what appears to be unique to HaRambam's works, namely giving titles to chapters of a work.

[42] HaRambam Shemoneh Perakim chapter 4

illnesses of the soul must know and understand the soul. There are five parts to the human soul, writes HaRambam – the nutritive, sentient, imaginative, appetitive, and rational. The goal of the development of the soul is to grow intellectually.[43]

The soul can be trained to be virtuous or driven by vices. A symptom of a sick soul is a disposition that "that consists in being deficient or excessive with regards to virtues."

> The health of the soul consists in its condition and of its parts being such that it always does good and fine things . . . A soul that is sick consists in its condition and that its parts being such that it always does bad and ugly things.[44]

Good actions, according to HaRambam, are, "Those that are balanced in the mean between two extremes, both of which are bad; one of them is excess while the other is deficient."[45]

The golden mean is always the ideal. In chapter four HaRambam notes how people often mistakenly believe that certain extreme behaviors are virtuous. For example, people will praise a man who is exceedingly courageous and places himself in dangerous situations without thought, or one who is so generous he gives all his money away. For HaRambam, these are symptoms of a soul that is not well. All extremes in behavior are symptomatic of illness. In order to heal such a soul, the person may have to behave in the other extreme for a short period of time.

In the same chapter HaRambam discusses the Andalusian attitude towards ascetic practices. He writes that the ascetics are mistaken in thinking that "by afflicting their bodies . . . they . . . thereby come near to God." Virtuous men sometimes adopt ascetic practices for a short period of time as a remedy or treatment of their soul or to set an example to the society in which they live. This, however, should not be construed as the ideal. The ideal of the Torah is to live always

---

[43] For a discussion on HaRambam's understanding of the difference between Neshama and Nefesh see my Mysticism of

[44] *Shemoneh Perakim* chapter 3.

[45] Ibid, chapter 4.

in a balanced middle path. One should enjoy that which the law permits and deny oneself that which the law forbids. To impose on oneself prohibitions that are permitted is foolish and again symptomatic of a soul that needs healing.

> The perfect man needs to inspect his moral habits every day ... whenever he sees his soul inclining to one of the sides he should rush and correct it.[46]

In chapter five of the *Shemoneh Perakim* HaRambam expands on an idea that he alluded to in chapter one. He states that one who seeks to perfect his soul must set his sight on a single goal, namely the pursuit of knowledge of God. HaRambam describes the challenges and difficulties of pursuing such a path and concludes with:

> If a man happens to exist in this condition, I will not say that he is inferior to the prophets of Israel. Such a man directs all the powers of his soul toward God.

As the Jews of Andalusia knew well, man's ultimate goal is the pursuit of knowledge of God. HaRambam quotes a verse in Mishle, "In all your ways know Him" (Mishle 3:6) and the Talmudic interpretation of this verse, "In all your ways, even with transgression."[47]

In chapter six HaRambam returns to discussing the nature of the soul. A healthy soul, writes HaRambam, does the right thing because it desires to do so and withholds itself from doing harmful or wrong things because such actions are repugnant to the soul. While one who abstains from an action that he desires to do is worthy, he or she must work on their soul until the action itself is distasteful. For the sake of illustration HaRambam teaches that an individual who has a desire to kill and commit murder but abstains from such an abhorrent act is of course praiseworthy - but terribly unhealthy. A healthy soul would not have such a desire to begin with. The same is true of one who desires to steal, commit promiscuous acts – but abstains from them. The healthy soul does not even desire such

---

[46] *Shemoneh Perakim* chapter 4.

[47] TB Berakhot 63a.

actions. The same principle does not apply to morally neutral actions such as eating Kosher food. Eating foods that are deemed forbidden by Jewish law are not immoral or bad but nevertheless forbidden. If one says, "I would love to eat a piece of pork, but I won't because the Torah law forbids it," the soul is reacting in a healthy manner.

Moral and ethical habits and behaviors are essential in one's pursuit of God, knowledge of God, and love and awe of God. Bad moral habits create a distance and in some cases a barrier between the seeker and God, as the verse states, "Only your sins have separated you from God" (Yeshayahu 59:2).

HaRambam concludes the *Shemoneh Perakim* by making clear that good habits and good character are learned, nurtured, and developed. No one is born with a good or bad character. God does not determine one's moral behavior. Regarding the biblical verses that seem to suggest that God guided Pharoah in his evil ways,[48] HaRambam explains that Pharoah did it to himself. He had reached a point of such evil that his freedom of choice and his ability to repent were denied. In other words, one has to exercise one's free will and learn and practice habits that heal the soul and bring about good character.

Final Thought About the Commentary on the Mishna

HaRambam's commentary on the Mishna is the only complete work that is written by HaRambam himself that has survived the perils of time and history. The Mimon family preserved the commentary manuscript along with other writings of HaRambam. Today most of the manuscript is on display at the National Library of Israel. It is incredibly inspiring to see HaRambam's own handwriting and the many personal corrections and edits he made to the original manuscript. One can see how over the years HaRambam continually updated his work. The manuscript had made its way to Aleppo, Syria where it was regarded as a treasure of the Jewish people. The presence of the manuscript is

---

[48] There are numerous verses that state that God had hardened Pharoah's heart.

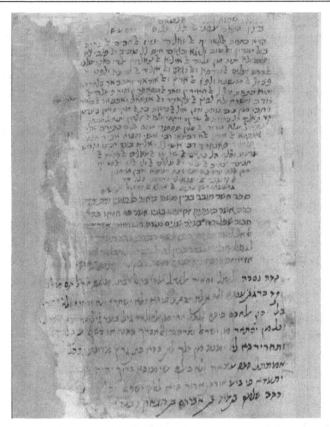

National Library Handwritten Manuscript of HaRambam

mentioned by Rabbi Yoseph Karo in his work called *Avkat Rochel*.

As the Mimon family expanded and flourished in various branches this treasure was regarded as a family heirloom, it was divided among the relatives. The manuscripts began to resurface in the seventeenth century in England and ended up in the Bodleian Library at the University of Oxford. In the early twentieth century the famous collector David Solomon Sassoon purchased at least two sections of the commentary. They were later sold to the National Library of Israel.

Even if this commentary had been the only work written by HaRambam, it would have secured his fame for perpetuity.

Rabbi Moshe Ben Mimon, HaRambam / Maimonides, Rambam

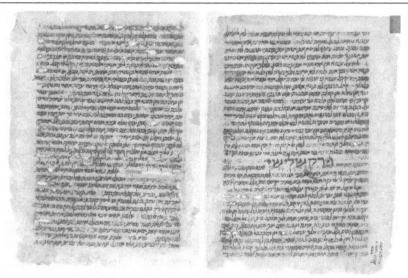

HaRambam's Commentary on the Mishna, Spain 1190

Judeo-Arabic as a Language of Choice

There is no doubt that the decision by HaRambam to write his *Commentary on the Mishna* and the Guide of the Perplexed in in Judeo-Arabic must have been carefully deliberated before the quill was put to the parchment. While HaRambam espoused the view that language is conventional,[49] which means that the Hebrew language developed

---

[49] For HaRambam, the Hebrew language is special because it is the language of the TaNaKH and because it is the holy tongue it is grammatically perfect, as Joseph ibn Kaspi asserts in *Asarah Kele Kesef*, edited by I. Last (Pressburg, 1903), or as HaRambam himself has asserted because it does not contain foul language, but it is nevertheless void of any metaphysical properties. See the Guide 3:8 and 2:30 also *MT Hilkhot De'ot* 2:4; *Keriat Shema* 3:4-5; *Perush HaMishna* Avot 1:16. This was the attitude of the scholars of Andalusia as is clear from Avraham ibn Ezra, Bereshit 2:7. European Jewry considered Hebrew language as having metaphysical qualities – a language containing the essence of what it describes. For this position see Nachmanides' *Perush al HaTorah* Shemoth 30:13 and his *"Ma'amar al Penimiyut HaTorah"* in *Kitbe HaRamban* volume 2, edited by C. Chavel, 467 (Jerusalem: Mossad HaRav Kook Publishers, 1964). For a comprehensive discussion in secondary sources see Twersky, *Introduction to the Code*, 324-330 and Faur, *Golden Doves*.

randomly without there necessarily being any logic associated with the phonetic sound applied to an object or idea, he nevertheless recognized the need to be mindful of his audience, the style he wanted to project, and the goals he set for his project. In the introduction to *Sefer HaMitzvoth* HaRambam notes how the biblical Hebrew language of the prophets is "too limited for us today."[50] This was the general consensus of the Jews of Al-Andalus, Muslim Spain.[51] Rabbi Yehudah HaLevi, author of the *Kuzari*, laments how the Hebrew language "shared the fate of its bearers, denigrating and dwindling with them."[52] Some two hundred years earlier Rabbi Saadia Gaon bemoaned the fact that the "nation of Israel forgot its language."[53] Similarly, Rabbi Avraham ibn Ezra notes how the Hebrew language was once elaborate and intricate but "it devolved, is forgotten, and irretrievably reconstruct-able."[54] The expert translator Yehuda ibn Tibbon alluded to the restrictive and "underdeveloped"[55] nature of the Hebrew language as one of the reasons why many Andalusians and Geonic authors chose to write in Judeo-Arabic rather than in Hebrew. Hebrew, he notes, "does not enable the writer to express thoughts succinctly and eloquently."[56] His son, the translator of HaRambam's *Commentary to the Mishna* and Guide of the Perplexed, repeats the same idea in the introduction to his *Perush HaMilot HaZarot*.[57]

While the world of Andalusia regarded the Hebrew language as

---

[50] *Sefer HaMitzvoth* Introduction.

[51] Menachem ben Saruk, *Mahberet*, edited by Z. Filopovsky, page 12; Avraham ibn Ezra, *HaMedakdek*, translated by A. Z. Rabinowitz, 28. For a comprehensive discussion on the issue see Abraham S. Halkin, "The Medieval Jewish Attitude Toward Hebrew," 232-248.

[52] Kuzari 2:68.

[53] Rabbenu Saadia Gaon, *Sefer HaGaluy*, edited by A. Harkavy, *Zikkaron LaRishonim* (Berlin, 1887), 154-156.

[54] Avraham ibn Ezra end of his Commentary on *Shir HaShirim*.

[55] Yehuda ibn Tibbon, Introduction to his Hebrew translation of *Hovot HaLevavot* by Bahya ibn Pakuda, edited by A. Zifroni. (Hebrew) (Jerusalem: Hotzaat Mahberet LeSifrut, 1964).[56] Ibid.

[57] Edited by J. Even Shemuel (Jerusalem: 1947), 11.

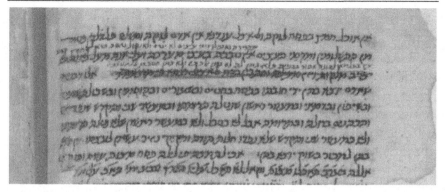

HaRambam kept editing and making corrections
to the manuscript until he died

Lashon HaKodesh [the sacred language] because of its linguistic purity and grammatical consistency, and some even embraced its metaphysical status – all being good reasons to render it unique and surpassing all other languages[58] – its limited linguistic scope could not be ignored. Therefore, HaRambam's language of choice was Arabic and more specifically Judeo-Arabic, simply because it was superior in that it was continually developed by its linguists and philologists. It afforded HaRambam philosophic precision and rhetorical capabilities that Hebrew did not have at its disposal. When the time came to translate HaRambam's works, Shemuel ibn Tibbon had to delve into the available biblical and Mishnaic Hebrew and develop its linguistic reach to do justice to the unforgiving and exacting ideas put forth by HaRambam.

The *Mishneh Torah*

HaRambam's *Mishneh Torah* garnered the greatest fame. This is a monumental work that organized and codified the entire corpus of Talmudic law. It was completed around 1180 C.E., when he was forty-

---

[58] See Menachem ben Saruk, *Mahberet* page 10; Saadia Gaon, *Sefer HaEgron* page 55; Shelomo ibn Gabirol, *Shirim*, ed. Bialik and Ravinsky page 176; Yehuda HaLevi, *Kuzari* 2:81, Rabbi Yoseph Kimhi, *Sefer HaGaluy* page 3, and others.

two years old. He continued to revise and edit it until his death twenty-four years later.

HaRambam offers several reasons for writing this code of Jewish law. He wrote to the sages of Lunel that he did not compose the *Mishneh Torah* for personal glory; rather he devoted his intellectual and creative output to provide a clear, practical code of Jewish law that is available to all who seek to know how to observe *halakha*.[59] HaRambam develops this idea further in his introduction to the *Mishneh Torah*. The study of *halakha*, writes HaRambam, is difficult and can be confusing. Few scholars have the time to assimilate and master the necessary material. Without such a code, he argued, Jewish law will be lost. In a response to Pinchas the Dayan of Alexandria, HaRambam notes how the impetus that inspired Rabbi Yehuda Hanasi to write down the Mishna in and around 135 C.E. was because the times were difficult and unsettled – much like his own day and age. Until Rabbi Yehuda Hanasi the study of Torah was transmitted orally from student to teacher. Jewish law prohibits reciting the written law orally and committing to writing the oral law. The writing of the Mishna by Rabbi Yehuda HaNasi constituted a breach of the said ruling and a substantive change in the nature of Halakhic transmission. HaRambam explains and justifies this literary transgression because of the historical political crisis of that time. The Roman government was increasing its reach and power and Jews were wandering and emigrating to distant lands. The risk of having even one generation lose access to the oral chain of transmission could be irreparable and a fatal blow to the body of Torah knowledge that was being preserved. HaRambam saw himself as continuing the work of Rabbi Yehuda HaNasi:

> In our days severe vicissitudes prevail, and all feel the pressure of hard times. The wisdom of our wise men has disappeared. The understanding of our prudent men is hidden. Hence the commentaries of the Geonim and their compilation of laws and responses which they took care to make clear, have in our times

---

[59] Letter to Jonathon of Lunel, Responsa 49.

become hard to understand so that only a few individuals properly comprehend them . . . on these grounds, I Moses the son of Mimon the Sefaradi bestirred myself . . . .[60]

Just like the Mishna of Rabbi Yehuda HaNasi was a reaction to changing political times and the possibility of losing the oral Torah, HaRambam saw the Mishneh Torah as a literary reaction to changing times and political crisis in his generation.

The *Mishneh Torah*'s clarity, organization, and scope make it a remarkable work of literature. The entire body of biblical and rabbinic law, the fundamentals of Jewish philosophy and beliefs, as well as a primer to the great mysteries of Jewish mysticism are carefully and sensibly organized in exactly one thousand chapters, in fourteen volumes, including all the laws that had no relevance in HaRambam's day and age or in the diaspora. The *Mishneh Torah* also includes the calendar specifications and calculations, the texts of the prayer books and Haggadah, the precise lettering of a Sefer Torah, as well as exact measurements of the building of the Bet HaMikdash and quantities relevant to sacrificial offerings.

HaRambam's Mishneh Torah is a code of Jewish law, and a code must be precise and concise. A well-written code requires a carefully thought-out logical structure where each ruling has its necessary place. HaRambam understood that this work would be thoroughly scrutinized. He therefore made sure that it was flawless as a code, offered clear guidance, enunciating principles, and provided closure to countless Talmudic and rabbinic ambiguities.

Instead of the traditional Aramaic-Hebrew of the Geonim, HaRambam wrote the *Mishneh Torah* in simple, easy-to-understand Mishnaic Hebrew. This shift made the Talmudic law universally accessible to the masses. This was not just a matter of cutting and pasting or charting data. Anyone even remotely familiar with Talmudic Law and the Talmud as a text will know it is not a code but a running discussion of countless viewpoints and ideas, tangents, and free-associated thoughts. The adjudication of Talmudic law involves numer-

---

[60] HaRambam, Introduction to Mishneh Torah, translation by Isadore Twersky, *Maimonides Reader* page 39

ous rules scattered throughout the Talmud and in responsa literature of the Geonim, as well as the application of variant teachings, texts, and traditions. All this material had to be mined and filtered – without the internet – while running from persecution, with limited access to libraries and books. The *Mishneh Torah* set out to decide and rule on Jewish law and practice based on conflicting variant and various ruling, opinions, and traditions.

The *Mishneh Torah* is organized and meant to be studied progressively. There is a longstanding Talmudic tradition that there are six-hundred thirteen biblical commandments, but the tradition does not include a list of the commandments. Numerous lists were created during the period of the Geonim, some more popular than others. HaRambam parted ways with those lists and wrote *Kitab Al-Faraid,* in Hebrew *Sefer HaMitzvoth* [the Book of Commandments], where he first lists his version of the six hundred thirteen biblical mitzvoth and then explains, based on fourteen principles, the criteria for their inclusion in the list. He then expands each of the mitzvoth, stating each mitzvah's biblical source and a summary of how it is observed and how it is expounded upon in rabbinic literature. He then divided biblical law into fourteen sections where he carefully, precisely, and authoritatively codified all rabbinic extensions and amplifications of the biblical law. Each grouping has a preface and reference of the biblical commandments discussed in the section. In other words, the student of the *Mishneh Torah* can find any topic and its ruling in a matter of moments.

HaRambam's *Mishneh Torah* took Jewish learning by storm. He organized the law and, instead of Talmudic Aramaic, he codified it in Hebrew. Instead of the elaborate debates and discussions of the Talmud, he cites only one deciding opinion – entirely dropping all variant points of view. He states the law without indicating its source or promulgator. By doing so he filled the need of providing a completely referenced and readable code of the entire Jewish law.

The rulings in the *Mishneh Torah* were gathered from the Babylonian Talmud and the less-studied Jerusalem Talmud. He reviewed all ancient texts as well as the less accredited texts such as the *Beraitot,* the *Tosefta,* and all the Halakhic midrashim as well as several shorter, less authoritative works such as *Avot de-Rabbi Natan, Avot de-Rabbi*

Eliezer, Massekhet Semachot, Kallah, Kallah Rabbati, Seder Olam, Targum Onkelos, Targum Yonatan, among others.

The physician and scholar Isaac bar Sheshet HaNasi of Saragossa (early thirteenth century) noted that those who opposed the publication of the *Mishneh Torah* bemoaned the fact that their monopoly on legal competence was now broken.[61] With the publication of HaRambam's *Mishneh Torah*, anyone – including lay people – can now find answers to legal *halakhic* questions without the need to consult a rabbi.

The *Mishneh Torah*'s originality was not limited to Jewish Law. Traditionally, Jewish law was studied and presented as separate and distinct from Jewish philosophy and beliefs. Law required precision while Jewish philosophy and dogma is more fluid. In the first section of the first volume of the *Mishneh Torah*, called *Hilkhot Yesodei HaTorah* [the Laws of the Foundations of Torah], HaRambam unequivocally presents the primary theological and metaphysical principles of Jewish faith. He then sprinkles Jewish theology, aggadah and esoterica throughout the *Mishneh Torah*.

The great work begins with belief in the absolute Unity of a singularly unique God, Creator of heaven and Earth, and ends with belief in the coming of the Messiah, a politically powerful individual who will reestablish the Davidic dynasty, rebuild the Bet Hamikdash, return all Jews to the land of Israel, and bring peace and prosperity.

The illustrious scholar and historian Professor Haym Soloveitchik described the Mishneh Torah as a great literary work of art. He writes:

> The *Yad* (*Yad HaHazaka* is another name for the Mishneh Torah), on the other hand, has commanded the attention of scholars for eight hundred years and has drawn into its vortex nearly everyone who has sat down to write on it . . . . .I know of no attempt to use the Mishneh Torah as the base of a layered text or as springboard for things beyond itself.

---

[61] See Daniel J. Silver, *Maimonidean Criticism and the Maimonidean Controversy 1180-1240*, 26; see also *The Wars of the Lord by Abraham Maimonides in Defense of His Father Moses Maimonides*, translation and introduction by Fred Rosner, 21 (Haifa: The Maimonides Research Institute Press, 2000).

Both the Mishneh Torah and the Shulkhan Arukh are towering works, but Mishneh Torah is that rarest of things – a book of law, a work of sequitur, discursive reasoning that is at the same time, a work of art. And a work of art creates its own imaginative universe. [62]

The books of the Mishneh Torah are:

Sefer Ha-Madda (The Book of Knowledge), which examines the fundamentals of Jewish faith including *Ma'aseh Merkava* and *Ma'aseh Bereshit*, Laws of Teshuva, and the prohibitions of idolatry.

Sefer Ahavah (The Book of Love [of God]), which covers prayers, blessings and devotional practices such as Tefillin, Mezuza, and Berit Mila. All the laws associated with a Sefer Torah is also included.

Sefer Zemanim (The Book of Seasons), which is devoted to the Sabbath and holidays and the fixing of the Jewish calendar.

Sefer Nashim (The Book of Women), which deals with family law, including marriage and divorce.

Sefer Kedushah (The Book of Holiness), which includes sexual prohibitions and dietary laws.

Sefer Hafla'ah (The Book of Utterances), which treats subjects such as oaths and vows.

Sefer Zera'im (The Book of Seeds), which deals with agricultural law and other commandments effective in the Land of Israel.

Sefer Avodah (The Book of Temple Service), which focuses on Temple worship.

Sefer Korbanot (The Book of Sacrifices), which details the laws of sacrificial offerings.

Sefer Taharah (The Book of Purity), which is devoted to the rules governing ritual purity.

Sefer Nezikin (The Book of Damages), which focuses on property damage and personal injury.

---

[62] Haym Soloveitchik, "Polemic and Art" in *Maimonides After Eight Hundred Years: Essays on Maimonides and His Influence*. Edited by Jay M. Harris (Harvard University Press, Cambridge, MA 2007) pages 335

Sefer Kinyan (The Book of Acquisition), which deals with property rights and includes sections on sales, neighborly relations, and partnerships.

Sefer Mishpatim (The Book of Civil Laws), which includes hiring, borrowing, loaning, and inheritance.

Sefer Shofetim (The Book of Judges), which covers the legal system, the political system, as well as the laws mourning.

Each book is divided into sub-sections by topic, and each topic is reflected in the sub-section's title, as in *"Hilkhot Shabbat"* ("The Laws

Rica and Ari Lieberman in Cordova, Spain circa 2021

of Sabbath"), which is included in The Book of Seasons. The sub-sections are internally divided into numbered chapters and paragraphs.

Moreh Nevuchim [The Guide of the Perplexed]

The *Moreh Nevuchim*[63] was completed in 1190 C.E., fourteen years before HaRambam passed away. This work is mistakenly characterized as Jewish philosophy. It is much more than that. In fact, traditional philosophic matters such as ethics, politics, and logic are hardly touched upon while the primary thrust of the work deals with biblical exegesis, hermeneutics, Divine providence, the nature and meaning of mitzvoth, prophecy, and the perfect worship of God. The Guide is an innovative work meant to be studied by the finest students. As HaRambam writes:

> The object of this treatise is to enlighten the religious man who has been trained to believe in the truth of our holy law, who conscientiously fulfills his moral and religious duties, and at the same time has been successful in his philosophic studies. Human reason has attracted him to abide within its sphere, and he finds it difficult to accept as correct the teachings based on literal interpretation of the law . . . hence he is lost in perplexity and anxiety.[64]

HaRambam felt Torah, revelation, and prophecy need not be a stumbling block for the philosophically sophisticated and disciplined student – when taught correctly. HaRambam unapologetically utilizes terms, concepts, and ideas that he drew from Jewish, Islamic, and Greek philosophical sources. He did not care to merge distinct ideas and thoughts, but rather he recognized that Judaism's most abstract and most profound beliefs required a clear, precise, and accu-

---

[63] *Moreh Nevuchim* was originally titled *Kitab Dalalat Al-Ha'irin*, translated into English as The Guide of the Perplexed.

[64] HaRambam, Introduction to The Guide of the Perplexed.

rate vocabulary that was provided by Aristotelian thought. For HaRambam, Aristotle's greatest achievement was his ability to express the world of the human spirit in clear terms and notions.[65] The student of the Guide immediately recognizes that HaRambam's teachings emerge from the great Jewish thinkers such as Saadia Gaon (882-942 C.E.), Shelomo ibn Gabirol (1120-1148 C.E.), Yehudah Halevi (1075-1141 C.E.), Avraham ibn Ezra (1089-1164 C.E.), Avraham ibn Daud (1110-1180 C.E.), and the many great scholars that preceded him.[66]

The impact of the Guide is difficult to assess. It influenced medieval thinkers such as Albert Magnus, Thomas Aquinas, Duns Scotus, Raymond Martini, and Meister Eckhart who regularly quote the Guide, as well as the most prominent modern-day thinkers such as Baruch Spinoza, Gottfried W. Leibniz, Isaac Newton, and James Joyce. I round out the list with modern thinkers such as Leo Strauss, Martin Buber, Franz Rosenzweig, Emil Fackenheim, Emmanuel Levinas, and Rabbi Joseph B. Soloveitchik. Sadly, but not surprisingly the Guide never made its way into the study halls of Lithuanian or Hassidic Eastern European Yeshivoth.

After being translated into multiple languages, the Guide became the source of significant controversy in Jewish European circles. The book was banned in Northern Spain, France, and Germany, and tragically it was turned over to the Dominican inquisitors in December of 1232 for public burning.[67] How such a thing could happen remains one of the great and most tragic mysteries of Jewish history.

The biblical text contains Divine and infinite truths, but it is a text that was written for the masses. The Torah, HaRambam notes, is expressed in equivocal terms so that the multitude will understand it and appreciate it according to their abilities, while the scholar will reveal and put forth its deeper meaning.[68] HaRambam believed that it

---

[65] Menachem Kellner, "Maimonides' Disputed Legacy." [66] Joel Kraemer, "Maimonides and the Spanish Aristotelian School," 62-64.

[67] The best work on the Maimonidean Controversy is written by Daniel Jeremy Silver, titled *Maimonidean Criticism and the Maimonidean Controversy: 1180-1240* (Leiden: Brill, 1965).

is the task of the teacher to reveal the text's truths by unveiling them with the finest tools available to the teacher. Like the "golden apple hidden in a silver lattice" (Mishle 25:11) the Torah's truths need to be revealed.[69] The "golden apples" must ideally be revealed orally from teacher to student.

HaRambam's mode of interpretation/revelation of the Torah's meaning is far from linear. In fact, he goes out of his way to contradict himself in order to purposely conceal the very truths he is trying to reveal. The Guide, HaRambam explains, was written as *rashei perakim* [chapter headings] which the exceptional student then must unravel and decode. Each student, depending on his or her level of understanding, will absorb the teachings personally. This is the way the secrets of the Torah must be taught, writes HaRambam – "conceal some parts" and "disclose other parts." Hakham José Faur, whose book *Homo Mysticus* presents an insightful and authentic reading of the Guide, describes the work as follows:

> Naïve readers believe that the Guide is a literary unit with a beginning, an end, and a middle. Rather, it is a puzzle that can be resolved in a variety of ways; for every solution there is a counter solution, and for every proof there is a counter proof. The prose is chilling and moody, the wit ice-cold. The style is non-linear, at times scintillating and exasperating. Abruptly, the road bifurcates, compelling the reader to make a critical decision either to pursue an avenue that may (or may not) lead from a linguistic suggestion to a shrewd, radical political analysis, finding at the end a trapdoor or to explore a perfunctory note, encoding perhaps, an unresolved message. Following Maimonides' train of thought is like moving at a vertiginous speed along a labyrinth, branching up and down in all directions. Throughout the text are concealed ideas affecting the ebb and flow of moods and thoughts. Stark primordial emotions insinuate themselves into the reader's con-

---

[68] Introduction to the Guide, 9; also Elliot Wolfson, "Beneath the Wings of the Great Eagle," 213.

[69] Faur, *Golden Doves* Introduction and pages 114-118.

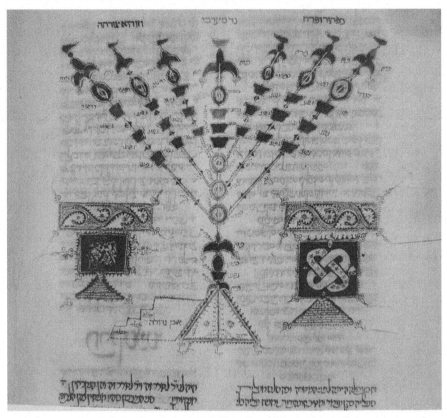

16th-century Reproduction of HaRambam's version of the Menorah

sciousness. The Guide functions like a multifaceted mirror, reflecting distant, unmapped regions in the reader's psyche. **What the reader finds at the conclusion of the road is a jazzy, kaleidoscopic portrait of himself/herself as reflected in the work of the great master. In this type of "reading" the most arduous task comes afterward; she/he will spend the rest of her/his life writing a postscript to his/her own Guide.** [The bolded text is my own for emphasis.][70]

---

[70] José Faur, *Homo Mysticus: A Guide to Maimonides' Guide for the Perplexed* (Syracuse University Press 1998), xi.

The goal is to make the student understand in accordance with the way of the Divine will, which is never revealed all at once. As the verse states, "*Sod Adonay lerey'av* [the secret of God is with them that fear Him]" (Tehillim 25:14). The student is constantly being challenged to make sense of the text and reveal the truth for himself/herself. Joel Kraemer describes the Guide's didactic approach:

> Maimonides gave keys for unlocking its secrets throughout the text. He guided by allusion rather than by imparting an authoritative body of teachings, as Plato saw knowledge not as information transmitted from teacher to pupil, but as a manner of being and thinking, communicated through dialogue.[71]

Leo Strauss, one of the pioneers in the study of Maimonides and the Guide in particular, writes:

> The Guide as a whole is not merely a key to the forest but is itself a forest, an enchanted forest, and hence also an enchanting forest. It is a delight to the eyes – for the tree of life is a delight to the eyes.[72]

The Letters of HaRambam

Iggeret HaShemad [the Letter of Apostacy]

HaRambam was not yet thirty years old when he began to assume the mantle of the rabbi of the entire Jewish people. In 1160 C.E. HaRambam penned *Iggeret HaShemad*, also known as *Iggeret Kiddush Hashem* [the Letter on Apostacy]. This letter was written while HaRambam and his family lived in North Africa, where it was not uncommon for the Jews to face the brutal choice between death or conversion to Islam. For the Muslim persecutors, conversion to Islam involved the recitation of the *Shahada* which stated, "The is no other God than Allah and

---

[71] Joel Kraemer, "Moses Maimonides: An Intellectual Portrait," 10-57.

[72] Leo Strauss, "How to Begin to Study The Guide of the Perplexed," in *Moses Maimonides: The Guide to The Perplexed*, translated by Shlomo Pines, xii (University of Chicago Press, 1963).

Mohamad is the Prophet." Members of the Jewish community sent a series of questions to the rabbis of Europe regarding those who surrendered under the intense oppression and chose to recite the *Shahada* (Islamic profession of faith) and remain alive. While we do not have a copy of the original letter, we can assume based on HaRambam's response that the following questions were asked:

- What is the religious status of those who recited the *Shahada* but remained practicing Jews in secret?
- Is the recitation of the *Shahada* considered idolatry for which one must choose death over transgression?
- Should the head of a Jewish household choose death over the recitation of the *Shahada* when he knows that if he does so his entire family will be raised as Muslims?

These questions were first addressed to an unknown European rabbi whose response was widely circulated throughout the Maghreb. This rabbi claimed unambiguously that the recitation of the *Shahada* by Jews and Islam as a religious practice is idolatry and any Jew faced with the choice of reciting the *Shahada* or death must choose death, based on the Talmudic *halakhic* ruling "be killed rather than transgress." He further notes that a Jewish court may impose capital punishment on anyone who does not choose death. Additionally, the Jews who recite the *Shahada* in public in order to appease their Muslim oppressors but observe the Torah in secrecy are rejected by God. Any and all commandments observed by these Jews in secret have no religious value, and their prayers are repugnant to God.

This response threw the communities throughout the Maghreb into a state of despondency and hopelessness. It denied these communities any prospect of continued association with Judaism, with Jewish culture, and with God of Israel. HaRambam, despite his youth, could not remain silent.

HaRambam asked how one could condemn an entire people without knowing the Jewish community and the potential disastrous consequences of such a ruling. The presumed sage who wrote that letter must be a fraud, an "empty vessel" as "one not even worthy of a reply."

The man of whom the inquiry was made offered a weak and senseless reply, of foul content and form. He made statements in it distinctly harmful.[73]

Regarding the respondent sage, HaRambam applies the verse: "His talk begins as silliness and ends as disastrous madness."[74]

The letter that HaRambam goes on to pen reveals important insights into his philosophy of *halakha*, vision as a communal leader, and how Andalusian culture varied from their counterpart European Jewish culture.

HaRambam begins the body of the letter by comforting the victimized Jew who may have recited the *Shahada* and now feel rejected by the community. He asserts that the fraudulent sage who further victimized the Jewish community is guilty of slander against God's most beloved. Greater men than this fraud have been punished for their sin of slandering the people of God:

> If this is the sort of punishment meted out to the pillars of the universe – such as Moshe Rabbenu, Eliyahu HaNavi, and Yeshayahu HaNavi, and the ministering angels because they briefly criticized the Jewish people, can one have an idea of the fate of the least among the worthless who let his tongue loose against Jewish communities of sages and their disciples, priests, and Levites and called them sinners, evildoers, gentiles, disqualified to testify, heretics who deny the Lord God of Israel? These are verbal quotations from his response; can you picture his punishment? . . . God will not abandon nor forsake His people "for He did not scorn, He did not spurn the plea of the lowly" (Tehillim 22:25).[75]

HaRambam then goes on to give examples of great Mishnaic and Talmudic sages who had to transgress their faith during times of persecution and continued to observe their Judaism in secrecy, choosing life over death. The choice of the victimized Jews of Maghreb was

---

[73] *Epistle on Martyrdom*, 15. See David Hartman, *Crisis and Leadership*.

[74] Kohelet 10:13.

[75] *Epistle on Martyrdom*, 19.

consistent with the choices made by the saintly rabbinic sages of the Mishna and Talmud.

In response to the claim that the Jewish victims of the forced declaration enjoy no rewards for the observance of mitzvoth, HaRambam cites several rabbinic teachings that assert the fact that the mitzvoth and good deeds observed by the evilest sinner had merit in God's eyes. Esav was rewarded for his observance of *kibud av* [honoring his father]; Ahab and Nebuchadnezzar also enjoyed merit in God's eyes for their observance of mitzvoth and good deeds. If this is indeed God's attitude toward willful evildoers, how much more kind, compassionate, and considerate will God be with those who were forced into sinning?

After discrediting the fraudulent responder HaRambam then embarks on a detailed *halakhic* discussion supporting his position. HaRambam understood that discrediting the letter would not suffice: His ruling must be based on a strict and careful reading of the *halakha*.

The first argument HaRambam puts forth is an important distinction between willful behavior and forced behavior. For the person who is forced to behave a certain way – even if Jewish law requires of that person to choose death – the transgression is always considered to have been performed under compulsion. Therefore, he or she will always be exempt from a court-imposed punishment or death. HaRambam is consistent in his ruling when he later codifies this law when writing his *Mishneh Torah*. Such a distinction is obvious, and HaRambam wonders how the fraudulent correspondent could have missed this point.

HaRambam's second *halakhic* argument is much more fundamental to the issue. For HaRambam, the victimized Jews were not obligated to consider death when asked to recite the *Shahada*. The *Shahada* is a mere declaration, nothing more than words:

> There has never yet been a persecution as remarkable as this one, where the only coercion is to say a few words. When our rabbis ruled that a person must surrender himself to "death and not transgress" it does not seem likely that they had in mind speech that did not involve an action.[76]

[76] *Epistle*, 30-31.

This last statement of HaRambam was challenged by Professor Haim Soloveitchik[77] who claims that the Mishna in Sanhedrin rules that one who declares "you are my God" to an idol has transgressed the prohibition of idol worship and must be put to death. Hakham José Faur[78] responded to Professor Haim Soloveitchik in a heated exchange and argued that the case described in the Mishna cannot be compared to the situation of the Jews in Maghreb. The Jews in Maghreb were being coerced. A declaration of words under compulsion is an empty act and lacks any religious meaning. "They know very well," writes HaRambam, "that the Jews who recite these words are doing this in order to escape punishment and to satisfy the oppressor with a simple confession."[79] HaRambam rules an action is fundamentally different and meaningful even under compulsion, while words under compulsion are meaningless. HaRambam concludes his letter:

> Anyone who suffers martyrdom in order not to acknowledge the apostleship of that man [Muhammad], the only thing that can be said of him is that he has done what is good and proper, and that God holds great reward in store for him. His position is very high, for he has given his life for the sanctity of God, may He be exalted and blessed. But if anyone were to ask me whether to surrender his life or acknowledge, I tell him to confess the *Shahada* and not choose death.[80]

HaRambam chose a much gentler tone in the letter to the victimized community than when he rules on this matter in *Mishneh Torah*. In the *Mishneh Torah* HaRambam writes that one who chooses death

---

[77] Haym Soloveitchik, "Maimonides' Iggeret ha-Shemad: Law and Rhetoric" in *Haym Soloveitchik Collected Essays II* (London: The Lipman Library of Jewish Civilization, 2019), 288-331. [78] Jose Faur, "Two Models of Jewish Spirituality" in *Shofar* volume 10 no. 3 (spring 1992), 5-46: see also Faur, "On Martyrdom and Jewish Law: Maimonides and Nachmanides" *in Bar Ilan Annual Vol. 30-31 Meir Simcha Feldman Memorial Volume* (2006), 373-408; also Yitzchak Blau, "Idolatry and Martyrdom" in *The Torah U-Madda Journal* Volume 17 2016-2017, edited by David Shatz, 35-46.

[79] Ibid, 30.

[80] Ibid.

when he or she is not obligated to do so has committed a capital offense.[81] Unlike his European brethren, HaRambam was unequivocal about the fact that when it comes to sanctifying God's name, acts of voluntary piety and martyrdom are forbidden.

> [In certain situations] Our sages ruled, "let him transgress and not die," and yet this man sees himself as better and of higher status than the sages, and more punctilious about the law. For saying a few words and the use of his tongue he surrenders himself to death and claims to have sanctified God's name – but by his action he is a sinner and rebellious, and he makes himself guilty against his life.[82]

The *Shahada* never posed a problem to the Jews of Andalus and Muslim lands. The first part of the *Shahada* is a declaration of God's unity. HaRambam and the Jews who lived in Muslim lands recognized that Islam is a true monotheistic belief system. In a letter he wrote to Ovadia the Convert, HaRambam writes:

> These Ishmaelites are in no way idolaters. It has already been excised from their mouths and hearts, and they properly regard God as a Unity, a Unity with no exception.[83]

This perspective has significant *halakhic* implications. For example, when dealing with Christians Jewish law requires that Jews keep in mind that they are dealing with idolaters but when dealing with Muslims they are dealing with monotheists. A Jew may not drink or derive any pleasure from wine made by Christians because their wine is used for idolatrous purposes. While the wine of Muslims may not be drunk lest the social interaction lead to more intimate relations, one may, however, sell or derive other forms of pleasure from Muslim wine because they are not considered idolaters.[84] For HaRambam, all

---

[81] *MT Hilkhot Yesodei HaTorah* 5:3-4.

[82] *Epistle*, 30.

[83] *Iggerot HaRambam* [Letters of Maimonides, Hebrew and Arabic] 2 Volumes edited and translated by Yitzchak Shailat, 238 (Ma'aleh Adumim: Ma'aliyoth Press, 1987).

[84] *MT Hilkhot Ma'achalot Assurot* 11:7.

the prohibitions that Jewish law imposes on relations between idolators are applied to Christians[85] and not to Muslims.

This letter affords for us, the students of HaRambam, a glimpse into the passions of this great thinker and rabbinic sage. For HaRambam the value of human life is supreme. While Jewish law demands the sacrifice of one's life under certain circumstances – if there is the slightest doubt as to whether or not real-life circumstances fit the template described by the rabbinic sages, HaRambam rules that life takes precedence. Life as an independent value is supreme and represents the Torah's overall goals.

HaRambam's treatment of the victims of Islamic fundamentalism in this letter remains to this day controversial. It represents a classic example of Andalusian real-life religious practice and European Ashkenazic real life religious practice.

The *Risala, Iggeret Teiman* [The Letter to the Jewish Community of Yemen]

In 1172 C.E., HaRambam wrote the *Risala*, known in Hebrew as *Iggeret Teiman* and in English as Epistle to [the Jewish Community of] Yemen. The chief rabbi of the Yemenite Jewish community, Rabbi Yaakov ben Netanel, had turned to HaRambam for guidance in the wake of the harsh circumstances that had befallen the Jewish community of Yemen at the time. Yemen had been conquered by a radical Muslim sect that sought religious reform and began persecuting the Jewish community who, up until that time, were a tolerated minority. HaRambam was asked to address the harsh economic and physical oppression the Jewish community was experiencing, as well as the existential and spiritual crisis that fell upon the Jews of Yemen. HaRambam recognized the urgency as well as the magnitude of the responsibility placed upon him to offer this community that was on the brink of destruction words of encouragement, empowerment and hope.

Like Judaism, Islam is a monotheistic religion, and like Judaism

---

[85] *MT Hilkhot Avoda Zara* 9:4.

it rejects in absolute terms all forms of idolatry. There was always a sense of religious affinity between the spiritual aspiration of Islam and Judaism. In fact, Rabbi Netanel ben Fayyumi, the father of Yaakov ben Netanel, wrote a book titled *Gan HaSekhalim* [the garden of the wise], where he treats the Quran as a divine text and regards Mohammad as a legitimate prophet. His goal was to prove that the purpose of the Quran is not to replace the Torah but rather complement it.

> Therefore, let every people practice what it has received, following their prophets, priests and leaders; and none is left without Torah for it is all from one God to whom they all return, and all pray to Him and look to Him.[86]

When the Jews were persecuted by the Christians in Europe there was always a sense that their oppressors were idolaters and pagans who would one day see the error of their ways. The Jews could accept the oppression when they knew they were preserving the true faith. The persecuted Jewish minority zealously embraced their persecution as an act of Kiddush Hashem [sanctifying God's name] in the face of pagan and idolatrous persecutors. They saw themselves as the legendary heroes who accepted their fate, such as Hana and her sons who were killed by the Greeks or Rabbi Akiva and the ten sages who were martyred by the Romans.

The new circumstances created confusion for the Jews of Yemen. Islam was not an idolatrous or pagan religion. Muslim culture, like Jewish culture, embraced literature, poetry, philosophy, theology, and scientific inquiry. Unlike European Jewry, there was an affinity between Jewish and Muslim culture. Sephardic Jews wrote poetry and religious commentary in Arabic. There is not one religious text or Jew-

---

[86] Natan'el al-Fayyumi, *Sefer Gan HaSikhlim* [Garden of the Intellects in Hebrew], 4th edition, edited by Yosef Kafikh, Introduction p. 10 and page 114 (Kiryat Ono, 2016). See Marc Shapiro, "On Books and Bans," *Edah Journal* 3:2 (2003): "The clearest support for Sacks' position is provided by R. Netanel ben al-Fayyumi (twelfth century), who maintains that 'God sent different prophets to the various nations of the world with legislations suited to the particular temperament of each individual nation.' Although Sacks is motivated by a post-modern vision, the medieval R. Netanel also claimed that God's truth was not encompassed by Judaism alone."

ish poem by an Ashkenaz Jew in Latin because Latin was regarded as the language of the idolator. The battle with Islam was not the great historical battle against idolatry.

This of course weakened the resolve of the Jews of Yemen. *Why suffer at the hands of a culture that shares the same religious goals?* was the question HaRambam was asked to address. Based on HaRambam's response one infers that the questioner, Rabbi Yaakov ben Netanel, was actually wondering whether or not Islam is the actual fulfillment of the Bible's messianic hope. And if indeed that is the case, why not convert to Islam? This concern was exacerbated by two critical issues. Apparently, astrological forecasts (which were taken seriously at the time) suggested that Israel would not be redeemed. This tale was compounded by the fact that Rabbi Saadia Gaon's prediction of the Messiah's arrival had come and gone without a messiah.

HaRambam addressed every issue in the correspondence with tact, clarity, and authority. He showed unequivocally that there is absolutely no credence to astrological predictions. Astrology, he writes, is charlatanism and baseless and has nothing in common with a sound view of how the world operates. He explains that Rav Saadia Gaon's messianic reckoning is nothing more than the rabbi's estimate, meant to comfort his community that was experiencing difficult times. Ironically, HaRambam himself goes on to offer a messianic date based on a tradition he received from his own father.[87] According to his father's calculations, the messianic era was supposed to begin taking place around 1220 C.E. and that the renewal of prophecy would take place in that year.[88] Of course this too was a rabbis wishful thinking in order to encourage his community.

Yet another aspect of this correspondence was the appearance of someone in Yemen who claimed to be the Messiah. While his name

---

[87] Notwithstanding the fact that in his *Mishneh Torah*, HaRambam rejects any sort of Messianic calculations because it does not contribute to the fear of God and might even detract from it.

[88] After HaRambam's death, his son Abraham had to respond to the Yemenite community about this tradition.

remains unknown, it seems from HaRambam's response that this false Messiah attracted many followers and whose false promises would not only generate further friction with the Muslim people but drag the Jewish community into deeper despair. HaRambam devoted considerable ink to depict this Messiah want-to-be as a mentally unstable liar.

The central feature of this letter to the Jewish community of Yemen is HaRambam's effort to afford the Jews living under Muslim rule with a credible historical and theological picture that offers comfort, strength, and resolve to withstand the difficult times. The literary greatness of this letter lies in its brilliant use of *halakha* and the clear articulation of philosophic arguments. HaRambam was a master rhetorician who could make a strong philosophical argument while at the same time offering comfort and hope to a suffering community. HaRambam skillfully uses the TaNaKH as a prooftext showing that despite Islam's apparent power and their monotheistic beliefs, Judaism and the Jewish people remain God's covenanted community.

HaRambam presented a three-tiered form of suffering the Jewish people have endured; the Yemenite experience represents the third and final stage of that torment. The first stage is described:

> Ever since the time of revelation every despot or rebel ruler, be he violent or ignoble, has made it his first aim and his final purpose to destroy our law and vitiate our religion by means of the sword, by violence, or brute force. Such were Amalek, Sisera, Sancherib, Nebuchadnezzar, Titus, Hadrian, and others like them.[89]

The first stage of Jewish persecution is characterized by the use of physical and violent force by the Jewish people's enemies. In the second stage the nations of the world employ physical force against the Jewish people but they also introduce arguments meant to undermine Jewish faith and beliefs.

> The second class consists of the most intelligent and educated among the nations, like the Syrians, Persians, and Greeks. They

---
[89] Hartman, *Crisis and Leadership*. Also *Epistle of Yemen*, 97.

also endeavor to demolish our Law and to abrogate it by means of arguments they invent and controversies that they create.[90]

The second stage described above is the sort of battle waged by early Christianity. The third and most insidious tier devised by the enemies of Israel is an effort to undermine the religious faith and belief system by imitating it.

> After that a new class arose . . . that resolved to lay claim to prophecy and to found a new law, contrary to Divine religion, and to contend that it also came from God, like the true claim. Thus, doubts will be generated, and confusion will be created since one is opposed to the other and both supposedly emanate from one god, and it will lead to the destruction of both religions.[91]

This last stage is the battle the Jews of Yemen faced. Mohammad claimed to have received a Divine law that supersedes the Torah. He claimed that Jesus of Nazareth was indeed an emissary of God, negating the Torah, and now Islam negates both Christianity and Judaism. HaRambam brilliantly uses the Book of Daniel as a prooftext for his historical construct of the battle the Jewish people have faced since their encounter with God at Mount Sinai.

HaRambam notes how Daniel foretold of the rise of Christianity: "The children of the brazen among your people shall make a bold claim of prophecy, but they shall fall."[92] This verse, argues HaRambam, describes the emergence of Christianity from within the Jewish people. Similarly, he argues, the rise of Islam is also predicted in the Book of Daniel:

> This was predicted by the Divinely inspired prophet Daniel, according to whom, in some future time, it would happen. Sometime later a person would appear with a religion similar to the true one, with a book and an oral communication, who will arro-

---

[90] Ibid, 98.
[91] Ibid, 98.
[92] Daniel 11:14.

gantly pretend that God has granted him a revelation and that he conversed with God and other extravagant claims . . . [93]

HaRambam continues using the Book of Daniel to bring comfort and hope to the readers of his letter. He uses the well-known visual image that Daniel presents where he prophesied the four great empires. The "great sea," writes the prophet, stirred up by the "four winds of heaven" and from the waters emerged the "four beasts." Each of the beasts was identified with an empire that sought the destruction of the Jewish people. The fourth and last empire displaced the earlier empires. HaRambam brilliantly notes how the fourth and last beast most resembles the human image. This, writes HaRambam, is proof that Islam, identified with the last beast, uses a strategy to overtake Judaism by resembling it and confounding its followers. Daniel, writes HaRambam, prophesied Islam's rise and also prophesied its downfall:

> And behold, the horn had two eyes similar to the eyes of a human, and a mouth speaking the big things. This obviously alludes to the person who will found a new religion similar to the Divine religion and make claim to a revelation and to prophecy. He will produce much talk and endeavor to alter our Torah and abolish it . . . But God informed Daniel that He would destroy this person, notwithstanding his greatness and his long endurance, together with the remaining adherents of his predecessors. For the three empires that warred against us will ultimately perish. The one that sought to overpower us with the sword, the second that claimed it had arguments against our faith, and the third that claimed to have a religion similar to ours.[94]

The rise of Islam in HaRambam's presentation of history was foreseen by the prophet – as well as Islam's downfall which occur in Daniel's vision. The similarity between Islam and Judaism is a sign that the prophet's vision indeed came about and is a proof of Judaism's authenticity.

---

[93] *Epistles*, 100.
[94] Ibid, 100-101.

HaRambam concludes his letter by writing that these persecutions and confounding religious philosophical experiences are tests and trials. Their purpose is to separate "the wheat from the chaff" within the Jewish nation. Only the worthy will enjoy the ultimate redemption.

Ma'amar Tehiyyat HaMetim [the Letter of the Resurrection of the Dead]

In 1190 C.E. HaRambam wrote *Makalah Fi Tehiyyat HaMetim* known in Hebrew as *Ma'amar Tehiyyat HaMetim* [Treatise on Resurrection]. Note the distinction between *iggeret* and *ma'amar*. Both terms translate into English as letter; the difference, however, is significant. An *iggeret* is a response to a correspondent while a *ma'mar* is a letter initiated by the author.

HaRambam felt compelled to write this essay later in life as a reaction to his detractors who were slandering his religious integrity by stating that he did not believe in the resurrection of the dead. This criticism was leveled against HaRambam by Samuel ben Ali, a popular Babylonian scholar. He based his accusations on the fact that the *Mishneh Torah* chapters that speak of the world-to-come and life after death make no mention of the corporeal resurrection of the dead. For ben Ali this meant that HaRambam was a denier of this principle of faith and his works had to be rejected.

In the Treatise on Resurrection of the Dead HaRambam discusses the nature of God's Unity, the messianic age, resurrection, and *olam haba* [the world-to-come]. He asserts without equivocation that belief in the bodily resurrection of the dead is a cardinal tenet of Jewish faith. Like his predecessors, Rav Sa'dia Gaon and Rav Hai Gaon, HaRambam understood that truth not only emerges from the senses and science but also from revelation and tradition.[95] One who denies resurrection of the dead, writes HaRambam, denies the possibility of all miracles, even those described in the Torah. While resurrection cannot

---

[95] See Shalom Carmy's article "The Sovereignty of Dogma.".

be explained philosophically or scientifically, one must resort to the truth of revelation as a principle put forth by our prophets.

This essay leaves the student of HaRambam unconvinced. Uncharacteristically, nowhere in the essay does he explain the purpose of resurrection. He notes that the physical resurrection of the dead will be temporary, and the resurrected will again die which further begs the question – for what purpose? This question is amplified in the context of HaRambam's greater philosophical output. For him all biblical and rabbinic references to physical rewards for observing the Torah (such as rainfall, material prosperity, good health, and national independence) are all for the sake of that observance. The more one observes God's law the easier God will make the observance of the law and the pursuit of proximity to God.

> For a man cannot engage in the service of God when he is ill or hungry or thirsty or during time of war; and God therefore declared that all these would be removed, and they would be healthy and at peace so that their knowledge of God might be perfected and they will merit the world-to-come. For it is not the purpose of the Torah that the land be richly productive or that people live long or have healthy bodies [for their own sake but] rather they will be supported by all these things in fulfilling the true purpose of Torah.[96]

This same idea is reiterated throughout HaRambam's writings, including the *Mishneh Torah*.[97] This notion is also true on a national level. The political liberation that the messianic era will usher in is meant to afford the people of Israel conditions to achieve human perfection and spread the knowledge of God throughout the world.

> Hence, all of Israel, their prophets, and sages longed for the advent of Messianic times that they might have relief from the wicked tyranny that does not permit them to properly occupy themselves with the study of Torah and the observance of the

---

[96] Introduction to *Perek Helek*.

[97] *MT Teshuva* 9:1.

commandments; that they might have ease to devote themselves to getting wisdom and thus attain life in the world-to-come.[98]

The entire purpose of the Messianic age is not for power, glory, wealth, or any sort of physical reward. On the contrary, all rewards are ultimately spiritual in nature. The entire purpose of Torah is to elevate the human being and extricate him from his or her physical and material impulses into a state of spiritual consciousness. To glorify the physical and base impulses of the human being by making them the purpose of Torah is to corrupt the entire purpose of the covenant with God.

Rabbi Aharon HaKohen of Lunel, a student and admirer of HaRambam, defended his teacher in 1202 and argued that physical resurrection must be understood allegorically. Bringing the body back is more of a punishment to the soul than it is a reward. The masses who are not philosophically inclined may very well understand this principle of faith literally, but those who are educated philosophically recognize its deeper meaning.

This conclusion is familiar to the students of HaRambam. In the Guide he sets forth the idea that an educated Jew recognizes the dual realm of one's belief system.

> Among the things to which your attention ought to be directed is that you should know that in regards to the correct opinions through which the ultimate perfection may be obtained, the Law has communicated only their end and made a call to believe in them in a summary way – that is to believe in the existence of God, may He be exalted, His unity, His knowledge, His power, His will, and His eternity ... In the same way the Law also makes a call to adopt certain beliefs, beliefs that are necessary for the sake of political welfare. Such, for instance, is our belief that He, may He be exalted, is violently angry with those who disobey Him, and that it is therefore necessary to fear Him and dread Him and take care not to disobey Him.[99]

---

[98] Ibid, 9:2; also MT *Laws of Kings and Their Wars* chapter 11.

[99] Guide 3:28, 512, Pines translation.

The Unity of God is a belief that needs no qualification, but the belief that God gets angry is a belief that is not literal and whose purpose is for the masses.

Letters: A Final Thought

HaRambam's deep love of God led him to develop a love of all people as well. Despite his personal and familial suffering at the hands of Muslims, the ravages inflicted by the Christians, as well as the personal and professional attacks by his own people, HaRambam wrote with religious conviction, philosophic objectivity, and compassion for his followers, readers, and even detractors.

HaRambam refused to dilute his faith. He was an astronomer, mathematician, physician, philosopher, scientist, logician, and theologian – but most of all he was "simply a man of God."[100]

The words of Professor Rabbi Isadore Twersky most aptly describe the scope and nature of HaRambam's influence on Judaism, Jewish learning, and Jewish culture:

> Maimonides is perhaps the most famous and resplendent figure of medieval Judaism. His name is a direct result of the quality and quantity, scope and originality, magnetism and fascination of his writings.
>
> He was a prolific author of amazing vigor and precision, of intellectual moral and religious force, of analytical sharpness and aesthetic delicacy.
>
> In truth his reputation needs no inflation or exaggeration for his stature is nearly *sui generis* (unique) and his commanding influence has been almost universally recognized.
>
> His literary oeuvre was not only remarkably comprehensive but also endlessly repercussive.

---

[100] Etienne Gibson, "Homage to Maimonides," in *Essays on Maimonides: An Octocentennial Volume*, edited by Salo Wittmayer Baron, 35 (New York: Columbia University Press, 1941).

He wrote epoch making works in the central areas of *halakha* and religious philosophy, – an achievement that is unquestionably, almost overpoweringly, characterized by monumentality, using the term very literally.

His mighty historical image assumes heroic proportions rather early in his posthumous career, and it is this historic figure which dominates the stage.[101]

Despite his position of prominence HaRambam responded to letters and inquiries that came to him from all over the world. No subject was too small or insignificant for him. His countless letters have been collected and edited by scholars. Each letter is a new window into the man and his leadership.

The Supremacy of Jewish Law

In his introduction to his *Commentary on the Mishna*, HaRambam explains the nature of Jewish law and the role of those who adjudicate *halakha*. There he quotes a Talmudic statement that he refers to as a midrash:

> The holy One, blessed be He, has nothing in this world but the four cubits of *halakha* [law].[102]

What appears to be a clear-cut Talmudic statement affirming the supreme importance of Jewish law is for HaRambam a launchpad into an exploration of Jewish thought.

> One should delve discerningly into this matter, because if one examines it superficially, one will find that it is far from the truth, as for the four cubits of *halakha* alone represent the ultimate objective, while the other sciences and bodies of knowledge are to be cast away. And it would follow that during the time of Shem and Eber and after them [before God revealed himself to Avraham] when

---

[101] Twersky, *Introduction to the Code*.
[102] TB Berakhot 8a.

there was no *halakha*, the Holy One blessed be He had no part in the world at all!! If one delves discerningly into this matter, however, one will observe therein wonderous wisdom and one will find that it comprises a collection of eternal truths. I will explain this for you so that it may serve as an example for you in all other matters that you come across. Therefore, pay close attention . . .[103]

HaRambam here establishes the groundwork for what is the foundation of Andalusian Jewish culture. The goal of the religious seeker cannot possibly be limited to the observance of Jewish law but must include the pursuit of a wide range of knowledge such as sciences, physics, philosophy and more. To drive his point home HaRambam transports his reader to the time of Shem and Eber when Jewish law was not yet in existence. It cannot be that God had no interest or stake in the world because Jews were not observing Jewish law. If that were the case, the world would not have existed.[104]

HaRambam continues and makes a case for expanding the definition of *halakha* beyond its colloquial usage. The tradition HaRambam inherited taught that the purpose of life is contemplation and the pursuit of intellectual truths, the highest of which is knowledge of God, proximity to God, and love of God. Man is both physical and spiritual. The seeker is caught between the physical forces within himself / herself and the spiritual forces that seek to realize his/her ultimate purpose. "The purpose of this world," writes HaRambam, "is to help man become wise and good." Wise in speculative knowledge and good in terms of making this world a better place. One must be wise in order to be good, and good in order to be wise.

Therefore, from all that we have said, it becomes clear that the purpose in the creation of everything in this existing world is to serve the perfect individual who is full of wisdom and good deeds. If you delve into and learn these two things, namely wisdom and good deeds, from the explicit or only the alluded teachings of the sages, of blessed memory, then you will know the correctness of their state-

---

[103] HaRambam, Introduction to *Commentary on the Mishna*.
[104] Guide 2:25.

ment that "the Holy One, blessed be He, has nothing in His world but the four cubits of the Law."[105]

Halakah is therefore not simply one's practical conduct but also the pursuit of knowledge. That is why HaRambam's *Mishneh Torah* includes the Book of Knowledge and is full of theological and philosophical teachings. In the Guide HaRambam writes:

> The Law as a whole aims at two things: the welfare of the soul and the welfare of the body.[106]

He continues:

> As for the welfare of the soul, it consists in the multitudes acquiring correct opinions corresponding to their respective capacity . . . As for the welfare of the body, it comes about by the improvement of their ways of living with one another . . . The second aim is the more certain one and it is the one regarding which every effort has been made precisely to expound it and all its particulars. For the first aim can only be achieved after achieving the second aim.[107]

For HaRambam the observance of Jewish law, mitzvoth, and good deeds require great effort and attention. While the first aim may be more noble[108] it can only be attained by making the second aim of supreme importance.

The Nature of Man's Role in Society

HaRambam states based on the sciences that he had studied that "man, by nature, is political."[109] This idea is an underlying principle in much of HaRambam's philosophical works and the reason for much of his creative output. He wrote to the sages of Lunel that he

---

[105] Ibid.
[106] Guide 3:27.
[107] Ibid.
[108] Ibid.
[109] Guide 2:40.

did not compose the *Mishneh Torah* for personal glory, but because he cannot understand how a people such as the Jews do not have a clear practical code of Jewish law that is available to all who seek to know how to observe *halakha*.[110] The entire Torah is to be understood in the framework of man's nature as a political being. What this means is that mankind lives within society and for society to self-sustain it must employ political means.

> It has been explained with utmost clarity that man is political by nature and that it is his nature to live in society. He is not like other animals for which society is not a necessity.[111]

To avoid conflict and conflicting goals within society, mankind requires a regimen establishing norms and patterns of behavior that offer the members of the society a common vision. Therefore, writes Ha-Rambam "the law, although it is not natural, enters into what is natural."[112] Torah and the corpus of Jewish law is indeed such a regimen and operates in such a way that affords its followers a shared goal.

> ... If on the other hand you find a law, all of whose ordinances are due to attention being paid, as was stated before, to the soundness of circumstances pertaining to the body and also the soundness of belief – a law that takes pains to inculcate correct opinions about God, may He be exalted, in the first place, and with regard to the angels, and that desires to make man wise, to give him understanding, and to awaken his attention, so that he should know the whole of that which exists in its true form – you must know that this guidance comes from Him, may He be exalted, and that the law is Divine.[113]

This passage is not only an endorsement of Torah but an indictment of religious fanaticism that forbids the pursuit of knowledge and the right of people to learn truth. Divine law is not simply a sys-

---

[110] Letter to Rabbi Jonathon of Lunel, *Letters* 49.

[111] Guide 2:40.

[112] Ibid.

[113] Ibid.

tem that sustains a degree of social order; rather, its goal is the transformation of the individual, a means to actualize one's spiritual potential, and the development of society. This explains HaRambam's view on the biblical mitzvah to appoint a king. Many medieval commentaries, particularly European ones,[114] understood the appointment of a king as a biblical compromise addressing the needs of the people. A state needs governance, and the most orderly form of governance at the time was a monarchy. The king imposes the law of the state. The Jewish state was governed by a three-part system: The Sanhedrin [the Supreme Court of Israel] legislated the law while the High Priest and priesthood conducted the service in the Temple and the king enforced the religious and civil law.

For HaRambam, the Messiah of Israel will be a king:

> If there arises a king from the house of David who meditates on the Torah, occupies himself with the commandments as did his ancestor David, observes the precepts prescribed in the written and oral Torah, prevails upon Israel to walk in the way of Torah and to repair its breaches, and fights the battles of the Lord, it may be assumed that he is the Messiah. If he does these things and succeeds in building the Bet HaMikdash and gathers the dispersed of Israel, he is beyond all doubt the Messiah.[115]

The Messianic era, according to the Jews of Andalus, will not be an era of miraculous events. On the contrary, writes HaRambam, "The sole difference between the present and the messianic days is delivery from servitude to foreign powers."[116]

> The sages and prophets did not long for the days of the Messiah that Israel might exercise dominion over the world, or rule over the heathens, or be exalted by the nations, or that it might eat and drink and rejoice. Their aspiration was that Israel be free to devote

---

[114] Avraham ibn Ezra also objected to the monarchy and of course he was originally from Andalus.

[115] *MT Hilkhot Melakhim* 11:4.

[116] Ibid 12:2.

[117] Ibid.

itself to the Law and its wisdom with no one to oppress or disturb it, and thus be worthy of life in the world-to-come...[117]

HaRambam's literary legacy is all expansive. Everything is there. Ben Bag Bag said about the Torah, *"Hafoch ba vahafoch ba ki kulo ba,"* [turn it over and turn it again for everything is in it].[118] I permit myself to apply his dictum to the writings and legacy of HaRambam.

HaRambam and Creating a Jewish Community

As has been persuasively shown, HaRambam does not assign any special ontological status to the Jewish people.[119] *Behira*, the idea that God chose the Jewish people, has nothing to do with their being better or different. Instead, HaRambam identifies with the rabbinic teaching that God chose the Jewish people because they chose God. Although the *behira* was not for intrinsic reasons, the election of the Jewish people finds expression in the liturgy and in the responsibilities that such an election demand.

> The Holy One blessed be He said to Israel: "You have made Me a unique object of your love in this world, so I shall make you a unique object of My love in this world."[120]

When seen in the context of HaRambam's views on *ta'amei hamitzvoth* [his persistent search for providing reasons for the commandments],[121] dramatic insights into community building emerge. For HaRambam, being chosen by God is a dynamic process initiated by man in search of God. By encouraging the pursuit of *ta'amei hamitzvoth* he presents a model that by its very nature encourages research, thought, and dialogue. It engages all members of the community in a religious quest to find meaning in the law of the Torah. Yeshayahu Lei-

---

[118] Pirke Avot 5:6.

[119] Kellner, *Maimonides on Judaism and the Jewish People*.

[120] TB Haggiga 3a and TB Berakhot 6a.

[121] See Guide 3:26, 31, and 49. See Twersky's *Introduction to the Code*, 374-430.

bowitz, the renown Maimonidean, noted that the pursuit of *ta'amei hamitzvoth* is not pursuit of knowledge as much as it is a pursuit of God.[122] Like Avraham our forefather, we too choose God because we, the seekers, have come to the conclusion that His laws are perfect. The observance of the commandments becomes the stage upon which a relationship based on knowledge is forged. That choice and the knowledge it offers is then communicated, shared, and expounded to others, thereby creating a dynamic learning community.

HaRambam categorically rejects the position of those who see the election of the Jewish people as absolute or because the Jewish people are intrinsically special irrespective of their personal choices. This absolutist attitude rejects the process of uncovering reasons for mitzvoth and leads to observing mitzvoth without finding meaning in them as highest form of religious expression. For HaRambam such an attitude is not only contrary to the Torah's intended spiritual goals but reflect an illness of the soul:

> There is a group who consider it a grievous thing that reasons should be given for any law. What would please them most is that the intellect would not find meaning for the commandments and prohibitions. What compels them to feel this way is a sickness of the soul. A sickness to which they are unable to give utterance and of which they cannot furnish a satisfactory account.[123]

Understanding Judaism and Jewish law exclusively in terms of absolutist faith reflects a worldview that finds it unnecessary to engage God's outside world to better understand the way of the Torah. Mitzvoth become a means to creating an isolated community of individuals whose common language is dogmatic. The more they separate themselves from the world around them the more deeply they experience the fullness of their spirituality. When non-comprehension becomes the highest expression of religious fervor, then actions that

---

[122] Yeshayahu Leibowitz, *The Faith of Maimonides*, translated by John Glucker, 15-25 (Tel-Aviv: MOD books, 1989). See *MT Hilkhot Me'ilah* 8:8 and Twersky's essay in *Introduction to the Code*, 407-408.

[123] Guide 3:31.

seem the least comprehensible appear to be the supreme demonstration of religious faith.

For HaRambam the ultimate goal is to create an inclusive community, casting as large a net as possible. Inclusion involves the ability to explain the nature of one's practices and beliefs in terms of concepts that can be understood by a diverse public of seekers.[124] Jewish law and Jewish practices are experienced most fully when they can be scrutinized and explained through the lenses of a range of various disciplines.

The mitzvoth of being in a constant state of love of God and awe of God involve the ability to move beyond the traditional disciplines and integrate them into a religious lifestyle.

> And what is the way that will lead to the love of Him and the awe of Him? When a person contemplates His great and wonderous works and creatures and from them obtains a glimpse of His infinite wisdom he will straightway love Him, praise Him, glorify Him, and long with an exceeding longing to know His great name . . . And when one ponders these matters one recoils in awe and realizes how small, lowly, obscure, unintelligent one is when standing in the presence of Him who is perfect in knowledge.[125]

HaRambam continues:

> In harmony with these sentiments, I shall explain some large and general aspects of the Sovereign of the universe that they may serve the intelligent individual as a door to the love of God . . .[126]

HaRambam's ability to articulate and communicate the teachings of Torah and the rabbinic sages is very much a function of his use of the most contemporary intellectual tools available to him at his time.

---

[124] In his seminal work *Major Trends in Jewish Mysticism*, pages 28-29, the noted scholar Gershom Scholem draws a completely different conclusion. He wonders how HaRambam expected anyone to remain religious and observant of the law if he expected the law to be examined philosophically.

[125] *MT Hilkhot Yesodei HaTorah* 2:1; the same idea is reflected in Guide 1:26, 33, 46.

[126] Guide 1:26.

There is no doubt that the Andalusian culture and the path HaRambam chose as the most ideal is indeed the most difficult. And yet in the tradition of the great rabbinic sages of the Talmud – despite the highest regard for the past and the precedent, his teachings are always presented along with an exploration of new insights in light of emerging ideas. Like his Sephardic predecessors dating back to Rav Saadia Gaon, HaRambam understood that intellectual openness, while challenging, is the most direct path to God.

At the end of the day, for HaRambam, being a part of the covenantal community is essential to the spiritual life of the believing Jew and the spiritual seeker. It is the seeker's daily relationship with God that is structured within the context of communal participation that inspires the pursuit of the path to enlightenment.

Could HaRambam Have Been a Mystic?

Could HaRambam have been a mystic? It depends on how one defines mysticism. HaRambam was certainly not a kabbalist. The legend that irritably keeps finding its way into conversations and articles suggesting that late in life HaRambam met a kabbalist who convinced him to retract everything he wrote, repent, and convert to a kabbalistic lifestyle never happened. This tale was convincingly disproven by Gershon Scholem[127] and more recently revisited by Michael Shmidman[128] but unfortunately continues to find traction amongst amateur kabbalists. Stories like these are found in post-expulsion documents (early 15th century) some 200 hundred years after HaRambam died. It is not surprising that kabbalists sought to position themselves in relationship to HaRambam. By the 15th century the Mishneh Torah, HaRambam' legal code was a staple of Jewish learning and embraced by both the proponents and opponents of HaRambam' philosophy.

According to the leading scholars in the field such as Elliot Wolf-

---

[127] Scholem, Gershon, "*Mi Hoker li-Mekubal,*" Tarbiz 6 (1935), 90-98. See also Miess in *Bikkurim ha-Ittim* 11 (1831), 131-142.

[128] Shmidman, "On Maimonides' Conversion," 379-384.

son and Alexander Altman Jewish mysticism must be understood as a multidisciplinary religious field as opposed to a historical phenomenon. If Louis Jacobs is correct when he defines mysticism as a religious practice that seeks direct experience of the Divine rather than a secondhand acceptance of theological propositions,[129] how can one deny that HaRambam was indeed a mystic? The primary thrust of his life's work is to provide a path that leads to a correct love and awe of God, knowledge of God, and proximity to God while maintaining philosophic integrity and observing the law of the Torah.

Nothing, however, is more compelling than the case made by Professor Aviezer Ravitzky. He shows how HaRambam's most trusted student who translated the Moreh HaNevuchim from its original Arabic to Hebrew and earned HaRambam's seal of approval, Shemuel ibn Tibbon, read the Guide as an esoteric text revealing the mystical secrets of Judaism to the world.[130]

HaRambam himself states the purpose of the *Guide of the Perplexed*:

> For my purpose is that the truths be glimpsed and then again concealed, so as not to oppose that divine purpose which one cannot possibly oppose, and which has been concealed from the vulgar among the people those truths especially requisite for His [God's] apprehension. As the verse states: "The secret of the Lord is with them that fear Him."[131]

Professor David Blumenthal and Dr. José Faur were among the first modern scholars to place HaRambam, and by extension the Andalusian mystical tradition he recorded, among the great Jewish mystical works. More recently Abraham Elkayim and Dov Schwartz edited a volume[132] dedicated to HaRambam and his relationship to

---

[129] Louis Jacobs, "The Place of Mysticism in Modern Jewish Life," *European Judaism: A Journal for the New Europe*, Volume 2, 32.

[130] Ravitzky, "Samuel Ibn Tibbon," 87-123.

[131] Rabbi Moshe Ben Maimon, *Maimonides The Guide of the Perplexed* Introduction, translated by Shelomo Pines, page 7. See also Guide 2:2 and 2:29

[132] Published by Bar Ilan University in honor of Professor Moshe Halamish.

kabbalah and mysticism. Professor Gideon Freudenthal has made significant advances in this field and has identified insightful inroads in reading the mystical trends in HaRambam' writings.

The Andalusian (Southern Spanish) mystical tradition teaches that God is absolutely separate from and not dependent upon His creation, and yet the possibility of an intimate relationship with God is real. It is a tradition that teaches how Judaism, Jewish law, and Jewish thought are the most direct avenues to the infinite. God is available to all "who seek Him with sincerity."

It is a mystical tradition predicated on the possibility of unmediated and personal communion with God. The mystic, like Moshe Rabbenu of old, does not merely want to do what God commands; the mystic wants to communicate and commune with God, and wants to know the answers to life's ultimate questions. Judaism as preserved by the Andalusian tradition provides ample venues for the non-mystic and the non-expert to know and experience the transcendent.

Unfortunately, for most, the name HaRambam or Maimonides or simply Rambam is synonymous with absolute rationalism and neo-Aristotelian thought. The impression from Rabbi Dr. Natan Slifkin's title of his recent book *Rationalism vs Mysticism* or Menachem Kellner's book *Maimonides' Confrontation with Mysticism* is that rationalism and mysticism cannot co-exist.

To ignore HaRambam's mystical teachings simply because they are rational, and because they are subtle, and/or because they are vehemently against the kabbalistic enchanted mythological practices, is a gross omission.

The unfortunate problem is that most equate kabbalah with mysticism. The schools of kabbalah primarily operated in the realm of mythology, superstition, magic, astrology, and the like. They were, at best, careless when it came to ascribing corporeality to God. All of these practices are wholly and totally rejected by HaRambam. For this reason, the kabbalah schools of southern France banned HaRambam' books, especially the Guide. Mysticism does not have to mean one suspends one's reason and rational thinking.

The differences between kabbalah and Andalusian mysticism are great and beyond the literal reading of their texts. They pertain to different stages of one's spiritual development. For the Jews of Andalus, the mystical tradition of Judaism is theocentric – it revolves around the ultimate reality, which is God. It is a process of constant de-anthropomorphizing, constantly removing any form of corporeality or imagery or even language when it comes to God. One could argue kabbalah is anthropocentric. It places man at the center of reality and magic, superstition, angels, language, amulets, and sorcery as his tools to control or manipulate God's will. The Torah posits categorically that God is the ultimate reality and is therefore independent of anything that man, priest, or spirit may do or say or chant. God's will is all that truly exists.

One of the primary teachings of the mysticism of Andalusia is that an authentic mystical experience can only take place in a mind, spirit, and practice that is completely purged of corporeality and superstitions.[133] Anything short of that is an impediment to union with God, love of God, and awe of God.

That HaRambam was indeed a deeply committed mystic who sought proximity with God, and taught through his writing how to inspire, induce, and stimulate a profound love and awe of God, is evident from the fact that he sought to teach not only *about* prophecy but also how to achieve human perfection and prophecy.

His own descendants read and taught his works through mystical lenses, as Paul Fenton has convincingly shown.[134] Around 1270, mystical commentaries on HaRambam's Guide began to emerge. In those

---

[133] HaRambam writes that his intellectual forbearers all came from Andalusia, and they were steeped in Greek philosophy as long as the philosophy did not question the foundations of Jewish law (Guide 1:71). Guttman notes how ibn Daud had produced his work *Sefer HaQabbala* [the Book of Tradition] ten years before HaRambam wrote the *Mishneh Torah*, where he described the ultimate pleasure of Man is to know God; his use of Aristotelian language is evident. See Guttmann, *The Philosophy of Judaism*, 152.

[134] Paul Fenton, *Deux Traites*.

early years there were more mystical commentaries on the Guide than there were philosophical commentaries.[135] According to David Blumenthal, this is also the way the Jews of Yemen read Rambam's works.[136]

Because HaRambam cannot be ignored by the world of Torah, modern day kabbalists such as the Chabad movement have attempted to interpret HaRambam in accordance with their thinking. They see HaRambam as one who merged intellect, heart, and law with the pursuit of God.[137] Their challenge, however, is HaRambam's attitude toward secular education, which Chabad does not endorse and his understanding of *ta'amei hamitzvoth* [providing rational reasons for the Torah commandments]. Of course, Chabad prefer their own supernatural and magical explanations. More fundamentally, they find it hard to explain how HaRambam, a pillar of Judaism, can totally ignore the Zohar and its teachings.

Dr. Marc Shapiro[138] shows how some Hassidic masters tried to base some of HaRambam's *halakhic* rulings on the Zohar, despite the fact that the Zohar came to light after he had finished the *Mishneh Torah*. The Rebbe of Kotzke is a good example of one who made attempts at reinterpreting HaRambam rational reasons for mitzvoth in a more Hassidic fashion. For example, HaRambam writes that the incense in the Bet Hamikdash was to counter the bad smell of the rotting meat. The language HaRambam uses is *re'ach ra* [bad smell], which the Rebbe of Kotzke reads as *ru'ach ra* [evil spirits].[139] The attempt to bring HaRambam into the kabbalistic camp is also evident in the writings of Rabbi Moshe Chaim Luzzato. He makes use of HaRambam's notion of Divine overflow but again falls short; the greater content of Luzzatto's thought is magic, super-stition, and kabbalistic in nature.[140]

---

[135] Idel, "Maimonides' and the Kabbalah," 201.

[136] Blumenthal, "Maimonides' Philosophic Mysticism." *David R. Blumenthal: Living with God and Humanity*, 85–109.

[137] See Gottlieb, "Hassidic Maimonidean Theology," v263-287.

[138] Shapiro, *Studies in Maimonides*, 88-92.

[139] Ibid, 92-93.

[140] Hansel, "Philosophy and Kabbalah," 213-227.

HaRambam, the mystic emerges when his writings are studied as a pedagogic guide on how to observe a spiritual, experiential progression of love of God culminating in the highest levels of Divine knowledge, providence, and love and awe of God.

A Glimpse at the Man: HaRambam

We are obsessed with understanding HaRambam's ideas, philosophy, and his various works yet we neglect attempting to know the man, Rabbi Moshe ben Mimon. What was his temperament and disposition like? Did he have a patient and pleasant personality, or was he a social misfit, a genius who cannot relate to the average person? Most, if not all of the material that speaks to his character and personality are hagiographic in nature and are written by people who lived many years after HaRambam had already died.

HaRambam's *halakhic* and philosophical material betray his humanity while his letters and personal correspondences present a more relatable person, one who is occupied both mentally and physically by his onerous work schedule.

The short letter below affords us a completely different perspective on the man. This letter was discovered in the Taylor-Schechter Genizah[141] Collection and translated and edited by Professor Paul Fenton.[142] The original letter is written in Judeo-Arabic, the common language of the Jews of medieval Egypt. The letter describes the visit

---

[141] Plates 1-11. The Taylor-Schechter Genizah Collection contains Jewish writings found in Egypt from the late ninth century that give a detailed picture of economic, cultural, and social life in this region. These documents include all sorts of writings, from literature to court documents and personal notes.

[142] Paul Fenton, "A Meeting with Maimonides," 1-4. Thank you to Mordechai Ovits for bring this to my attention. For other such Genizah letters that describe HaRambam's personality see S. D. Goitein, "Moses Maimonides, Man of Action: A Revision of the Master's Biography in Light of Geniza Documents" in *Hommage À Georges Vajda: Etudes d'Histoire et de Pensée Juives*, edited by G. Nahon and C. Touati, 155-67 (Louvain: Peeters, 1980).

to the home of HaRambam by a man and his son.[143] The author of the letter was commissioned to deliver a note to the great master, HaRambam, and he expected to simply deliver the note and leave. To his surprise, HaRambam invited him and his son al-Galal into his home. He was greeted warmly by his host and his son Avraham. The guest is overwhelmed by HaRambam's hospitality and proudly de-

---

[143] This was ratified by Professor Goitein per Professor Paul Fenton.

scribes how the master even confided in him regarding the content of the letter that was delivered. All the while Avraham, HaRambam's son, entertained al-Galal by teaching him how to address the great master HaRambam. In this letter we learn that HaRambam enjoyed lemon candy and that he lived in a roomy home. The last line of the letter is precious.

Meeting With Maimonides (Plates I-II)

> We set out for Rabbi Moses' house
>
> He remained at the entrance to the house while I and al-Galal proceeded to enter. I kissed his noble hand, and he received us with a most cordial welcome. He said to me, "Come and be seated young man," beckoning me to sit on the edge of the Iwan, opposite where he himself was seated.
>
> I sat down while he read the message, I gave him from beginning to end. He was delighted with the presents and started to play with Galal – may God protect him.
>
> Then there transpired that which a book would prove insufficient to describe. Next, platters were brought, and he began to eat lemon cakes. We stayed just for a while but he detained me in order that we confer a moment confidentially. In the meantime, Rabbi Avraham, may God protect him, had taught al-Galal a term with which to address Rabbi Moshe. Upon his reciting it Rabbi Moshe laughed with amusement and played with the child.

HaRambam the Savior of Judaism

Shemuel ibn Tibbon (see next chapter), HaRambam's loyal student and faithful translator who lived in the 13th century among European Jews attributed to HaRambam the title of "savior." He writes:

Then God saw the poverty of knowledge of His people and the

amount of ignorance concerning everything relating to wisdom, and He raised up a savior, a wise and understanding man, wise in crafts and with an understanding of "whispering." Since the days of Rav Ashi until his own, no one was known to have risen up among our people who was like his with regard to every aspect of wisdom. He is the true sage, the divine philosopher, our master our teacher, Moshe the servant of God son of the great sage Rabbi Mimon..."[144]

---

[144] Shemuel Ibn Tibbon, Perush Kohelet, (Commentary on Kohelet) translated and edited by J. Robinson, in *Philosophy and Exegesis in Samuel ibn Tibbon's Commentaries on Ecclesiastes* (PHd Dissertation, Harvard University 2002)

My prayer to God is this:
That You be bound in love with someone
Unmoving as stick and stone.

For only having suffered love's agony
Of pain and separation
Shall You come to feel and value
My love for You
MOHAMMED H. RAZI[1]

Yehuda ben Shaul ibn Tibbon
(1120-1190 C.E.)

Shemuel ben Yehuda ibn Tibbon
(1150-1232 C.E.)

It CAN BE STATED without equivocation and without sounding hyperbolic that Yehuda ibn Tibbon and his son Shemuel as well as a select few other translators who originated in Andalusia and escaped to Europe are responsible for preserving whatever it is we have of Andalusian Judaism, scholarship, mysticism, and culture. The ibn Tibbon family are the most famous because they translated some of the most important works that came out of Andalus. One wonders how much of the Judeo-Arabic intellectual and religious culture would have survived history without their efforts.

Yehuda ibn Tibbon was born in Granada in 1120 C.E. and left Spain on account of the Almohad persecutions. He settled in a small town called Lunel, in Southern France. He supported his family as a

---

[1] "Rabiah Balkhi: Medieval Afgani Poet," in *Middle Eastern Muslim Women Speak*, ed. Elizabeth Warnock Fernea and Bassima Kattan Berzirgen (Austin 1977) page 81

physician and died in Marseille in 1190 C.E. Once in Sothern France he began to translate the great works of the Jewish scholars from Andalusia whose writings were in Judeo-Arabic or purely Arabic into Hebrew. Judeo-Arabic refers to the Middle-Arabic dialect utilized by Jews living in Arab lands up until the late 12th century. In its written form it utilizes Hebrew script rather than Arabic and as a spoken language it includes Hebrew expressions.

As was mentioned earlier the Jewish scholars of Andalus espoused the view that language is conventional[2] this means that the Hebrew language developed randomly without there necessarily being any logic associated with the phonetic sound applied to an object or idea. They nevertheless recognized the need to be mindful of their audience, and the style they wanted to project. Yehuda ibn Tibbon alludes to the restrictive and "underdeveloped"[3] nature of the Hebrew language as one of the reasons why many Andalusians and Geonic authors chose to write in Arabic rather than in Hebrew. He writes:

> These books were composed in the Arabic language, since that was the language of the nation in whose midst they dwelled –

---

[2] For HaRambam the Hebrew language while special because it is the language of the TaNaKH and because as Joseph ibn Kaspi asserts in *Asarah Kele Kesef*, edited by I. Last (Pressburg, 1903) that it is the holy tongue because it is grammatically perfect or as HaRambam himself has asserted because it does not contain foul language it is nevertheless void of any metaphysical properties. See the Guide 3:8 and 2:30 also MT Hilkhot Deot 2:4; Keriat Shema 3:4-5; Perush HaMishna Avot 1:16. This was the attitude of the scholars of Andalusia as is clear from Abraham ibn Ezra Bereshit 2:7. European Jewry considered Hebrew language as a metaphysical language containing the essence of what it describes. For this position see Nachmanides Perush al HaTorah Shemoth 30:13 and his "Ma'amar al Penimiyut HaTorah" in *Kitbe HaRamban* edited by C. Chavel (Jerusalem, 1964) volume 2 page 467. For a comprehensive discussion in secondary sources see Isadore Twesky, *Introduction to the Code of Maimonides (Mishneh Torah)* (Yale University Press, 1980) Pages 324-330 and Faur Jose. *Golden Doves with Silver Dots: Semiotics and Textuality in Rabbinic Tradition*. Scholars Press, 1999

[3] Yehuda ibn Tibbon, Introduction to his Hebrew Translation of Hovot HaLevavot by Bahya ibn Pakuda ed. By A. Zifroni

most of the authors from among the ranks of the wise leaders (Geonim) and sages (*Hakhamim*) were in the kingdom of Ishmael; an since that was an expansive and clear language, lacking nothing and being that the sacred tongue (Hebrew) did not put but the books of the bible into our hands and isn't sufficient for all we need to discuss; and since only the exceptional ones from among our nation could understand it as such they elected to compose their discourses in Arabic.[4]

Hebrew, he notes "does not enable the writer to express thoughts succinctly and eloquently."[5] His son the translator of HaRambam's Guide repeats the same idea in the introduction to his *Perush HaMilot HaZarot*.[6]

The world of Andalusia regarded the Hebrew language as "*Lashon HaKodesh*" the sacred language because of its linguistic purity and grammatical consistency. Some even embraced its metaphysical status - all being good reasons to render it unique and surpassing all other languages[7] and yet its limiting scope could not be ignored. Therefore, the language of choice was Arabic and more specifically Judeo-Arabic simply because it was superior in that it was continually developed by its linguists and philologists. It afforded the Andalusian scholars philosophic precision and rhetorical capabilities that Hebrew did not have at its disposal. When the time came to translate the Guide of the Perplexed from Arabic into Hebrew Shemuel ibn Tibbon had to delve into the biblical and Mishnaic Hebrew at his disposal and develop its linguistic reach to do justice to the Guide's unforgiving and exacting ideas.

---

[4] Yehudah ibn Tibbon translation of Jonah ibn Janah's *Sefer Harikma* , Introduction. Ed. By Michael Wilensky, (Jerusalem Academy of Hebrew Language Press, 1964)

[5] ibid

[6] Edited by J. Even Shemuel (Jerusalem, 1947) page 11

[7] See Menachem ben Saruk Mahberet page 10; Saadia Gaon Sefer HaEgron page 55; Shelomo ibn Gabirol Shirim, ed. Bialik and Ravinsky page 176; Yehuda HaLevi, Kuzari 2:81, Rabbi Yoseph Kimhi Sefer HaGaluy page 3 and others

Yehuda ibn Tibbon had one son, Shemuel, and two daughters. He educated his son in accordance with the Andalusian curriculum which included the Hebrew and Arabic languages and grammar, Torah, Talmud, mathematics, sciences, and philosophy.

While in Southern France Yehuda ibn Tibbon forged a strong friendship with the Talmudic scholar and chief rabbi of the region, Rabbi Meshullam ben Yaakov HaKohen (also known as Rabbenu Meshullam) and his sons Asher and Aharon.

His Impact in Europe

Yehuda ibn Tibbon had the utmost respect for Rabbenu Meshullam and the circle of scholars that he found himself to be among. They were well versed in Talmudic studies, but they lacked knowledge in languages and other studies. He writes in his introduction to his translation of *Duties of the Heart*:

> In the lands of Edom (Christian Europe) there are great scholars who have mastered the science of Torah and Talmud since days of old, but they did not attend to other sciences because the craft was solely Talmudic studies and because they did not possess books of other sciences.[8]

Yehuda ibn Tibbon made no pretensions about being an author. He was an exceptionally gifted scholar who exercised great humility. From his son Shemuel we know that although he had written original, insightful, biblical interpretations, he was happy to be known as a translator of existing knowledge that emerged from the Judeo-Arabic traditions of Andalusia. He competently translated works that required adapting Hebrew to philosophical ideas and concepts. He created "almost out of nothing, a Hebrew philosophical vocabulary, an accomplishment that required great creativity and competence."[9]

---

[8] Yehuda ibn Tibbon, Introduction to his Hebrew Translation of *Hovot HaLevavot*.

[9] Gidon Freudenthal, "Abraham Ibn Ezra and Judah Ibn Tibbon as Cultural Intermediaries."

The first text he translated from Arabic to Hebrew, at the request of Rabbenu Meshullam, was Bahya ibn Pakuda's *Duties of the Heart*'s first Gate on the Unity of God. He translated the remaining Gates many years later. He wrote in the introduction:

> Having now learnt that one of the sages of Sefarad, namely Rabbi Bahya ben Rabbi Yoseph, of blessed memory, wrote a book about the doctrine of the duties of the heart, based on the idea of the unity of God, he [Rabbi Meshullam] craved to see it. As soon as the work reached him, he instructed me to translate for him its ideas into the Hebrew language.

This sparked a series of other translations. Ibn Tibbon's next project was to translate Shelomo ibn Gabirol's *Tikkun Middot Hanefesh* [improvement of the moral qualities of the soul], which he completed around 1161 C.E. He then translated Ibn Janah's *Sefer HaRikma*. In the introduction to that book, he warns his readers not to ascribe difficulties they will surly encounter to his translation "for they arise from the profundity and complexity of the subject matter."[10] According to Gidon Freudenthal, as educator and tutor Yehuda ibn Tibbon accompanied his written translations with an oral component propagating the philosophical-spiritual legacy of Andalusia.[11] Yehuda ibn Tibbon went on to translate Yehuda HaLevi's *Kuzari* and Rav Saadia Gaon's *Emmunot VeDe'ot*. Neither of those translations have an introduction of the translator.

Shemuel ibn Tibbon

Shemuel ibn Tibbon is most famous for his elegant and precise translation of HaRambam's *Moreh HaNevuchim* [the Guide of the Perplexed] from Arabic into Hebrew. After Rabbi Jonathon of Lunel, one of the community leaders in Southern France had commissioned Shemuel to translate HaRambam's Guide, the young scholar / translator wrote to HaRambam asking him to resolve a number of philosophical

---

[10] Yehuda ibn Tibbon, *Sefer HaRikmah*, introduction to the translation.

[11] Freudenthal, "Abraham Ibn Ezra and Judah Ibn Tibbon as Cultural Intermediaries," 71.

issues he was struggling with in the Guide.¹² There were four correspondences that went back and forth between HaRambam and Shemuel and of the four only two survived. The surviving letter from HaRambam to Shemuel ibn Tibbon was written in 1199, just five years before his death.¹³ HaRambam wrote as follows:

> Years ago, I had already heard of the honored prince, the sage, your father Yehudah and we are all aware of the breadth of his knowledge and the clarity of his language, both in Arabic and in Hebrew. Learned men from Granada, and one from Toledo, came here and told us about his great honor. We were also given examples of your father's wisdom and I was shown all of the books that he translated, from the grammar books to the works of wisdom literature. But I did not know that he had a son. However, since your letters in both Hebrew and Arabic arrived and I considered them and saw the placed that caused you doubt in the Guide of the Perplexed and places where you thought there might have been a scribal error, I quoted an ancient poem: 'The father's excellence has passed to the son.' Blessed is the one who compensated your father for his wisdom by giving him a son like this.¹⁴

Shemuel ibn Tibbon also translated into Hebrew other works of HaRambam, as well as works of Averroes and Aristotle. Unlike his father, Shemuel ibn Tibbon was also an original author in his own right. He wrote the first full commentary on Kohelet according to HaRambam's philosophy which he titled *Ma'amar Yikavu Hamayim*. He considered this work as a completion of the Guide. He writes:

---

[12] Initially the rabbis of Lunel had asked HaRambam to prepare a translation of the Guide but he declined and he himself had suggested Shemuel do the job. This correspondence is published in Shailat's Iggerot HaRambam (Volume 2, letter #6)

[13] See Doron Forte "Back to the Sources: Alternative Versions of Maimonides Letters to Samuel ibn Tibbon and Their Neglected Significance" in *Jewish Studies Quarterly* 23 (2016) pages 47-49

[14] See Shailat, Iggerot HaRambam, Volume 2, pages 525

For HaRambam explained the meaning of all books of the Hebrew Bible but with regards to Kohelet I have not found that he did so.[15]

His *Ma'amar Yikavu HaMayim* was intended to be an appendix of sort to the Guide. He also wrote several smaller philosophical exegetical works in order to "enlighten the eyes of the intellectuals."[16] His works found a receptive audience in Southern France and in other parts of Christian Europe.

Shemuel ibn Tibbon further developed the technical vocabulary that his father began formulating in order to translate Arabic philosophical works as precisely as possible.

Shemuel ibn Tibbon was born in Lunel among the scholars of Southern France. Despite his father's wish that Shemuel practice medicine he was very active in business. As a young man he visited Marseille to engage in commerce. He traveled to Alexandria at least twice and while in Egypt he acquired HaRambam's letter to Yemen and a copy of the *Mishneh Torah*. He returned to Marseille and settled down to raise a family.

His influence was broad. Shemuel was regularly quoted by Rabbi David Kimhi, his son-in-law Jacob Anatoli, and Rabbi Menahem HaMeiri. In Italy his writings were regularly consulted and commented on by the scholars of that region. A litmus test of his influence may be how he was singled-out by the anti-philosophy circles in Christian Europe. Rabbi Yaacov ben Sheshet wrote a critique of his *Ma'amar Yikavu HaMayim* while Rabbi Solomon ben Avraham of Montpellier accused him of revealing the secrets of the Guide to the uninitiated. He earned the reputation as the expert in HaRambam's philosophy.

In addition to having translated HaRambam's Guide he also translated HaRambam's commentary on Mishna Avot along with its introduction called *Shemoneh Perakim* [the Eight Chapters]. He also translated HaRambam's Treatise on Resurrection.

---

[15] Shemuel ibn Tibbon, Ma'amar Yikavu HaMayim, Introduction, ed L. Bisliches (Pressburg, 1837)

[16] Ibid

Shemuel ibn Tibbon was known for the precision of his translations as well as his ability to clarify points. He, unlike his father who sought to produce the most literal translation possible, first considered the larger context of a passage before translating.[17] He used rabbinic as well as biblical expressions and followed the Arabic syntax. Like his father, he coined new terms and expressions. When possible, he always consulted with the authors.

Shemuel ibn Tibbon's *Perush HaMilot HaZarot* is the first of its kind. It is a philosophical lexicon written in Hebrew. It serves as a glossary for HaRambam's Guide and other philosophical works he translated. For example, when HaRambam uses the expression *Ma'aseh Bereshit* [the account of the Creation] he is referring to something very specific.

> The master HaRambam has indicated that this is what the sages called *Ma'aseh Bereshit*. He meant by this that the secrets of *Ma'aseh Bereshit* represent chapter headings in natural science, which is the science that investigates all aspects of things that are governed by nature, i.e., all celestial and sublunary bodies and their accidents. The final source of all books in this science are those written by Aristotle. These include the following: 1) "the Discourses on Nature" [physics] in which natural things are discussed in general. 2) "On the Heavens of the World" in which the spheres, planets, and starts along with the four elements and their mixtures are discussed in general. 3) "On Generation and Corruption" in which the causes of generation and corruption, their attributes and quiddity, are discussed in particular. 4) "The Signs of Heaven" [meteorology] in which accidents and things that come into existence in the upper part of the atmosphere are discusses. Some of these things when they come into existence are also found on land and sea . . . .[18]

Shemuel ibn Tibbon was not afraid to offer his own creative inter-

---

[17] S. J. Pearce, *The Andalusi Literary and Intellectual Tradition: The Role of Arabic in Judah ibn Tibbon's Ethical Will* (Indiana University Press, 2017)

[18] Shemuel Ibn Tibbon, *Perush HaMilot HaZarot*, entry *Ma'aseh Bereshit*.

pretations even when they went against his master HaRambam. About HaRambam's mastery Shemuel ibn Tibbon writes, "In any branch of learning we have not known since Rav Ashi."[19] And yet he did not place HaRambam beyond error. In his introduction to his translation of HaRambam's commentary on Avot, Shemuel ibn Tibbon criticizes HaRambam's interpretation of Yirmiyahu 9:22-23 as it is presented at the end of the Guide, and he offers his own interpretation. While HaRambam insists that man's final objective on earth is to do good and act in Godly ways, ibn Tibbon argues man's final objective is strictly intellectual. Another example where they disagree is his commentary on Yaakov's dream as is recorded in Bereshit chapter 28.

> And he dreamed and behold a ladder set up on the earth, and the top reached the heavens; and behold the angels of God were ascending and descending on it; and behold the Lord stood above it and said, "I am the God of Abraham your father and the God of Isaac."[20]

In his Guide HaRambam notes how Yaakov's vision of the ladder is an example of a biblical allegory that he interprets: The angels are prophets who first ascend the ladder of knowledge and then descend with Divine wisdom with which they better the society and the world around them. The ladder is set on Earth and its rungs extend into the celestial realm, ascending and descending the various celestial intelligences. God, at the top of the ladder, is the first cause, the prime mover. Shemuel ibn Tibbon is the first to build on HaRambam's approach to these verses and take it in a new direction. In *Ma'amar Yikavu HaMayim*, in chapter eleven, he emphasizes the educational aspect of HaRambam's reading. According to ibn Tibbon, the angels ascending the ladder are philosophers who engage in the study of metaphysics and mysticism. The angels that descend are separate intelligences from the Divine that help humans reach their final perfection.

---

[19] Quoted by Aviezer Ravitzky in his article, "Samuel Ibn Tibbon and the Esoteric Character of the Guide of the Perplexed," 87-123.

[20] Bereshit 28:12-13.

Lucena
Home to another important archaeological find, an ancient Jewish necropolis was discovered near the village of Lucena just 15 years ago. It has an astonishing 380 tombs, all facing towards Jerusalem.

HaRambam placed his seal of approval on Shemuel ibn Tibbon's translation of the Guide. He referred to him as "his worthy translator"[21] to the scholars of Lunel. HaRambam always replied in detail to all of Shemuel ibn Tibbon's queries about style and ideas contained in the Guide.

How Shemuel ibn Tibbon Understood the Guide

Shemuel ibn Tibbon, HaRambam's most trusted colleague, understood the Guide of the Perplexed as an esoteric profoundly mystical text. He understood that HaRambam's unique style was a means to revealing the hidden message of the Torah.

---

[21] *Kovetz Teshuvoth HaRambam*, Pt. 2, page 44a and "Letter to Jonathan of Lunel" in Shailat, *Letters*.

... wisdom that no man was permitted to teach publicly, but only to transmit chapter headings to those who have understanding and are worthy of it, so that they may form those principles and understand the whole issue.[22]

Shemuel ibn Tibbon highlighted the esoteric character of the Guide. He viewed himself as occupying a unique role from which to present HaRambam's daring goal of presenting the purest form of Jewish mysticism to the world.

Judaism and Jewish culture owe a debt of gratitude to both Yehuda and Shemuel ibn Tibbon. They played key roles in the transmission of the Andalusian tradition into Christian Europe.

Yehudah ibn Tibbon's Ethical Will to his Only Son Shemuel

Sometime around 1172 Yehudah ibn Tibbon began writing a letter to his only son Shemuel and he just kept writing, editing, and emending the letter until his death in 1190. He called this letter *Iggeret HaMusar*,[23] the Epistle of Admonition. The father would keep returning to the letter as if it was a running monologue to his son. The passage of time in the writing of the letter is evident from the content. At the beginning of the letter, he is writing to a youthful young man falling behind in his studies and behaving stubbornly while making intemperate business decisions. The letter then speaks to a young man about to get married while the latter part of the ethical will is clearly speaking to a man the author regards as an equal. The occasional insult lobbied at his son is understood as a reprimand of a father expecting excel-

---

[22] Quoted by Ravitzky, 109.

[23] The term iggeret can refer to many types of documents most of the time it refers to a private correspondence or a legal document, announcement or message. Ibn Janah does not translate it in his dictionary and neither does Yehudah ibn Tibbon in his *Sefer HaShorashim*. Rav Sa'adia gaon defines the term as an anthology (Kitab Jami) suggesting it is a text that may contain a range of things. Rabbi Avraham ibn Ezra in his commentary on Megilath Esther similarly translates iggeret as a text that contain multiple ideas.

lence from his only son. Indeed, excellence is an apt description of the success Shemuel would ultimately achieve.

Even though the ethical will, as we will see below, contains a great many themes it is primarily an aspiration and self-reflective directive of a father to his son.

The long letter comprises of a wide range of personal, religious, professional, and ethical advice. It represents the most cherished values of the father, the author, Rabbi Yehudah ibn Tibbon.

One empathizes with the father who berates his son for sloppy handwriting, and for his reluctance to study Hebrew, the sacred language of the bible and Arabic the language of his Andalusian heritage. The importance of mastering the Arabic language is a theme that Yehudah ibn Tibbon visits and revisits throughout the letter. For this father Arabic language is the wellspring of cultural prestige and the means to acquiring true knowledge. He writes:

> You have not cultivated your Arabic writing as expected: You began to study it seven years ago, when I forced you to learn it even though you did not want to. You know that the greatest men of our nation did not achieve their greatness or their lofty heights but through their Arabic writing. You know that the *Nagid* explained that the acclaim accorded to him – and to his son after him was because of it (their knowledge of the Arabic language). You see that the *nasi* Sheshet, achieved wealth and honor through his Arabic writing in this land as in the kingdom of Ishmael.[24]

He advises his son to practice writing in Arabic because Jews like Shemuel HaNagid achieved rank and success due to their ability to write and communicate well. He exhorts his son to maintain his Torah studies as well as the study of sciences and medicine.

> My son, take it upon yourself to copy out one page of After

---

[24] Yehudah Ibn Tibbon, Mussar Av translated by S. J. Pearce *The Andalusi Literary Intellectual Tradition: The Role of Arabic in Judah Ibn Tibbon's Ethical Will* (Indiana University Press, Bloomington and Indianapolis, 2017), Appendix Page 208

Proverbs and to consider its advice daily. On every Shabbath, read the weekly Torah portion in Arabic because it will be useful to you in developing your Arabic vocabulary[25] . . . Be steadfast in your fear of God and your observance of the commandments.[26] My son, study history from time to time with the sage Aaron ben Meshulam. It is a necessary science.[27]

He is to make sure to teach his children and teach other people's children. He is to read the TaNaKH and grammatical works on Shabbath and festivals and is not to neglect the study of Shelomo *HaMelekh's* Mishle. Youth, Yehudah ibn Tibbon writes, is the optimal time to learn new things. Pray every day and attend a minyan on time he exhorts.

The father consistently advises his son to stay healthy and eat well.

Amongst the most important things that will come up in my admonitions and my instructions to you is that you should pay attention to what you eat. You are killing me before my time! I was in a crisis of fear for you when I cared for you while you were ill. Every year – because of my own shortcomings you experienced illness, most of which was caused by bad food.[28] Do not eat food that will prevent you from eating more.[29]

If you feel symptoms of any illness in any of your organs, you should immediately try to do everything necessary to cure the illness. You know what Hippocrates said: 'When time is short, trial and error is dangerous.' Therefore, be quick and do not delay! Utilize known remedies and distance yourself from the unknown ones.[30]

Shemuel is advised to always double check what he writes. Even the Ba'al HaMa'or, the great scholar of their generation asked to have

---

[25] Ibid Page 211
[26] Ibid page 215
[27] Ibid page 218
[28] Ibid page 216
[29] ibid page 217
[30] Ibid 219

his writings checked.

> My son, when you write a text, review it and reread it because no man is impervious of carelessness. Do not let haste keep you from returning to any letter to revise it – even a short one. Take care to avoid mistakes in Hebrew and Arabic language, in verb forms, grammar, and in grammatical gender because sometimes familiarity with vernacular language can lead to mistakes in these areas. A man will be known his whole life by the mistakes written in his own hand.[31] The beauty of a written text is in the script and the beauty of the script is in the pen, in the ruling and in the ink. The beauty of a letter demonstrates the worth of the scribe.[32]

Yehudah ibn Tibbon showed great concern for his son's family life. He advises his son to treat his wife with respect and not follow the ways of those who treat their wives poorly. Later in the letter he expresses concern that he never hit his wife, a practice that was unfortunately all too common in Europe at that time.[33]

> My son, I must also insist that you honor your wife to the best of your ability because she is wise and a modest woman, the daughter of a wise and prestigious family. She is a god companion to you and your sons. She is not profligate, nor does she make large requests for food or dress or outerwear. Remember how well she cared for you when you were sick. She is honorable and unique. She has brought up your sons without a maidservant or manservant. Even if she were only your son's wet-nurse, she would be an honor and a credit to you, but she is all the more so because she, the daughter of a great family, is your soulmate. Do not raise your vice to her or debase her; that is the behavior of lesser men.[34]

---

[31] Ibid pages 212-213

[32] Ibid 213

[33] See Avraham Grossman, "Medieval Rabbinic Views on Wife Beating: 800-1300" in *Jewish History* 5, 1 (1991) page 53-62

[34] S.J. Pearce page 218

Yehudah ibn Tibbon advises his son about being a good and attentive father to his own children. He writes:

> My son, be attentive to your children as I was to you; be kind to them as I was to you; guide them as I guided you; and watch over them as I watched over you. Try to teach them Torah just as I tried. Just as I did for you, you should do for them. Do not ignore any of their maladies nor your own no matter how small; and thus God can save you and them from every illness and plague.[35]

> Why do I work if not for your benefit and your children's? May God allow me to see all of their faces happy! My son do not refrain from following in my footsteps in studying Torah and medical sciences – but mostly occupy yourself with Torah.[36]

Rabbi Yehdah ibn Tibbon advises his son to select his friends carefully. He writes:

> My son, you know that friendship with the wicked is harmful: as intractable as leprosy. The sage, peace be upon him said: Do not start down the path of evil people .... do not associate with someone whose friendship you do not value. The sage, peace be upon him said: 'If you walk with wise men, you will become wise.'[37]

Among the many themes touched upon, Rabbi Yehudah ibn Tibbon informs his son about business and being politically savvy.

> My son, be thoughtful about whose affection and wisdom you rely on. Never abandon your friends or mine. My son do not fight with other men and do not involve yourself in fights that are not your own. Do not try and win arguments against stubborn people, even in matters of Torah; and do not force your opinion on others.[38]

---

[35] Ibid page 219
[36] Ibid page 209
[37] Ibid page 210
[38] Ibid page 211

> You must be aware that you have not given me the courtesy of seeking my counsel or keeping me informed about any matter relating to your sales and purchases. And when I asked you about it you interrupted my questions and hid things from me .... You saw what happened to you in your dealings with Solomon, the son of Joseph the sage, when you departed from my method and ignored my advice. In Marseille, too: we were together in a strange land, and you bought a lot of merchandise of little value without asking my counsel or informing me. I did not find out anything about your activities or business until you offloaded the riverboat in the city of Arles. Even a non-Jew from my city would have kept me apprised of his purchases and sales.[39]

Shemuel is also reminded to be a good person.

> My son, be generous with your time and presence. Care for the sick and let your knowledge cure them. Since you receive payment from the rich you can treat the poor for free. God will grant you your reward and salary and you will build a reputation for kindness and sensibility in the eyes of both God and man; and you will be respected by both great and small and by Israel and by the other nations. Your good name will reach near and far ....[40]

A theme that keeps being repeated throughout the long letter is the importance of honoring one's father. The impression one gets from some parts of the letter is that Yehdah ibn Tibbon did not feel like his son was showing appropriate *Kavod*, honor to his father.

> My son, you have long known that the creator did not offer a reward for the observance of any of the Ten commandments except for the one about honoring one's parents, for which the reward is long life and good days. As it is said: 'Honor your father and mother as the Lord, your God has commanded you.' And in rebuke: If I am a father where is my honor?[41]

---

[39] Ibid page 214
[40] Ibid page 212
[41] Ibid page 206

> ... but you have adopted all these bad manners towards me and made light of my honor which the creator commanded you to respect. May the Source forgive you completely in this world and favor you in the next, teach you to do His will, and cause you to find favor in the eyes of God and man.... Do not let what I have written here in my testament leave a bitter taste in your mouth. By the same measure you have not honored me up to this point, honor me now in what is left of my life, and after my death by continuing in your pursuit of wisdom ... [42]
>
> Praise my Creator! I know that in every path you pursue you fear the heavens, except in the manner of honoring your father; in this you have violated all my orders to you and have not heard my voice.[43]

Rabbi Yehuda ibn Tibbon's ethical will is most famously known for the passages in which he speaks about his most treasured possession, his library:

> I have honored you, by buying you many books so that you would not have to borrow books from any other man which you see most other students doing, trudging about to borrow books and not always finding them. But you, praise God can lend and do not have to borrow books since you have two or three copies of most of your books. And what's more I have compiled anthologies for you in every discipline and I had hoped that your hand will be a cradle to each of them.[44]
>
> My son, make your books your companions, and your shelves and bookcases your paradise and orchard. Revel in their verdancy, pick their roses and gather up their fruits, spices, and myrrh.[45]

Yehudah ibn Tibbon draws on the well-known trope of the library as an enchanted garden. By doing this links his passion for books that

---

[42] Ibid 215

[43] Ibid page 2125

[44] Ibid page 207

[45] Ibid page 210

he so dearly wants to impart on his son with a familiar image that is used in Andalusian poetry. The library and the books are a physical symbol of the overriding message and culture the father want to impart on his only son. The library is the anchor that grounds and places supreme value on the intellectual, philosophical heritage of Andalus. The very fact that so many people sought the opportunity to borrow and see the ibn Tibbon library speaks to the cultural intellectual capital of his library. It clearly evokes the sense of a culture lost. In his ethical will Yehudah ibn Tibbon encourages his son to share his books with students, colleagues, and friends reminiscent of the great libraries of Andalusia.[46]

Yehudah ibn Tibbon links the value of lending books with the core value of study. And while lending books may lead to the loss of books it is nevertheless a valuable method of growing and learning.

> Neither take your studies with your teacher for granted nor cease to study with the younger men., even if you do not leave your teacher's study until late at night. You should always share everything that you have learned from me and from your teachers with other worthy student to keep your knowledge fresh at hand; by teaching them you will learn it by heart and by answering their questions you will remove any doubt. Nor should you refuse to lend books to anyone who does not have any or the ability to buy them, as long as you are sure he will return them to you. You know what our sages wrote: 'Wealth and happiness reside within Him and His righteousness remain forever.' So do not keep the benefit of your possessions from others or guard your books closely. Cover your books with lovely tapestries and guard them against moisture, bookworms, and damage, because they are your treasure. When you lend a book to anyone, inscribe his name in the catalogue before it leaves your house; and when it is returned, cross it out with a pen. On Passover and Sukkoth recall all of the books that you have out.[47]

---

[46] It is said that the library of Cordova had over 400,000 books. Ramjaun Ibrahim, *Libraries in Al-Andalus or Medieval Spain*, (2020)

[47] S.J. Pearce page 219

The father, author of this letter, while at times harsh reminds his son how he always be there for him:

> Even now, my son, I am never far away from you; not for a day for two and not for ten or twenty days. Take all of this to heart and act on it.[48]

This ethical will is a true treasure of Andalusian culture and a reminder of the lost era of enlightenment. It serves numerous purposes and contains a range of elements that conform to a variety of genres. The ethical will is about 30% poetry, it is biographical and didactic.

A Fitting Final Thought

I thought it fitting to end this short book with a passage written by Shemuel ibn Tibbon which supports the overall theses of this work and other published material of mine namely that HaRambam was more of a transmitter than he was an innovator. The Andalusian intellectual, spiritual, legal, and mystical tradition is the more authentic representation of Talmudic rabbinic Judaism.

Rabbi Shemuel ibn Tibbon saw himself as responsible for introducing what he believed to be an authentic philosophical approach of Judaism to European Jewry.[49] Throughout his writings he presents HaRambam as a "cultural hero"[50] who restored the true essence of Judaism which had gradually lost its core intellectual nature after the close of the Talmud. Shemuel ibn Tibbon is heir to a tradition that the intellectual Jewish tradition began with Moshe Rabbenu and con-

---

[48] Ibid 217

[49] Carlos Fraenkel, "Beyond the Faithful Disciple: Samuel Ibn Tibbon's Criticism of Maimonides" in *Maimonides After 800 Years: Essays on Maimonides and His Influence* edited by Jay M. Harris (Harvard University Press, MA 2007) pages 33-63

[50] This is the way Bernard Septimus describes Shemuel ibn Tibbon's presentation of HaRambam see Septimus, *Hispano-Jewish Cultural Transition* (Cambridge MA, 1982) Page 46

Statue of Yehuda ibn Tibbon in Granada Spain

tinued until the close of the Talmud and was then interrupted until it "was restored to its present glory through HaRambam's teachings."

The sages of the Mishna and the Talmud also wrote down hints and riddles, scattered and dispersed in their midrashim that pering to the wisdom he possessed in these subjects and his ability to apply the art of concealment. After the sages of the Talmud however, only very few were stirred to compose a book or write a word about these sciences; the composing of books about legal judgements and what is forbidden and permitted was sufficient for them. Then God saw the poverty of knowledge of his people and the amount of ignorance concerning everything related to wisdom, and He raised up a savior, a wise and understanding man, wise in crafts and with an understanding of whispering. Since the days of Rav Ashi until his own, no one was known to have risen up among our people who was like him with regards to every aspect of wisdom. He is the true sage, the divine philosopher, our master and our teacher, MOSES, the servant of God, son of the great RABBI MAIMON. And the Lord stirred his spirit to write books of great nobility. He wrote books in the field of Talmud as well as another great and noble book which he called Mishneh Torah ... but all of this was insignificant in his eyes until he composed yet another treatise, a priceless pearl, which he called according to its utility *Moreh HaNevuchim* (Guide of the Perplexed) [The purpose of this book] is guidance provided to the perplexed with regard to the true meaning of the verses written in the Torah, the Prophets and Writings as HaRambam has explained .... [51]

Shemuel ibn Tibbon likens HaRambam to Moshe Rabbenu "our master and our teacher Moshe the Servant of God." He is the great authority who returns Judaism to its original legal and philosophical religion.

---

[51] Shemuel ibn Tibbon, Perush Kohelet, His commentary on Kohelet edited and translated by J. Robinson, *Philosophy and Exegeses in Samuel Ibn Tibbon's Commentary on Ecclesiastes*, (Ph.D. Dissertation, Harvard University Press 2002) pages 230-231

Primary Sources

MAIMONIDES

Moreh HaNevukhim, Dalalat al Ha'irin [Guide of the Perplexed]. Hebrew translated by Joseph Kafikh. Jerusalem: Mossad HaRav Kook, 1972.

Moreh Nevukhim. Hebrew translation of Shemuel ibn Tibbon with commentaries of Efodi, Shem Tov, Crescas, and Abravanel. Jerusalem: 1960.

The Guide of the Perplexed. Translated with introduction and notes by Shlomo Pines, Chicago: University of Chicago Press, 1963.

Moreh Nevukhim LeRabenu Moshe ben Maimon. .Ttranslation by Michael Schwartz. Tel Aviv: Tel Aviv University Press, 2002.

Le Guide Des Egares. French translation by Salomon Munk with Preface by Clade Birman, One Volume .Verdier, 1979.

Perush HaMishna. Hebrew translation by Joseph Kafikh, 3 Volumes. Jerusalem: Mosaad HaRav Kook, 1969

Sefer HaMitzvoth. Hebrew translation by Joseph Kafikh. Jerusalem: Mossad HaRav Kook, 1971.

Sefer HaMitzvoth. English translation by C. Chavel. Lindon, 1967.

Mishneh Torah, Shabsi Frankel Edition, 16 Volumes.

Mishneh Torah, Rambam La'am, Mossad HaRav Kook Edition.

Mishneh Torah, The Code of Maimonides, Yale Judaica Series. English translation general editor, Leon Nemoy. New Haven, CT: Yale University Press.

Epistles of Maimonides, Epistle on Martyrdom, Epistle to Yemen, Essays on Resurrection. Translated by Abraham Halkin, discussions by David Hartman. Philadelphia: Jewish Publication Society of America, 1985.

Haqdamot HaRambam LaMishna [Maimonides' Introductions in his Commentary on Mishna]. Edited and translated by Yitzchak Sheilat. Ma'aleh Admim: Ma'aliot Press, 1977.

Iggerot HaRambam [Letters of Maimonides] 2 Volumes. Edited and translation by Yitzchak Sheilat. Ma'aleh Adumim: Ma'aliot Press, 1987.

A Maimonides Reader. Edited by Isadore Twersky, New York: Behrman House, 1972. Pages 424-436.

Introduction to *Perek Helek*

Letter of Astrology

Letter to Obadiah the Proselyte

Rabbi Saadia Gaon

Rabbi Alfasi

Avraham ibn Ezra

Shemuel Ibn Gabirol

Selective Bibliography

Abramson, Shraga. *Topics in Geonic Literature: Researches in the Literature and Responsa of the Geonim in Print and Manuscript* (Hebrew). Jerusalem: 1974.

Allony, Nehemiah. *The Egron: The Book of the Principles of Hebrew Poetry by Rav Sa'adyah Gaon.* Jerusalem: 1969.

Altmann, Alexander. "The Ladder of Ascension" in *Studies in Mysticism and Religion Presented to Gershon G. Scholem on his Seventieth Birthday by Pupils, Colleagues and Friends.* Edited by Ephraim E. Urbach, R.J. Zwi Werblowsky, and Chaim Wirszubski, pp. 1–32. Jerusalem: Magnes Press, 1967.

"Maimonides' Attitude Toward Jewish Mysticism" in *Studies In Jewish Thought: An Anthology of German Jewish Scholarship,* edited by Alfred Jospe. Detroit: Wayne State University Press, 1981.

Biblical and Other Studies, editor. Cambridge: Harvard University Press, 1963.

Assaf, Simcha. *Sa'adya Gaon's Siddur: The Book Collecting Prayers and Benedictions* (Hebrew). Jerusalem: 1941.

Ashtor, Eliyahu. *The Jews of Moslem Spain.* Philadelphia, Jerusalem: JPS Society, 1992.

Barton, Simon. *A History of Spain.* London: Palgrave Macmillan, 2004.

Ben-Meir, Ruth. "Samuel Ibn Tibbon's Preface to the Commentary on Ecclesiastes," *Maimonidean Studies*, 4: 13-44 [Hebrew section]. New York: Yeshiva University Press, 2000.

Ben-Shammai, Haggai, "The Long Introduction and the Short Introduction to Rav Saadya Gaon's Translation of the Torah" (Hebrew) *Tarbiz* 69 (2000), pp. 199-210.

"Sa'adya Gaon's Ten Articles of Faith" (Hebrew) *Da'at*, 37 (1996). pp. 2-26

Berman, Joshua. *Ani Maamin: Biblical Criticism, Historical Truth, and the 13 Principles*. Jerusalem: Maggid Press, 2020.

Blumenthal, David "Maimonides' Philosophic Mysticism." *Living with God and Humanity*

Cohen, J. and Simon U. editors *Rabbi Abraham Ibn Ezra, Yesod Morah VeSod Torah* (Ramat Gan, Bar Ilan University Pres 2002)

Forte, Doron "Back to the Sources: Alternative Versions of Maimonides' Letter to Samuel Ibn Tibbon and Their Neglected Significance," in *Jewish Studies Quarterly* 23 (2016)

Levin, Isaac "Cling to the Ladder of Wisdom: The Influence of Neoplatnic Psychology on the Poetry of Abraham ibn Ezra" in Te'Udah Volume 8 (1992)

Studies in the Works of Abraham ibn Ezra (Hebrew) editor I. Levin (Tel Aviv University Press 1992)

Lewis, Bernard, translator. *The Kingly Crown: Keter Malkhut* by Solomon ibn Gabirol. Notre Dame University Press, 2002.

Bialik, Hayim Nachman, and Y. H. Ravnitzky, editors. *Shirai Shelomo ben Yehudah Ibn Gabirol* 2 Volumes. Tel Aviv: Dvir Press, 1925.

Brody, Robert. *The Geonim of Babylonia and the Shaping of Medieval Jewish Culture*. New Haven: Yale University Press, 1998.

Sa'adya Gaon. New York: The Littman Library of Jewish Civilization, 2016.

Carmi, T. *The Penguin Book of Hebrew Verse*. New York: Viking Press 1981.

Carmy, Shalom. "The Sovereignty of Dogma: Rambam and/or The Mishnah" in *The Legacy of Maimonides: Religion, Reason, and Community*. Yamini Levy and Shalom Carmy, editors. New York: Yashar Books, 2006.

Cole, Peter, translator. *Selected Poems by Shemuel Hanigid*. Princeton: Princeton University Press, 1996.

Selected Poems of Solomon Ibn Gabirol. Princeton: Princeton University Press, 2000.

Cohen, Joseph and Uriel Simon, editors. *Rabbi Abraham Ibn Ezra, Yesod Morah Vesod Torah.* Ramat-Gan: Bar Ilan University Press, 2002.

Davidson, Hebert, A. *Moses Maimonides: The Man and His Works.* Oxford: Oxford University Press, 2005.

Davidson, Israel. *Saadia's Polemic Against Hiwi al-Balkhi: A Fragment.* in *Texts and Studies of the Jewish Theological Seminary of America* 5. New York: JTS, 1915.

Daud, Abraham ibn, and Gerson D. Cohen. *The Book of Tradition: (Sefer Ha-Qabbalah).* 1967.

Faur, José. *Golden Doves with Silver Dots: Semiotics and Textuality in Rabbinic Tradition.* New York: Scholars Press, 1999.

"Two Models of Jewish Spirituality" in Shofar Volume 10 no. 3 (Spring 1992)

Fenton, Paul. "A Meeting with Maimonides" in *Bulletin of the School of Oriental and African Studies Volume 45 number 1.* University of London, 1982.

Fraenkel, Carlos "Beyond the Faithful Disciple: Samuel Ibn Tibbon's Criticism of Maimonides" in *Maimonides After 800 Years: Essays on Maimonides and His Influence* edited by Jay Harris (Harvard University Press, MA 2007)

Freudenthal, Gad. "Les Sciences dans les communautés juives médiévales de Provence: Leur appropriation, leur rôle," in *Revue des Etudes Juives* 1993, 152: 29-136.

"Abraham Ibn Ezra and Judah Ibn Tibbon as Cultural Intermediaries: Early Stages in the Introduction of Non-Rabbinic Learning in Provence in the Mid Twelfth Century," in *Exchange and Transmission Across Cultural Boundaries,* edited by Haggi Ben Shammai, Shaul Shanked, and Sarah Stroumsa, 52-91. Jerusalem: The Israel Academy of Science and Humanities, 2013.

Gibson, E. "Hommage To Maimonodies" in *Essays On Maimonides: An Octocentennial Volume,* edited by Salo W. Baron. New York: Columbia University Press, 1941.

Gil, Moshe. *In the Kingdom of Ishmael.* Tel Aviv: Tel Aviv University Press, 1997.

"The Babylonian Yeshivoth and the Maghrib in Early Middle Ages," in *Proceedings of the Academy for Jewish Research,* Volume 57 (1990-1991)

Gluck, Andrew. *Keter Malkhut: The Kingly Crown by Solomon ibn Gabiro.* translated by Bernard Lewis. Indiana: University of Notre Dame Press, 2003.

Gottlieb, I. *Yesh Sedder La Miqura: Chazal U'Parshanei Yemei HaBeinayim Al Mukdam Ume'Uchar BaTorah.* Jerusalem Ramat Gan: Bar Ilan University Press 2009.

Groner, Tsvi. "The Legal Methodology of Rav Hai Gaon" in *Brown Judaica Series* 66. Chico: Scholars Press, 1985.

Grossman, Avraham. "The Relationship Between the Social Structure and Spiritual Activity of Jewish Communities in the Geonic Period," in *Zion* 53/3. 1998.

"Medieval Rabbinic Views on Wife Beating: 800-1300 CE" in *Jewish History* Volume 5,1 (1991)

Guttman, Julius. *Philosophies of Judaism.* New York: Schocken Press.

Halbertal, Moshe. *Maimonides' Life and Thought*, translated from the Hebrew by Joel Linsider. Princeton, Oxford: Princeton University Press, 2014.

Halkin, Abraham S. "The Medieval Attitude Towards Hebrew" in *Biblical and Other Studies,* edited by Alexander Altmann. Cambridge: Harvard University Press, 1963.

Hartman, David. *Crisis and Leadership: The Epistles of Maimonides.* Philadelphia: JPS, 1985.

Harkavy, Abraham E. *Fugitive Remnants of the Egron and Sefer HaGalui Hasarid VeHapalit Misefer Ha'Egron Umisfer HaGalui* (Hebrew translation), 154-155.

Husik, Isaac. *History of Medieval Jewish Philosophy.* New York: MacMillan Pub Co, 1969.

Ibn Pakuda, Bahya. *The Book of Direction of The Duties of The Heart.* Introduction and Translation by Menachem Mansoor. London: Routledge and Kegan Paul, 1973.

Jacobs, Louis "The Place of Mysticism in Modern Life" European Judaism: A Journal for the New Europe Volume 2:32

Kafikh, Yosef. *Sefer Yetzirah [Kitab al-Mabadi] Im Targum Uperush HaGaon Rabbenu Sa'adia ben Yoseph Fayumi.* Jerusalem: PUBLISHER, 1972.

Introduction and Translation of *Emunot DeVe'ot* by Saadia Gaon. Jerusalem: Sura Press, 1969.

Daniel Im Targum U'Perush Rabbenu Sa'adia Ben Yoseph Fayumi. Jerusalem: Mosad HaRav Kook, 1973.

Iyov Im Targum U'Perush Rabbenu Sa'adia Ben Yoseph Fayumi. Jerusalem:Mosad HaRav Kook, 1973.

Mishle Im Targum U'Perush Rabbenu Sa'adia Ben Yoseph Fayumi. Jerusalem:Mosad HaRav Kook, 1976.

Tehillim Im Targu U'Perush Rabbenu Sa'adia Ben Yoseph Fayumi. Jerusalem: Mosad HaRav Kook, 1966.

Kanarfogel, Ephraim. "Assessing The (Non-)Reception of Mishneh Torah in Medieval Ashkenaz," in *The Dwelling of A Sage Lie Precious Treasures: Essays in Jewish Studies in Honor of Shnayer Z. Leiman.* edited by Yitzhak Berger and Chaim Milikowsky. New York: Ktav Publishing House, 2020.

Kellner, Menachem. "Maimonides' Disputed Legacy" in *Traditions of Maimonideanism* edited by Carlos Fraenkel. Leiden: E.J. Brill, 2009.

Maimonides on Judaism and the Jewish People. Albany: SUNY Press, 1991.

Kobler, Franz. *Letter of the Jews Through the Ages: From Biblical Times to the Renaissance.* New York: Hebrew Publishing Company, 1978.

Kraemer, Joel. "Maimonides and The Spanish Aristotelian School" in *Christian, Muslims, and Jews in Medieval and Early Modern Spain: Interaction and Cultural Change,* edited by Mark D. Myerson and Edward D. English. Notre Dame: University of Notre Dame Press, 2000.

"Moses Maimonides: An Intellectual Portrait" in *The Cambridge Companion to Maimonides,* edited by Kenneth Seeskin, 10-57. Cambridge: Cambridge University Press, 2005.

Maimonides: The Life and Works of One of Civilization's Greatest Minds. Doubleday, New York, 2008.

Langermann, Tzvi, "Abraham Ibn Ezra." ResearchGate, October 2018.

Leibowitz, Aryeh. "The Pursuit of Scholarship and Economic Self Sufficiency: Revisiting Maimonides' Commentary to Pirkei Avot" in *Tradition Magazine,* Volume 40:3 Fall 2007.

Leibowitz, Yeshayahu. *The Faith of Maimonides* translated by John Glucker. Tel Aviv: Mod Books, 1989.

Levin, Israel. *Yalkut Ibn Ezra.* New York, Tel Aviv: Israel Matz Hebrew Classic Library Foundation, 1985.

"Cling To the Ladder of Wisdom: The Influence of Neoplatonic Psychology on the Poetry of Abraham Ibn Ezra" in *Teudah,* Volume 8. Tel Aviv: Tel Aviv University Press, 1992.

"Studies in the Works of Abraham Ibn Ezra" (Hebrew) in *Teudah,* volume 8. Tel Aviv: Tel Aviv University Press, 1992.

Levy, Yamin. *The Mysticism of Andalusia: Exploring HaRambam's Mystical Traditions* (New York: Maimonides Heritage Center Press, 2023.

"Maimonides on Authority, Obedience and the Pursuit of Reason," in *Mishpetei Shalom: A Jubilee Volume in Honor of Saul (Shalom) Berman* edited by Yamin Levy

Lewin, Benjamin, M. *Iggeret Rav Sherira Gaon*. Haifa:1921.

Makari, George. *Soul Machine: The Invention of the Modern Mind*. New York & London: W. W. Norton & Co., 2015.

Malter, Henry. *Sa'adia Gaon: His Life and His Works*. Philadelphia: Intellectbooks, 1921.

Margalioth, Mordechai, editor. *Hilkhot Hanagid*. Jerusalem: 1962.

Melamed, Ezra Tzion. *Mefarshei HaMikra*. Jerusalem: Magnes Press, 1978.

Mondschein, Aaron. "Shitta Schelishit Le Perusho Shel Rabbi Avraham Ibn Ezra" in *Or Le Yaacov: Mechkarim Bamikra U'bemegillah*. Tel Aviv: 5747.

Neubauer, Adolf. *Mediaeval Jewish Chronicles and Chronological Notes*. Oxford, Clarendon Press, 1887.

Pearce, Sarah J. *The Andalusi Literary and Intellectual Tradition: the Role of Arabic in Judah Ibn Tibbon's Ethical Will* (Indiana University Press, 2017)

Rapaport, Solomon Judah Lieb, "Toldot Rabbenu Nissim ben Yaacov," in *Bikkure Haitim*

Ratzaby, Yehuda. *Perushei Rav Sa'adia Gaon Lesef Shemoth*. Jerusalem: Mossad HaRav Kook, 1998.

Ravitzky, Aviezer. *The Thought of Rabbi Zerahhah b. Isaac b. Shealtiel Hen and Maimonidean-Tibbonian Philosophy in the Thirteenth Century* [in Hebrew]. Jerusalem: Ph.D. Dissertation, Hebrew University, 1978.

"Samuel Ibn Tibbon and the Esoteric Character of The Guide of the Perplexed," *Association of Jewish Studies Review*, 6:87-123.

Rosner, Fred. *The Wars of The Lord By Abraham Maimonides in Defense of His Father Moses Maimonides*. Translation and introduction by Fred Rosner. Haifa: The Maimonides Research Institute Press.

Schama, Simon. *The Story of The Jews*.: Ecco Publishers, 2014.

Schechter, Solomon. *Saadyana: Geniza Fragments of Writings of Rabbi Saadya Gaon and Others*. Cambridge: Deighton And Bell, 1903, 1903.

Schirman, Jefim, H. "Salomon Ibn Gabrol: Su Vida Y Su Obra Poetica" in *Seis Conferencias En Torno A Ibn Gabirol*. Malaga, Spain:, 1973.

Scholem, Gershom. *Kabbalah*. New York: Dorset Press, 1974.

Septimus, Bernard. *Hispano Jewish Society and Transition*. Cambridge: Harvard University Press 1982.

Silver, Daniel, J. *Maimonidean Criticism and the Maimonidean Controversy 1180-1240*. Leiden Netherlands: E.J. Brill, 1965.

Selective Bibliography

Simon, Uriel. *Four Approaches for the Book of Psalms: from Sa'adia Gaon to Abraham Ibn Ezra*. New York: State University of NY Press, 1991.

Sklare, David, E. *Samuel Ben Hofni Gaon and His Cultural World*. Leiden, New York, Koln: E.J. Brill, 1996.

Shailat, Yitzchak. *Iggerot HaRabam* 2 Volumes. (Maleh Adumin: Ma'Aliyoth Press, 1987).

Haqdamot HaRambam LaMishna (Maleh Adumim Press, 1987)

Shapiro, Marc. "On Books and Bans" in *Edah Journal* 3:2, 2003.

Soloveitchik, Haim, "Polemic and Art" In *Maimonides After Eight Hundred Years: Essays on Maimonides and His Influence*. Edited by Jay Harris (Harvard University Press, Cambridge MA 2007)

"Maimonides' Iggeret HaShemad: Law and Rhetoric" in *Haym Soloveitchik Collected Essays II* (London Lipman Library Press 2019)

Strauss, Leo. "How to Begin to Study *The Guide of the Perplexed*" in *Moses Maimonides: The Guide of The Perplexed*, translated by Shlomo Pines. University of Chicago Press, 1963.

Stroumsa, Sarah. *Sa'adya Gaon: Hogeh Yehudi BeHevrat Yam Tikhonit*. Tel Aviv: Tel Aviv University Press, 2001.

TaShma, Israel Moses, Encyclopedia Judaica, (Keter Publishing, NY McMillan 1973) entry "Ibn Migash"

Thompson, Linda. "Learning Language: Learning Culture in Singapore," in *Language, Education and Discourse: Functional Approaches*, edited by Joseph A. Foley, 76-96. London: Continuum, 2004.

Twersky, Isadore. *Introduction to the Code of Maimonides (Mishneh Torah)*. Yale University Press, 2010.

The Maimonides Reader. Cambridge: Harvard University Press, 1973.

"The Beginning of Mishneh Torah Criticism" in *Biblical and Other Studies*, edited by Alexander Altmann. Cambridge: Harvard University Press, 1963.

"Some Reflections on the Historical Image of Maimonides: An Essay on His Unique Place in History" (Hebrew) translated by Joel Linzer in *The Legacy of Maimonides: Religion, Reason, and Community* edited By Yamin Levy and Shalom Carmy. New York: Yashar Books, 2006.

Vajda, Georges. , "An Analysis of the Ma'amar Yiqqawu ha-Mayim by Samuel b. Judah Ibn Tibbon," *Journal of Jewish Studies*, volume 10: 137–149, 1959.

Wijnhoven, Jochanan. "The Mysticism of Solomon Gabirol" in *The Journal of Religion*, volume 45, April 1965.

Wolfson, Harry Austryn. "The Classification of Sciences in Medieval Jewish Philosophy" in *Hebrew Union College Jubilee Volume*. Cincinnati: Hebrew Union College, 1925.

Wolfson, Elliot. "Beneath the Wings of the Great Eagle: Maimonides and Thirteenth Century Kabbalah" in *Moses Maimonides (1138-1204): His Religious, Scientific, And Philosophical Wirkungsgeschichte in Different Cultural Contexts*, edited by Görge K. Hasselhoff and Otfried Fraisse. Wurzburg: Ergon, 2004.

Zulay, Menachem. *Sadia HaHaskola HaPaitanit Shel Rav Saadia Gaon*. Jerusalem, 1964.

Index of Principal Concepts, Terms, and Names

The names of those listed in the table of contents are *not* included in this index.

Agron (Ha'Agron) 33, 34, 36
Alexandria 75, 183, 203, 252
Andalusia 3-12
Anthropomorphism 64, 109, 138-139
Aristotle 120, 181, 252, 254

Babylonian Talmud 2, 5-6, 26-29, 37, 55, 59, 113, 114, 206
Bagdad 7
Brody, Robert 36, 38 58
Byzantine Empire 83

Commandments
  Biblical 31, 40-41, 44,
  In a Poem 52
  Observance of 16
  Rational vs 46-48
  Reason for 235-236
  Theurgic approach to 242
  Treatise on 69-70
Convert 22, 73, 219-221
Creation 43, 46, 48, 122, 137, 138, 174, 231, 240
Culture, Transmission 10-17, 86, 123, 15152-153

Dalalat Al-Hairin 179, 210

Emunot VeDe'ot 42-45, 47, 171
Ethical Will 257-258, 263-265
Expulsion 4, 238

Faur, Jose 11, 136, 179 n4, 201 n49, 212, 213, 218, 218 n77, 239, 248
Fayyum (Fayyumite) 36
Fostat, city 59, 73, 75, 180, 183, 185, 186, 187

279

God
- Awe of 132, 137, 171, 199, 237, 239, 241, 243
- Knowledge of 72, 137-138, 142, 174, 198, 199, 227, 231, 239
- Love of 122, 131, 133, 137-138, 145-146, 229, 231, 237, 241, 243
- Unity of 45, 133, 138, 140, 145, 229, 251

Golden Age of Spain 3, 8
Grossman, Abraham 39, 260

Hebrew Language 7-8, 12, 34, 36, 85, 90, 91-94, 103, 107, 171-171, 201-202, 248-249, 251
Heikhalot 69

Ibn Daud, Avraham 4, 56, 57, 64, 66, 74-75, 81, 86, 99, 109, 123, 211
Ibn Rumahis 74

Jerusalem Talmud 7, 17, 19, 24, 26, 29, 108, 110, 113-114, 206
Judeo-Arabic 34, 53, 67, 136, 150, 157, 187, 201-203, 243, 247-250

Kavanah 71, 132, 141
Khazar Kingdom 83, 85

Langerman, Tzvi 151, 156
Latin 4, 8, 80, 82, 100, 106, 120, 185, 221
Lucena, City and Yeshiva 8, 17, 86, 91, 111, 146, 149, 256

Mikra 12, 51, 132
Mishneh Torah 5-6, 10, 19, 31, 42, 59, 116, 207 see Section on Mishneh Torah

Moshe Rabbenu 5, 10, 41, 57, 60, 68, 162, 164-166, 179, 182, 188, 192, 195, 240, 266
Mukdam U'MeUchar 162
Muslim Conquest 7
Mysticism 8, 43, 86, 120-121, 137, 139, 205, 238-239, 240-242, 247, 255, 257

Peshat 50-51, 96, 157-159, 169
Philosophy, Study of 2, 7, 9-10, 12-13, 44, 121, 153, 170, 175, 177, 201, 230-231
Pidyon Shevu'im 75
Poetry 6, 18, 34, 51, 106, 124, 153, 221, 264
Pumpedita 57-61, 65-66, 74

Rabbenu Tam 155-156
Rabbi Yehuda HaLevi 86, 107, 149, 151-152, 174, 202, 211
Rabbi Yehuda Hanasi 77, 187, 192, 204-205
Rabbi Yoseph Karo 71, 116, 200
Reish Galuta 37
Resurrection 45, 47, 193, 195, 226-228, 253

Sanhedrin 25, 27, 42, 60, 113, 121, 131, 180, 234
Sefer Ha-Qabbalah 56, 57, 64, 66, 74, 75, 81, 86 231 n133
Sefer HaGalui 33, 53
Sefer Yesira 43-44
Shahada 214-219
Shinun HaMikra 12
Soul 16, 45, 47, 48, 140, 142, 197, 232, 236, 251
Study 32, 40, 60, 74, 79, 85, 92, 132, 172, 183-184, 196

Index of Principal Concepts, Terms, and Names

Sura 37, 59-60, 66, 74, 87

Talmud 2-4, 59, 114, 206
Teshuva 135, 143, 145, 208
Twersky, Isadore 4, 182, 191, 229

Umayyad Caliphate 3, 5-6, 86

Zaragoza 90-91, 103-104, 129

Made in United States
North Haven, CT
17 June 2025

69913240R00163